CW01572497

HISTORY IN THE MAKING
Series Editor: John Jones

4 Britain, Europe and Beyond

1700–1900

HISTORY IN THE MAKING

Martin Dickinson

Deputy Head,
Hinchingbrooke School,
Huntingdon

4 Britain, Europe and Beyond

1700–1900

Nelson

Thomas Nelson and Sons Ltd
Nelson House Mayfield Road
Walton-on-Thames Surrey
KT12 5PL UK

Thomas Nelson Australia
102 Dodds Street
South Melbourne
Victoria 3205 Australia

Nelson Canada
1120 Birchmount Road
Scarborough Ontario
M1K 5G4 Canada

© Martin Dickinson 1979

First published by Macmillan Education Ltd 1979
(under ISBN 0-333-19321-0)

This edition published by Thomas Nelson and Sons Ltd 1992

I(T)P   Thomas Nelson is an International
        Thomson Publishing Company.

I(T)P   is used under licence.

ISBN 0-17-435070-8
NPN 9 8 7 6 5 4

All rights reserved. No part of this publication may be
reproduced, copied or transmitted save with written permission or
in accordance with the provisions of the Copyright, Design and
Patents Act 1988, or under the terms of any licence permitting
limited copying issued by the Copyright Licensing Agency,
90 Tottenham Court Road, London W1P 9HE.

Any person who does any unauthorised act in relation to this
publication may be liable to a criminal prosecution and civil
claims for damages.

Printed in China

Changes in the teaching of history over the last decade have raised many problems to which there are no easy solutions. The classification of objectives, the presentation of material in varied and appropriate language, the use and abuse of evidence and the reconsideration of assessment techniques are four of the more important. Many teachers are now encouraging their pupils individually or in groups to participate in the processes and skills of the professional historian. Moreover such developments are being discussed increasingly in the context of mixed ability classes and the need to provide suitable teaching approaches for them.

History in the Making is a new course for secondary schools intended for pupils of average ability. It is a contribution to the current debate, and provides one possible way forward. It accepts many of the proven virtues of traditional courses: the fascination of the good tale, the drama of human life, individual and collective, the need to provide a visual stimulus to support the written word.

But it has built on to these some of the key features of the 'new history' so that teachers can explore, within the framework of a textbook, many of the 'new' approaches and techniques.

To this end each chapter in this volume has four major components.

1   **The text**   This provides the basic framework of the chapters and, although the approach is essentially factual, it is intended to arouse and sustain the interest of the reader of average ability.

2   **The illustrations**   These have been carefully selected to stand beside the written pieces of evidence in the chapter, and to provide (so far as is possible) an authentic visual image of the period/topic. Photographs, artwork and maps are all used to clarify and support the text, and to develop the pupil's powers of observation.

3   **Using the evidence**   This is a detailed study of the evidence on one particular aspect of the chapter. Did the walls of Jericho really come tumbling down? Was the death of William Rufus in the New Forest really an accident? What was the background to the torpedoing of the *Lusitania*? These are the sort of questions which are asked, to give the pupil the opportunity to consider not only the problems facing the historian, but also those facing the characters of history. Different forms of documentary evidence are considered, as well as archaeological, architectural, statistical, and other kinds of source material; the intention is to give the pupil a genuine, if modest, insight into the making of history.

4   **Questions and further work**   These are intended to test and develop the pupil's reading of the chapter, and in particular the 'Using the evidence' section. Particular attention is paid to the development of historical skills, through the examination and interpretation of evidence. The differences between primary and secondary sources, for example, are explored, and concepts such as bias in evidence introduced through specific examples. Some comprehension questions are included, but the emphasis is very much on involving pupils with the

materials, and helping them to develop a critical awareness of different kinds of evidence and their limitations. By applying the skills which they have developed, pupils may then be able to formulate at a suitable level and in appropriate language, ideas and hypotheses of their own.

History in the Making is a complete course in five volumes, to meet the needs of pupils between the ages of 11 and 16 (in other words up to and including the first public examination). However, each volume stands by itself and may be used independently of the others; given the variety of syllabuses in use in schools today this flexibility is likely to be welcomed by many teachers. *The Ancient World* and *The Medieval World* are intended primarily for 11–13-year-old pupils, *The Early Modern World, 1450–1700* for 12–14-year-old pupils, *Britain, Europe and Beyond, 1700–1900* for pre-GCSE pupils and *The Twentieth Century* for GCSE examination candidates.

It is our hope that pupils will be encouraged, within the main topics and themes of British, European and World history, to experience for themselves the stimulus and challenge, the pleasure and frustration, the vitality and humanity that form an essential part of History in the Making.

John Jones

Contents

Maps

Britain before the Industrial Revolution

1 Village life

Two Britains

Britain today is an industrial country. Most people's jobs are in some way connected with industry. Over seven million men and women, for example, work in factories. Nearly three million others work in the shops where the goods produced in the factories are sold. The factories upon which we depend are situated in towns, as are the homes of most of the fifty-five million people who live in Britain. (Only a small percentage of the total population live in country areas.)

In 1700, however, Britain was still an agricultural country. A population of five and a half million lived mostly in small villages, working on the land. With a population of 674 000, London was the only sizeable town by modern standards. There was a thriving woollen cloth industry, based on the domestic system (where people worked in their own homes), but factories were virtually unknown. Over the years changes had taken place in the way people lived, but only gradually. A medieval peasant transported by some time machine to the year 1700 would have found much that was familiar.

The difference between the Britain of 1700 and the Britain of today is explained primarily by the Industrial Revolution between about 1770 and 1850 which completely transformed the country. We shall be looking at some of the changes which took place during this period and some problems those changes created. Let us start, however, by taking a closer look at life in Britain before the Industrial Revolution.

Village life in the eighteenth century

For most people in Britain at the beginning of the eighteenth century, life centred upon the village where they lived and worked. A farm labourer spent the whole of his life in or around the village where he was born. Villages were sited where the soil was suitable for growing crops or where sheep could be reared. The majority of people lived, as they had in medieval times, in the south, but villages were small even where

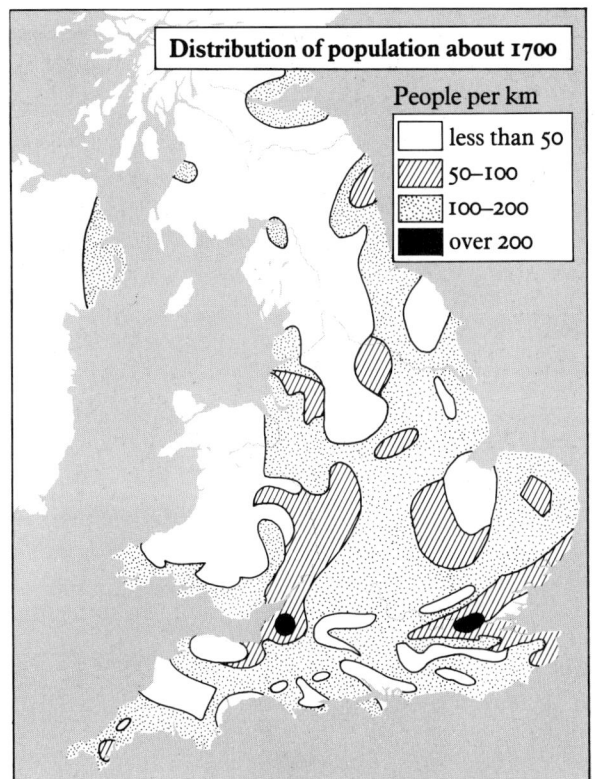

Distribution of population about 1700

People per km

- less than 50
- 50–100
- 100–200
- over 200

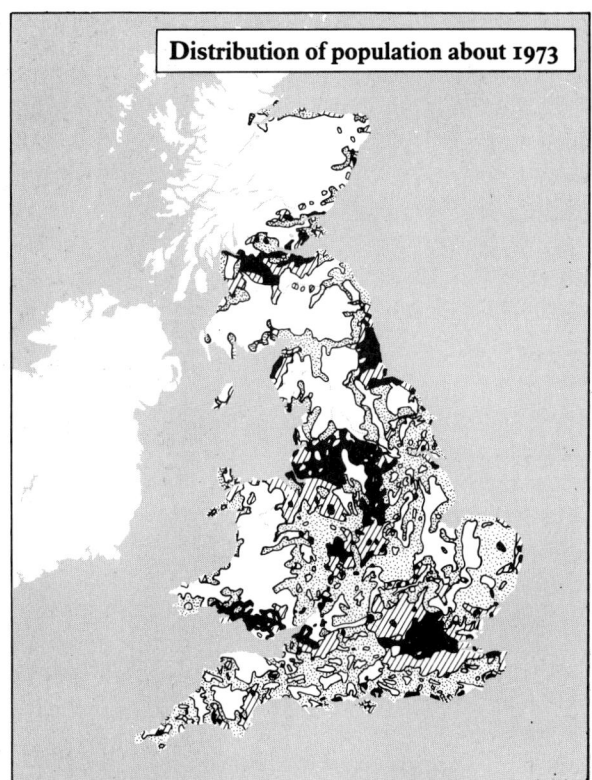

Distribution of population about 1973

the soil was fertile. A typical English farming village consisted of little more than a single street lined with farmhouses and cottages and surrounded on all sides by the lands worked by the villagers. The village church completed the picture.

If one house appeared larger and finer than the others then this belonged to the local squire, or lord of the manor, who owned more land than anybody else in the village. Generally the squire was also the local

The lord of the manor's house might have looked like this

Partridge shooting

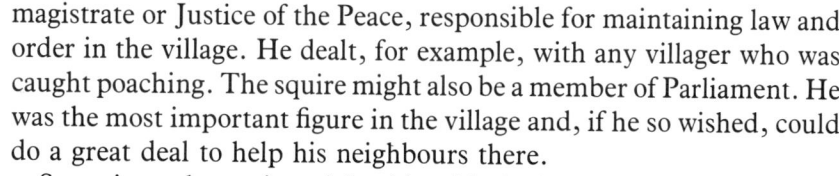

magistrate or Justice of the Peace, responsible for maintaining law and order in the village. He dealt, for example, with any villager who was caught poaching. The squire might also be a member of Parliament. He was the most important figure in the village and, if he so wished, could do a great deal to help his neighbours there.

Sometimes the squire might ride with the local hunt or go shooting, both of which sports were becoming increasingly popular. He would also entertain his friends and important neighbours to lavish meals. We know Squire Custance of Ringland in Norfolk frequently invited the local rector, Parson Woodforde, to dinner because Parson Woodforde kept a careful record of these meals:

We had for dinner a Calf's Head, boiled Fowl and Tongue, a Saddle of Mutton roasted on the Side Table, and a fine Swan roasted with Currant Jelly Sauce for the first Course. The second Course a couple of Wild Fowl called Dun Fowls, Larks, Blamange, Tarts, etc., etc. and a good Desert of Fruit after amongst which was a Damson Cheese.

A rector visiting a farmer's sick wife. When the picture first appeared in 1783 the caption read:
'He came he sympathised with looks of Love,
Pray'd for health on earth, Peace and Joy above;
The greatful farmer would a present make,
The priest refused, for Wife and children's sake.'

The rector was another important person in the village, and besides attending to his religious duties he would supervise the farming of his land. Unlike some clergymen, Parson Woodforde evidently took an active interest in his farm:

1776, 14 Sept. Very busy all day with my barley, did not dine till 5 in the afternoon, my harvest men dined here today, gave them some beef and some plumb pudding and as much liquor as they would drink. This evening finished my harvest, and all carried into the Barn – 8 acres [three hectares].

As they had done for centuries, the tenant farmers provided the rector with a tenth of their produce. These tenths were known as tithes and they could cause a lot of resentment. These lines were published in Stamford in 1831:

There's not a thing upon the farm but shows some kind of fear
When'er he hears the name of Tithes or finds the Parson near; ...
Now, ducks and geese that swim the pond, call help from all around;
When next you meet him, drag him in; – 'tis but a Parson drowned.

The tenant farmers rented their land but other farmers owned theirs. The different holdings varied in size, but most consisted of less than forty hectares and many of less than ten hectares. Some villagers would work as labourers on the larger holdings. At the beginning of the eighteenth century it was still common for these labourers to live in with the farmer and his family. Later, as farmers became more prosperous and less anxious to be constantly rubbing shoulders with their labourers, this custom declined. The cottagers in the village might also work as labourers for part of the year. But they supported themselves mainly by growing vegetables and a little corn on their small plot of land or by grazing a few animals on the village common.

Life was precarious for labourers, cottagers and for the smaller farmers. They simply survived from one year to the next with nothing put by to support them in bad times or in their old age. Many a family was compelled to seek help from the parish authorities because the man of the house had fallen sick. At the end of the century the soaring cost of food brought hardship for many. Here is the case history of a labourer from Presteigne in Radnorshire who had a wife and five children to support:

Earnings 6/- [30p]/week – first relief from parish in 1794-5.
Occasional income from his wife's baking.
Expenses. Half a bushel [18 litres] of wheat per week cost 6/- [30p].
House rent was 30/- [£1.50] a year.
The family breakfasted on 'onion pottage', and had bread or potatoes for dinner and supper. Very rarely was meat or butter eaten.

The open-field system

In 1700 perhaps half the arable land (land on which crops were grown) in England and virtually all that in the Scottish Lowlands still consisted of great open fields undivided by fences and hedges. In a village where this was so, farming would, in many respects, have changed little since medieval times.

Very often the village had three big fields. These were divided into

A labourer's cottage

strips of land separated only by uncultivated ridges known as balks. Each strip probably represented a day's ploughing and where the soil was not too difficult to work would be about a third of a hectare in size. A farmer's holding consisted of a number of strips in each of the fields. Every year crops were grown in two of the fields; wheat might be sown in one and barley in the other. At harvest time each farmer took in that share of the yield grown on his strips. After the crops were harvested, the fields could be used for grazing.

Each year one field was left fallow. Nothing was sown in it. The following year one of the other fields was left fallow and the year after that the remaining field. This was a simple way of ensuring that the soil remained fertile.

In addition to these fields the village had a meadow and a common. The crop of hay which the meadow produced was shared out in the same way as the wheat or barley. This hay was of great importance to the farmers because they had nothing else to feed their animals with during the winter. The village common was not cultivated at all but simply used for grazing animals and keeping the villagers supplied with wood.

In an open-field village nobody could be allowed to differ from the agreed way of farming the land. If a farmer grazed his animals in the open fields before the agreed time then he was taking an unfair advantage over the other farmers in the village and he was fined. 'None shall break the Stuble Feilde on the East side of West Wood with their Sheep before St John daye upon paine for every defeault . . . 3 shillings 4 pence [17p].' This sort of regulation was common in the open-field villages. Each one had its elaborate code of rules and its officials to make sure they were obeyed. One farmer for example, would undertake the job of pinder. This involved rounding up all stray animals and confining them in the pinfold until the owners recovered them, which they could only do on payment of a fine.

The open-field system had worked reasonably well for centuries. It did, however, have its weaknesses. Because all the cattle and sheep in the village grazed together, disease could spread very easily. One Oxfordshire farmer told: 'I have known years when not a single sheep kept in open fields escaped the rot.' Leaving one field fallow every year was an effective but wasteful way of keeping the soil fertile. It meant that in a three-field village only two-thirds of the land was being used in any given year. At the same time many villages did not have enough winter food for their animals and so had to kill some of them in the autumn. Some farmers' holdings were split up into far too many separate pieces of land. An extreme case was that of Richard Derby of Hanslope in Buckinghamshire. His ten and a half hectares were divided up into no less than twenty-four different lots! Finally, although the open-field system did not prevent changes in farming methods, it did not make it easy for a farmer to experiment, because his land was mixed up with everybody else's. It had to be farmed in the same way, unless the village rules were changed.

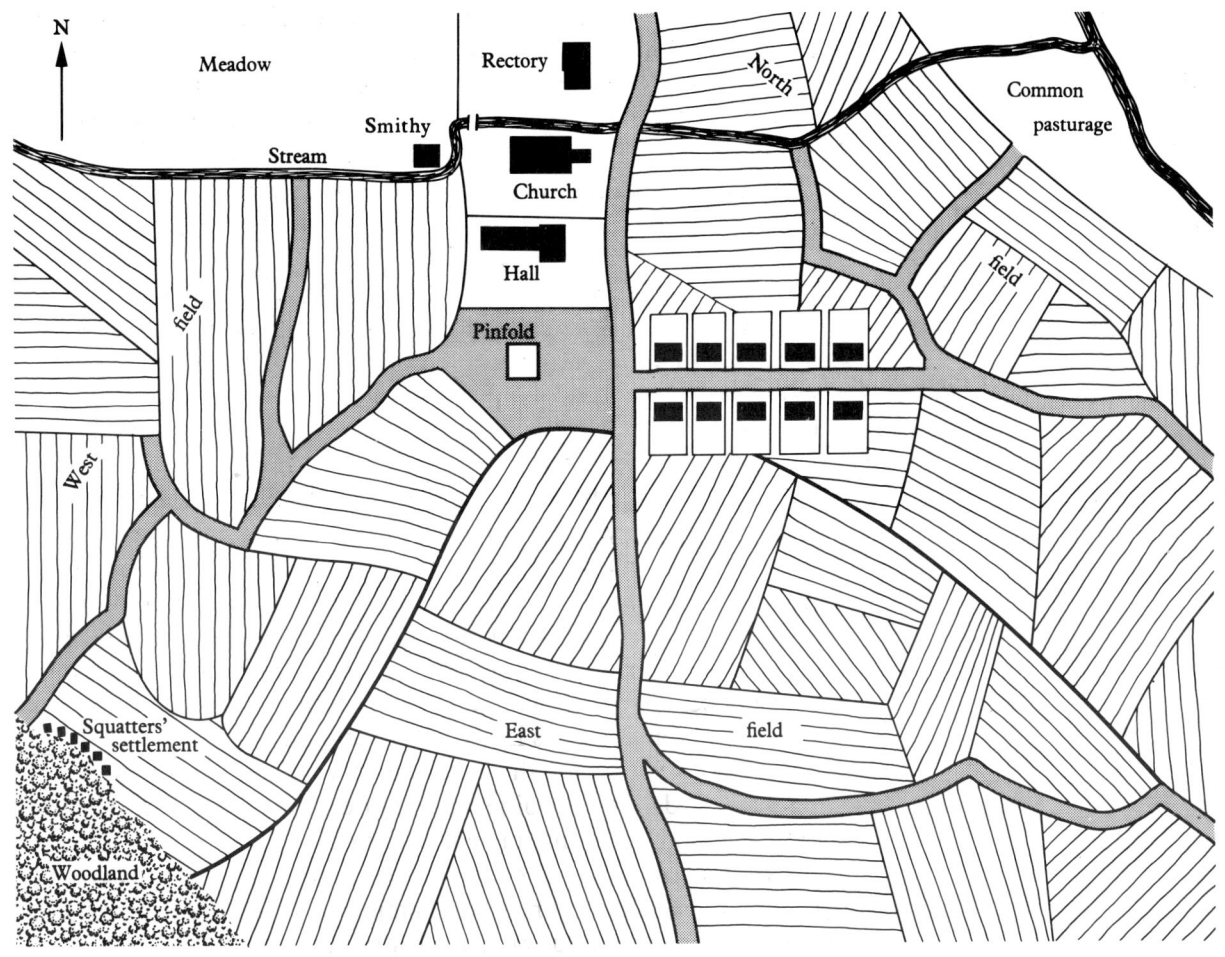

The open field system; a village
before enclosure

These inefficiencies did not matter so long as the land was producing enough food, but in the eighteenth century the population increased more rapidly then ever before. At the end of the century around nine million people lived in England and Wales. These extra people had to be fed and so the land had to produce more food. To do this it had to be farmed more efficiently. The result was an Agricultural Revolution.

The domestic system

As we have seen most people in Britain before the Industrial Revolution worked on the land. Industry did exist, however. Woollen cloth manufactured in this country had been sold abroad for generations.

Most industry was based on the domestic system. Instead of working in factories people worked in their own homes. Woollen cloth was spun and woven in cottages and farmhouses throughout the country. In the West Country, East Anglia and Yorkshire – the main centres of this country's most important industry – spinning and weaving had become full-time occupations. Elsewhere they enabled farmers and labourers and their families to earn some extra money in their spare time.

Daniel Defoe
1660–1731

The organisation of the industry varied from place to place but a general pattern can be traced. The man in charge was the clothier who arranged for the raw wool to be distributed or put out to the spinners to spin it into yarn. The yarn would then be collected and given out to the weavers to weave it into cloth. It took several spinners to supply one weaver with sufficient yarn and as a result the clothiers were compelled to employ spinners from farther and farther afield. The writer Daniel Defoe (1660–1731) commented:

... the weavers of Norwich and of the parts adjacent, and the weavers of Spitalfields in London ... employ almost the whole counties of Cambridge, Bedford, and Hertford; and besides that, as if all this part of England was not sufficient for them they send a very great quantity of wool one hundred and fifty miles by land carriage to the north, as far as Westmorland, to be spun; and the yarn is brought back in the same manner to London and to Norwich.

In this way the clothiers employed hundreds, and sometimes thousands, of workers. Putters-out were employed to travel round distributing and collecting material and paying wages. They did not usually go to the workers' homes but would operate from depots set up throughout the area covered by the clothier. The workers would have to carry their material to and from the barn, inn or shop which served as their local depot. If foreign trade hit bad times the clothier would simply put out less wool and spinners and weavers would be thrown out of work. This was a cause of complaint amongst the workers. The employers complained of the theft of material and of the delays caused by the custom of keeping 'Saint Monday' free for the ale-house.

The organisation of other textile industries, such as cotton and silk, was basically the same. The metal manufacturing industries of South Yorkshire and the West Midlands were based on the activities of, on the one hand, the men who supplied the metal and, on the other, the workers who fashioned the metal into knives, swords, nails and similar products, in small sheds attached to their homes. Some industries, like coal mining or iron smelting, could not be based on the home.

Sir Thomas Lombe's mill at Derby

There were hints of the factory system which was to develop. In the textile industries some processes such as dyeing or fulling were carried out in small mills because they required bulky and expensive equipment. In Yorkshire, wool was manufactured in the clothiers' homes, which came to resemble small factories. Defoe noticed this in Halifax:

... if we knock'd at the door of any of the master manufacturers, we presently saw a house full of lusty fellows, some at the dye-vat, some dressing the cloths, some in the loom, some one thing, some another, all hard at work, and full employed upon the manufacture. . . .

In 1717 Sir Thomas Lombe set up a silk mill at Derby which housed 300 workers. The building was greatly admired and became the pattern for the cotton factories when they were built.

However, until the Industrial Revolution, most industry remained securely based on the home.

Inside the ale-house

Using the evidence: relief of the poor

In Britain today widows, the old and those who are unemployed or unable to work because of sickness are all entitled to financial assistance from the government. During the period covered by this book none of these benefits were available and so bereavement, old age and unemployment made countless families desperately poor. Nor was this all. If a family's financial difficulties coincided with a time when the price of bread was high, because of a bad harvest, then things would be even worse.

In England and Wales the one source of help for the poor, charity apart, was provided by the parish authorities. Each parish was responsible for its own poor and so a needy person could turn for assistance to the parish overseers of the poor. Here are some entries from the Wimbledon parish records:

(1) 25 Oct 1747 Jo Skinner 2 shirts and a coarse sheet.
    26 Dec 1747 Jo Skinner a shirt and a pr of shoes.
    13 Mar 1748 Jo Skinner allowed relief at the discretion of the officers.
    12 Apr 1748 Jo Skinner to be allowed no relief, for it is the opinion of the vestry that he is capable of doing something for a livelihood.
    14 May 1748 Jo Skinner allowed no relief, for it is the opinion of the vestry that (he) is capable of getting (his) own living.
    19 June 1748 Jo Skinner allowed 1s. 6d. [7½p] p.w. pension, 4 lbs [1·8 kilograms] of meat every week, a kettle to boil his meat in, a pr of drawers and 1 pr of stockings.
    25 Sept 1748 Pension list settled for winter. Jo Skinner 1s. 6d.
    29 Jan 1749 Jo Skinner allowed 2 shirts.
    24 Sept 1749 Jo Skinner 1 shirt, but it is to be stopped out of his pension at 6d. [2½p] p.w. for 5 weeks.
    26 Dec 1749 Jo Skinner allowed 1 shirt and 1 pr of shoes.

This type of assistance (known as outdoor relief because the recipient was not required to enter a workhouse) was the most common kind of poor relief. From the 1790s, however, the amount spent on outdoor relief began to shoot up because of the widespread distress caused by bad harvests, fluctuations in trade and an overpopulated countryside. Criticism of outdoor relief grew and in 1832 a Royal Commission was appointed to investigate the whole question of poor relief. Its Report, published in 1834, argued that, as a general rule, people should be discouraged from seeking help. Neighbouring parishes should, therefore, unite to finance the building and running of a communal workhouse into which the poor would have to go if they wished to receive any assistance. These workhouses, the Report stated, should be run along very strict lines.

The Report's recommendations formed the basis of the Poor Law Amendment Act of 1834. The idea of setting the poor to work in workhouses was not new. Numerous workhouses had been built during the course of the eighteenth century. However, the Poor Law Amendment Act sought to encourage the building of more and to introduce a greater degree of harshness into the running of them. Below is a workhouse diet sheet recommended by the Commissioners.

In 1837, the sparseness of workhouse diets prompted Charles Dickens to write one of his most celebrated scenes. Oliver Twist was an orphan in the care of the local workhouse:

(2) Dietary for able-bodied men and women

		Breakfast		Dinner				Supper		
		Bread	Gruel	Cooked Meat	Potatoes	Soup	Suet, or Rice Pudding	Bread	Cheese	Broth
		oz	pints	oz	lbs	pints	oz	oz	oz	pints
Sunday	Men	6	1½	5	½			6		1½
	Women	5	1½	5	½			5		1½
Monday	Men	6	1½			1½		6	2	
	Women	5	1½			1½		5	2	
Tuesday	Men	6	1½	5	½			6		1½
	Women	5	1½	5	½			5		1½
Wednesday	Men	6	1½			1½		6	2	
	Women	5	1½			1½		5	2	
Thursday	Men	6	1½	5	½			6		1½
	Women	5	1½	5	½			5		1½
Friday	Men	6	1½				14	6	2	
	Women	5	1½				12	5	2	
Saturday	Men	6	1½			1½		6	2	
	Women	5	1½			1½		5	2	

Old people of 60 years of age and upwards may be allowed one ounce of tea, five ounces of butter and seven ounces of sugar per week, in lieu of gruel for breakfast, if deemed expedient to make this change.

Children under nine years of age to be dieted at discretion; above nine, to be allowed the same quantities as women.

Sick to be dieted by medical officer.

[Note: one pint = 0·57 litres; one ounce = 31 grams.]

A London workhouse, 1809

Charlie Chaplin in a scene from Shanghaied, *one of the films which made him wealthy and famous*

(3) The evening arrived; the boys took their places. The master, in his cook's uniform, stationed himself at the copper; his pauper assistants ranged themselves behind him; the gruel was served out; and a long grace was said over the short commons. The gruel disappeared; the boys whispered to each other, and winked at Oliver, while his next neighbours nudged him. Child as he was, he was desperate with hunger, and reckless with misery. He rose from the table, and advancing to the master, basin and spoon in hand, said, somewhat alarmed at his own temerity:

'Please, sir, I want some more.'

In his autobiography Charlie Chaplin describes his days in the Lambeth workhouse during the 1890s:

(4) Although we were aware of the shame of going to the workhouse, when Mother told us about it both Sydney and I thought it adventurous and a change from living in one stuffy room. But on that doleful day I didn't realise what was happening until we actually entered the workhouse gate. Then the forlorn bewilderment of it struck me; for there we were made to separate, Mother going in one direction to the women's ward and we in another to the children's.

How well I remember the poignant sadness of that first visiting day; the shock of seeing Mother enter the visiting room garbed in workhouse clothes. How forlorn and embarrassed she looked! In one week she had aged and grown thin, but her face lit up when she saw us. Sydney and I began to weep which made Mother weep, and large tears began to run down her cheeks. Eventually she regained her composure and we sat together on a rough bench, our hands in her lap while she gently patted them. She smiled at our cropped heads and stroked them consolingly, telling us that we would soon all be together again. From her apron she produced a bag of coconut candy which she had bought at the workhouse store with her earnings from crocheting lace cuffs for one of the nurses. After we parted, Sydney kept dolefully repeating how she had aged.

Not surprisingly people were deterred from seeking help.

In practice, however, local officials found that they did not want to commit every person they assisted to the workhouse. Outdoor relief was cheaper, more humane and, in times of heavy unemployment, more practicable. For these reasons it remained the form of assistance given to the majority of paupers. Here is a board of guardians (the body elected to administer poor relief in a Union) at work in 1862 in depressed Lancashire:

(5) A clean, old, decrepit man presented himself.
   'What's brought you here, Joseph?' said the chairman.
   'Why; aw've nought to do – nor nought to tak to.'
   'What's your daughter, Ellen, doing, Joseph?'
   'Hoo's eawt o' wark.'
   'An' what's your wife doing?'
   'Hoo's bin bed-fast aboon five year.'
   The old man was relieved at once; but, as he walked away, he looked hard at his ticket, as if it wasn't exactly the kind of thing; and, turning round, he said, 'Couldn't yo let me be a sweeper i' th' streets, istid, Mr Eccles?'

A clean old woman came up, with a snow-white nightcap on her head.
   'Well, Mary, what do you want?'
   'Aw could like yo to gi mo a bit o' summat, Mr Eccles – for aw need it.'
   'Well, but you've some lodgers, haven't you, Mary?'
   'Yigh, aw've three.'
   'Well; what do they pay you?'
   'They pay'n mo nought. They'n no wark – an' one connot turn 'em eawt.' This was all quite true.
   'Well, but you live with your son, don't you?' continued the chairman.
   'Nay,' replied the old woman, '*he* lives wi' me; an' he's eawt o' wark, too. Aw could like yo to do a bit o' summat for us. We're hard put to't.'
   'Don't you think she would be better in the workhouse?' said one of the guardians.
   'Oh, no,' replied another, 'don't send th' owd woman there. Let her keep her own little place together, if she can.'

Questions and further work

1 Explain the following: (a) open fields (b) balks (c) fallow (d) village common (e) pinfold.
2 Explain the disadvantage of each of the following facts about the open-field system:
   (a) the village animals all grazed together
   (b) one field was left fallow every year
   (c) there was insufficient winter food
   (d) farmers' holdings were divided into separate pieces of land
   (e) all the land in the village had to be farmed in the agreed way.
3 Documents 1, 4 and 5 tell us about people receiving poor relief. Which was written by:
   (a) a person who received help
   (b) a keeper of parish records
   (c) an outside observer?
4 Which document best helps us to understand the feelings of the poor themselves? Explain why.

5 Many people in the eighteenth and nineteenth centuries thought that the poor went hungry because of their own laziness or dishonesty. Was this true of Joseph and Mary in Document 5? Tell in your own words the parts of their stories which support your answer.

6 What was outdoor relief? Why was it more practical than indoor relief in times of economic depression?

7 In 1837 *The Times* reprinted the first four chapters of Dickens's novel *Oliver Twist* as part of its campaign against the Poor Law Amendment Act of 1834. Why do you suppose it did this?
Here are three statements about *Oliver Twist*. Decide whether each of them is true or false and say why.
(a) *Oliver Twist* is of value to the historian because it gives the case history of someone affected by the 1834 Act.
(b) *Oliver Twist* is of value to the historian because it tells what one person living in 1837 thought of the Poor Law Amendment Act.
(c) *Oliver Twist* is of no value to the historian because it is only a story.

8 Documents 3 and 4 describe life in a workhouse. Give two reasons why they cannot be directly compared with one another.

9 Discover if there was a workhouse in your area. If so, the building may still be standing and older people will probably have some stories about the days when it was in use. Their memories will help you to find out how attitudes towards the poor have changed during the last fifty years or so.

A workhouse dinner in the late 1830s as drawn by the artist Phiz

2 Town life

London in the eighteenth century

As it is today, London in the eighteenth century was a combination of many things. It was the capital and seat of government. It was a bustling modern city which already had an efficient postal service: '... you may send a letter from Ratcliffe in the east to the farthest part of West-minster for a penny, and that several times in the same day'. With its parks and gardens, theatres and coffee houses, tea gardens and taverns, London was a place for relaxation and amusement. It was also a thriving port, by far the most important in the country. Below London Bridge, which until 1738 was the only bridge across the Thames, the river was crowded with shipping presenting a spectacle rivalled only by the scenes at Amsterdam. Nor was this all, because London was also a centre of industry. Around the City and south of the river numerous industries had grown up, many of them connected with goods which passed through the port. Many textiles were dyed and printed in London before they were shipped abroad. Certain London-made goods had a special reputation. Her cutlery was said to rival that of Sheffield and her clocks and watches were acclaimed as the best in the world.

On top of all this, London was big. Most other towns were little more than overgrown villages by comparison. To people living at the time it seemed massive, bigger than it actually was. Daniel Defoe wrote: 'Suppose the City of London to contain fifteen hundred thousand people as they tell us it does...'.

The greater part of London's huge population lived in grossly

Covent Garden market

Above; Ranelagh Gardens in Chelsea were famous as a place of entertainment for the well-to-do

Below left: the River Thames at Limehouse

Uxbridge House in Mayfair was built for the Duke of Queensbury

overcrowded conditions. Only the wealthy could afford to live in the elegant houses which lined the streets and squares of Mayfair and other western districts. Elsewhere much of London was far more squalid than in the nineteenth century. The streets were narrow, unpaved and piled with stinking rubbish. Conditions were particularly bad north and east of the City and south of the river. These districts were a maze of alleys and courtyards overflowing with tumbledown houses. Inside the houses whole families frequently crowded into a single room. The very poor lived in cellars or garrets: 'The room occupied is either a deep cellar, almost inaccessible to the light, and admitting of no change of air; or a garret with a low roof and small windows . . .'.

Below: the inside of a London slum. This engraving by William Hogarth was first published in 1747.

Disease spread like wildfire in such conditions. Typhus, smallpox and other diseases claimed thousands of victims every year. Children were particularly vulnerable. During the period 1730–50 only one child in four born in London reached the age of five. Nor was disease the only threat to the wellbeing of London's inhabitants, particularly after dark. Then, anybody making their way along the dimly-lit streets risked falling down an unprotected coal shoot or down some unfenced cellar steps. In the poorer districts people frequently risked being attacked and robbed. In 1730 the shopkeepers and tradesmen of Covent Garden sent a complaint to the Westminster magistrates:

Several people of the most notorious characters and infamously wicked lives and conversation have of late . . . taken up their abode in the parish. . . . There are frequent outcries in the night, fighting, robberies and all sorts of debaucheries committed by them all night long to the great inquietude of his majesty's subjects. . . .

Top right: a thief at work in
Willesden Church

Bottom right: 'Gin Lane'. The
message of Hogarth's famous picture
is horrifyingly clear.

The Gin Age

Violence and crime were encouraged by the availability of cheap gin. The years 1720–51 are known as the Gin Age for at this time cheap gin could be bought almost anywhere in London. In 1726 the Middlesex magistrates reported that: 'All chandlers [the chandler's shop served as a general store for the poor], many tobacconists, and such who sell fruit or herbs in stalls and wheelbarrows sell geneva [gin], and many inferior tradesmen begin now to keep it in their shops for their customers . . .'. By 1750 every fourth house in the parish of Saint Giles was a gin shop.

Because gin was so easily available people literally drank themselves to death. London's death-rate during the Gin Age was higher than at any other time in the century. Moreover, gin was cheap but not cheap enough for many of the poor to be able to drink as they wished without resorting to crime or neglecting to buy food. Faced with starvation many families sought help from the parish authorities. Neglected children supported themselves by begging and petty pilfering.

Improvement came after 1751 when Parliament passed an Act which increased the price of spirits and forbade certain people like grocers and chandlers to sell them. Because gin was no longer so easy to obtain far less was drunk. In 1757 one man wrote: 'We do not see the hundredth part of poor wretches drunk in the streets since the said qualifications as before.' The Gin Age was over.

Changes in town life

In other ways life in London improved in the second half of the eighteenth century. Gradually streets were widened, paved and lit properly. In the process of the street improvement some of the cramped and dilapidated houses disappeared. The houses which replaced them were lighter and healthier. The health of London's inhabitants was also improved by better medical attention. From 1769 onwards dispensaries were set up to provide the poor with free medicine. The dispensary doctors also gave advice. They taught, for example, the value of cleanliness and fresh air.

However, life did not improve for everyone. In 1816 a dispensary doctor working in the parish of Saint Giles discovered cellars in which forty people were living and cellars and rooms which were shared with pigs and asses.

Using the evidence: a map history of Hull

Old maps tell us a lot about the past. The following maps have all been drawn from old maps of Hull. Together they help us to trace the development of a provincial port between about 1350 and 1869.

(1) *Hull in the fourteenth century*

*This map shows the town as it was about fifty years after King Edward I had, in 1299,
granted it the title of Kingston upon Hull.*

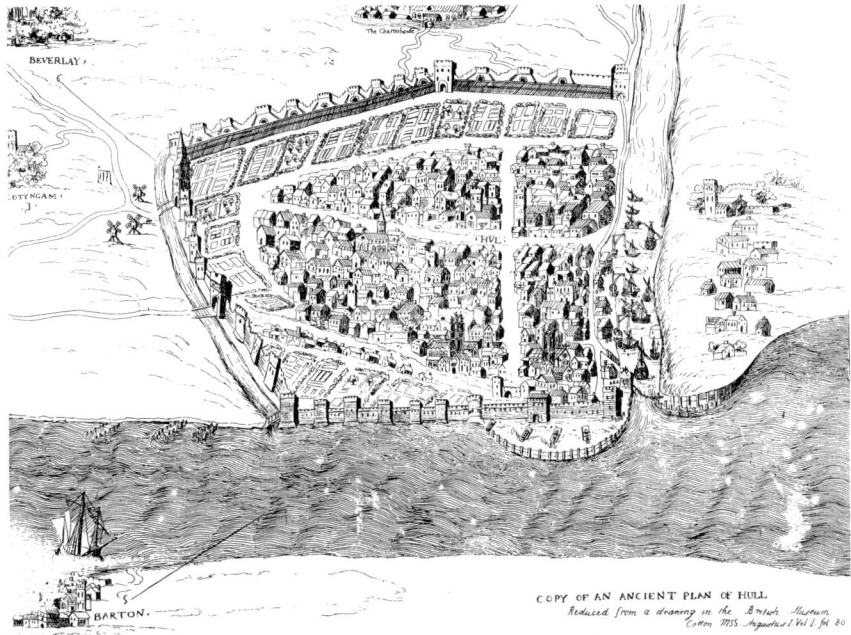

COPY OF AN ANCIENT PLAN OF HULL.
Reduced from a drawing in the British Museum
Cotton MSS. Augustus I Vol I fol 80

(2) *Hull in 1784*

*This map shows Hull's first dock, known to begin with simply as The Dock, which was opened
in 1778. The west walls, shown as still standing, were by now in a state of decay. The
fortification known as the Citadel was built at the end of the seventeenth century and was used
by the army until 1848.*

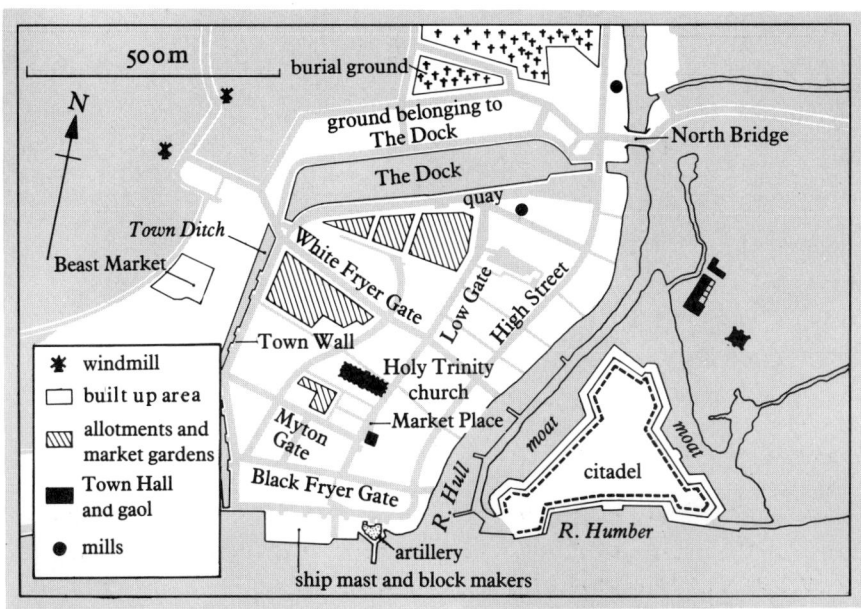

(3) *Hull in 1842*

Hull's first railway, the Hull and Selby line, was opened in 1840.

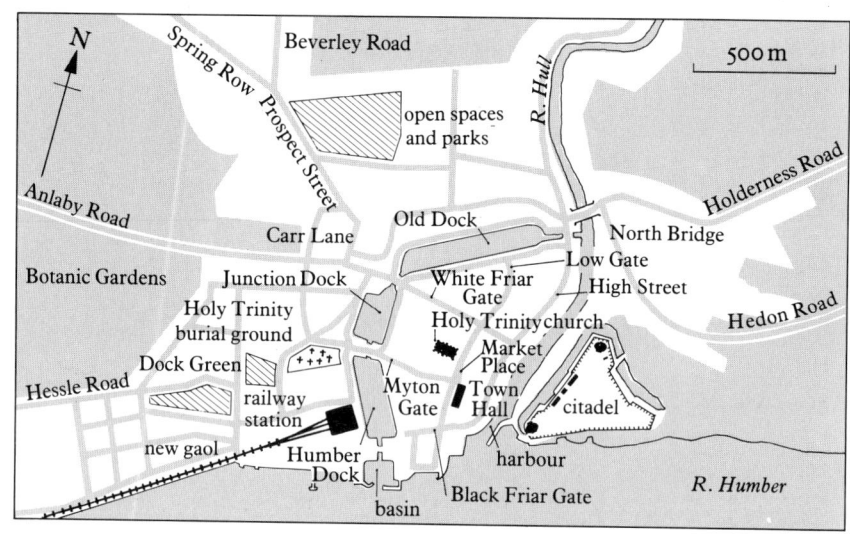

(4) *Hull in 1869*

Railway Dock was opened in 1846, Victoria Dock in 1850 and West Dock in 1869.

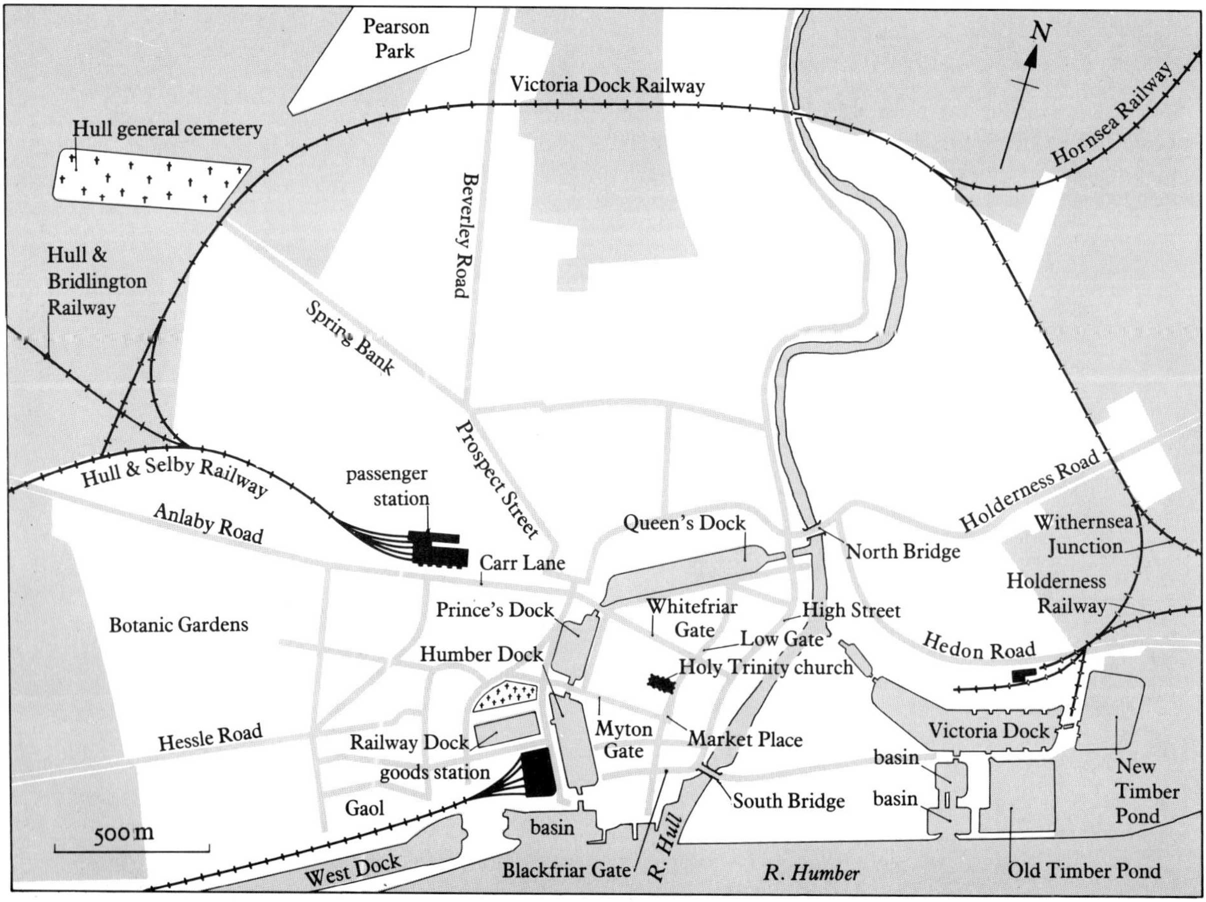

Questions and further work

1 Hull in the fourteenth century was a thriving port. For England the fourteenth century was a time of wars against Scotland and France. Does Map 1 support these two statements?

2 Compare Maps 1 and 2. What has been knocked down to make way for The Dock? Can you suggest why Hull's trade should have been expanding at this time?

3 What do Maps 1 and 2 tell us about Hull's rate of growth between 1350 and 1784?

4 Map 3 shows two new docks, Humber Dock and Junction Dock. In which order do you think they were built? Why do you think The Dock is now known as Old Dock?

5 Hull's first railway, the Hull and Selby line, joined up with the Leeds and Selby line. What do you suppose was the significance of this? What evidence is there on Map 4 that the railways contributed to the continued expansion of Hull's trade?

6 Map 4 shows railway lines to Bridlington, Hornsea and Withernsea. What benefit does this suggest the railways brought to the people of Hull?

7 Queen Victoria and Prince Albert visited Hull in 1854. What evidence of their visit can be seen in Map 4?

8 As Hull grew the town developed first along the main roads and along the river Hull. Why do you suppose this was?

9 Since 1869 Queen's Dock, Prince's Dock, Humber Dock and Railway Dock have all fallen into disuse so that all of Hull's docks are now located along the river Humber, like West Dock and Victoria Dock. Can you suggest why this has happened?

Foreign trade and the Empire

The expansion of foreign trade

Britain's foreign trade increased dramatically during the eighteenth century. Exports and imports both increased. The chief export was textiles. In 1750 woollen cloth was still by far the most important textile made in Britain. By the end of the century, however, as a result of the explosive growth of the Lancashire cotton industry, the export of cotton goods almost equalled that of woollens. Groceries, including sugar, spices and tea, formed the largest group of imports.

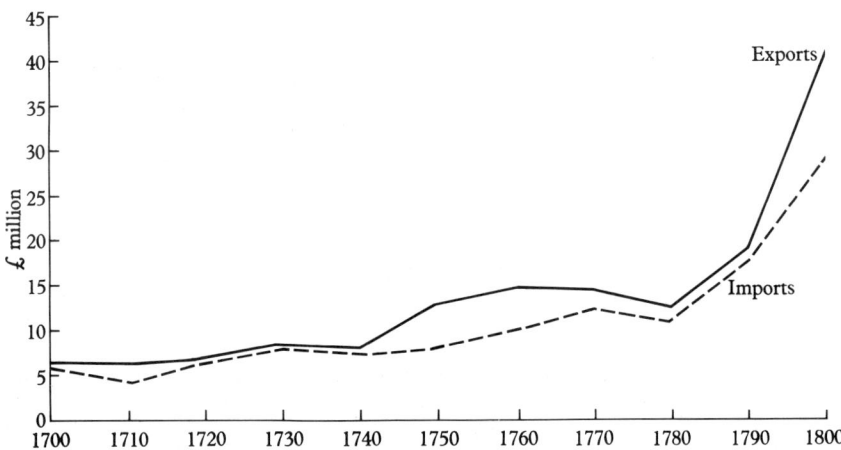

The value of exports and imports 1700–1800

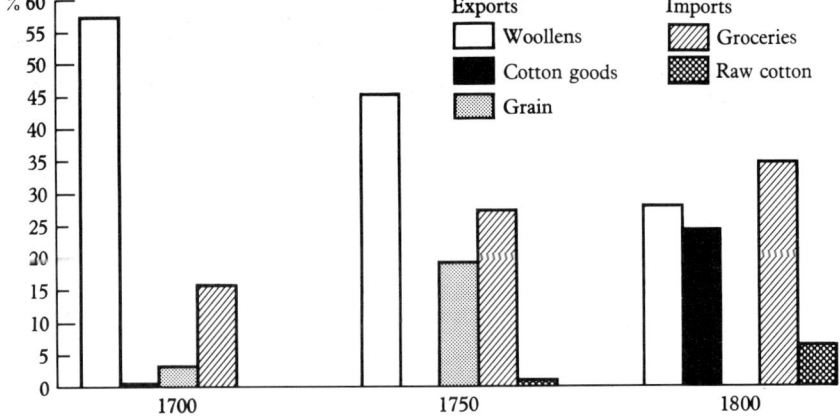

Some important goods traded between 1700–1800. (The figures are given as percentages of total exports and imports for England and Wales.)

Tea drinking achieved wide popularity during the course of the century. An excessively high import duty ensured that much of the tea consumed was brought into the country by smugglers. Parson Woodforde's *Diary* (see chapter 1) includes a number of references to a smuggler called Richard Andrews:

1777 29 March ... Andrews the Smuggler brought me this night about 11 o'clock a bagg of Hyson Tea 6 Pd [2·7 kilos] weight. He frightened us a little by whistling under the Parlour Window just as we were going to bed. I gave him some Geneva and paid him for the tea at 10/6 [52½p] per Pd ... £3. 3. 0 [£3.15].

At this time contraband tea probably accounted for two thirds of all tea imports. Other goods smuggled into the country to avoid import duties included wines, spirits and tobacco, while raw wool was illegally shipped to France to take advantage of the high prices it fetched there. Smuggling took place all along the coast and flourished in remote areas like Cornwall and the Isle of Man. When we look at trade figures for the eighteenth century we should remember that these take account only of goods legally entering and leaving the country. They provide us with only part of the trading picture.

Tea in the drawing-room

Smuggling contraband ashore

The port of Bristol about 1700

In 1700 by far the greater part of Britain's trade was with Europe. This was not the case in 1800. Foreign trade did not simply grow. It changed direction. More and more of the merchants' dealings were with the colonies. Trade with the West Indies and North America increased at a spectacular rate. This brought prosperity to the west coast ports of Glasgow, Whitehaven, Liverpool and Bristol, which were better placed than London for the Atlantic trade. Liverpool, in particular, became an important trade centre. Its population increased from around 6000 in 1700 to over 80 000 by the end of the century.

The prosperity of the western ports was based largely on the slave trade. During the eighteenth century it was dominated by British merchants. Slavers set out for West Africa laden with goods such as rum, trinkets and guns. At the trading posts which had grown up along the Slave Coast these goods were exchanged for Negro slaves provided by native rulers and suppliers. Packed with slaves, the ships then sailed across the Atlantic. Many slaves died on the journey. Those who survived were sold to the owners of plantations in the West Indies or on the American mainland. Depending on where the slaves were sold the

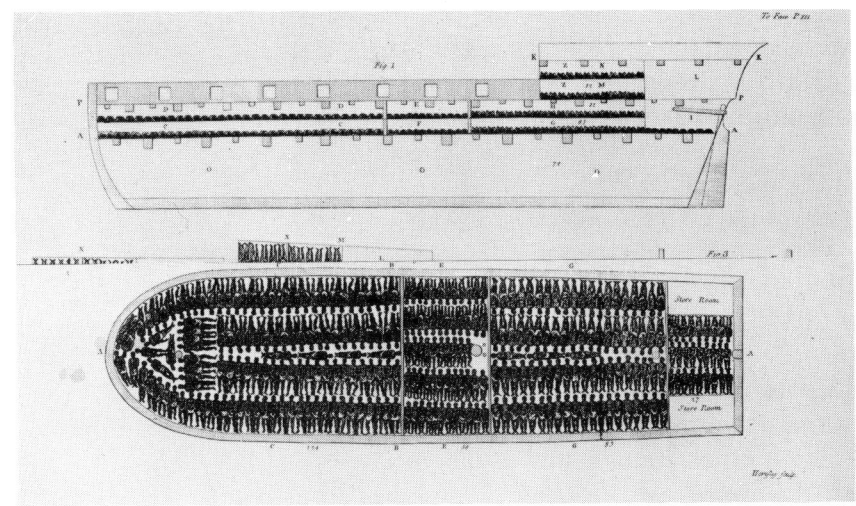

*Thomas Clarkson and other
supporters of Wilberforce's campaign
to abolish the slave trade prepared
this diagram of a slave ship in 1789*

ships were then filled with sugar, rum or tobacco before returning home to complete the third side of the triangular trade.

The slave trade involved much cruelty. It was also highly profitable. Slaves were sold in the West Indies for roughly five times what they had cost on the African coast. The journey may have been long (the round trip took between nine and twelve months) but from the merchants' point of view it was very worthwhile.

Foreign trade and the government

The government took a great interest in foreign trade. It wanted Britain to become wealthier and therefore more powerful and its trading policies were designed to bring this about.

The most important aim was to ensure that the goods leaving the country were worth more than the goods coming in (that is, to create a favourable balance of trade). As a general rule, therefore, imports were discouraged by increasing import duties, while exports were encouraged by reducing export duties. Important home industries, such as the woollen cloth industry, were 'protected' from foreign competition and encouraged to send their products overseas. (The export of raw wool was banned so that foreign manufacturers of woollen cloth were not given raw materials which would help them compete with British manufacturers.)

The government was also anxious that wherever possible goods should be carried in British-owned ships. This was not simply a question of wanting British merchants to prosper. In time of war merchant ships and seamen were called upon to assist the Royal Navy, and therefore the larger the reserve of merchant ships the more secure were the country's defences. The Navigation Acts, passed in 1651 and 1660, were designed to increase Britain's share of the carrying trade. They were aimed principally against the Dutch who, as late as 1728, were described by Daniel Defoe as 'the Carryers of the World'. The

Acts stated that goods coming into this country were to be carried either in British ships or in ships belonging to the country where the goods came from. The 1660 Act listed the goods to which this ruling applied. The list included many items from Europe, such as timber and naval stores from the Baltic, and the important colonial products, such as West Indian sugar and Virginian tobacco.

A further restriction was placed on the colonial goods listed. They could only be exported to Britain. The goods might then be re-exported to other countries but Britain was to have first claim upon the products of her colonies and was to act as middleman between the colonies and any other country which bought their produce.

In the eyes of the government Britain's colonies had an important role to play in helping the mother country to prosper. They could supply Britain with raw materials she did not possess and they could buy British-made goods. Many restrictions were placed on the colonies to ensure that Britain derived the maximum benefit from her overseas possessions. These restrictions were not always effective. In 1699, for example, the Board of Trade reported that: '. . . New England and other northern colonies have applied themselves too much, besides other things, to the improvement of woollen manufactures amongst themselves.' It was thought undesirable that any of the colonies should produce goods which might compete with British goods. The same year, therefore, an Act was passed which banned the export of woollen manufactured goods from the American colonies and even the transportation of such goods from one colony to another. The Act proved difficult to enforce and woollen manufacturing continued in the American colonies.

The clash of empires

In the course of the eighteenth century Britain became the most prosperous trading nation in the world. Her most serious commercial rival was France. At the beginning of the century both countries held possessions in North America and the West Indies and controlled trading posts in West Africa and India. Both saw these possessions as vital to their prosperity. A bitter struggle for supremacy overseas developed as each country sought to ruin the other's trading position by attacking the rival colonies. The struggle reached its height during the Seven Years War (1756–63). This was a triumph for Britain and left her in control of the most important of the European overseas empires.

During this war British and French forces clashed in each of the four areas mentioned above, but nowhere was Britain more dramatically successful than in North America. The map shows the areas of French and British influence in North America in 1756. New France, as Canada was known, was thinly populated. It had only a population of 55 000 whereas there were one and a half million settlers in the Thirteen Colonies.

Fighting between the British and the French had been going on for

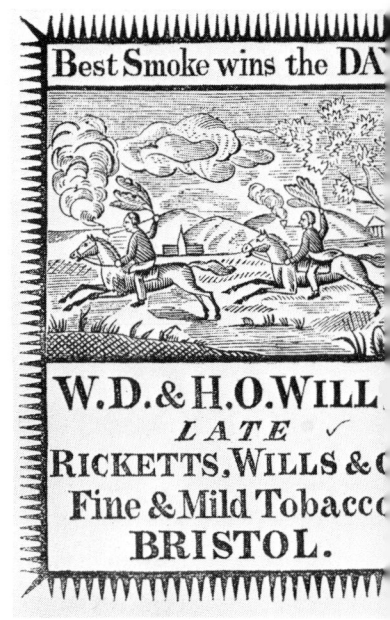

A nineteenth-century tobacco label. North American Indians smoked tobacco in long-stemmed pipes. The habit reached Europe in the sixteenth century and Virginian tobacco became one of Britain's main imports.

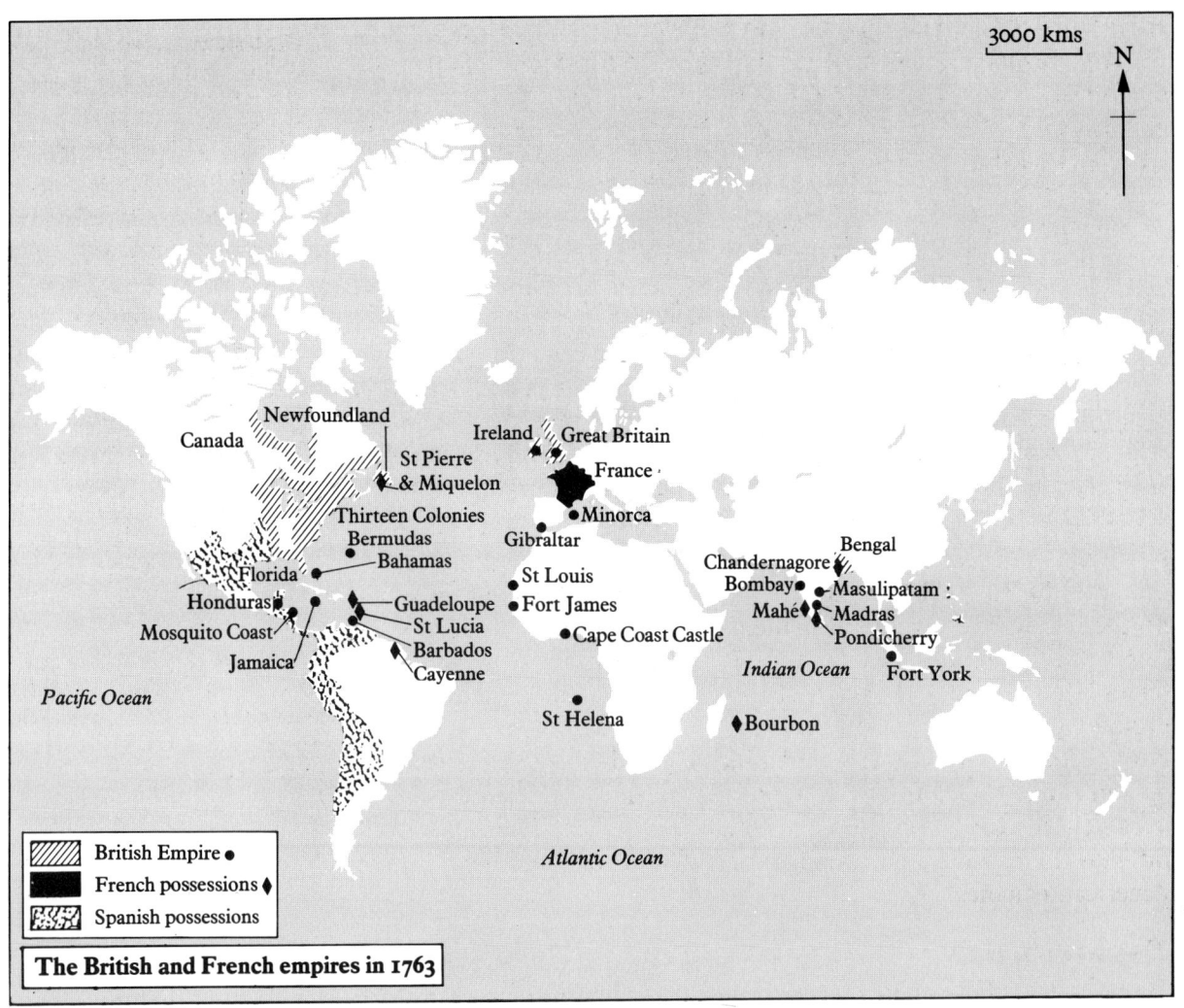

3000 kms

N

Newfoundland
Canada
St Pierre
& Miquelon
Ireland   Great Britain
France
Minorca
Thirteen Colonies
Bermudas   Gibraltar
Bahamas
Bengal
Chandernagore
Bombay   Masulipatam
Florida   St Louis   Mahé   Madras
Honduras   Fort James   Pondicherry
Guadeloupe
Mosquito Coast   St Lucia   Cape Coast Castle   Fort York
Jamaica   Barbados   Indian Ocean
Cayenne
Pacific Ocean

St Helena   Bourbon

Atlantic Ocean

///// British Empire •
■■ French possessions ♦
▨▨ Spanish possessions

The British and French empires in 1763

two years by the time war was officially declared in 1756. The French were moving down the River Ohio in an attempt to link up with the French settlements above New Orleans. As they moved southwards they constructed forts. Fort Duquesne for example, was built in 1753. If the French carried out their plan the settlers in the Thirteen Colonies would be unable to advance any farther westwards and this they wished to do. The people of Virginia, in particular, were anxious to move into the fertile lands of the Ohio valley. Clashes followed in which the French were supported by the native Indians.

With Britain and France officially at war, William Pitt, who directed Britain's war effort between 1757 and 1761, decided that Britain should take the whole of Canada. In this way the French threat would be dealt with once and for all, and Britain would benefit from Canada's fish and fur trades and valuable supplies of naval stores.

Pitt's plan was to use the navy to blockade the French home ports and so prevent the French from sending reinforcements across the Atlantic.

A British infantry soldier

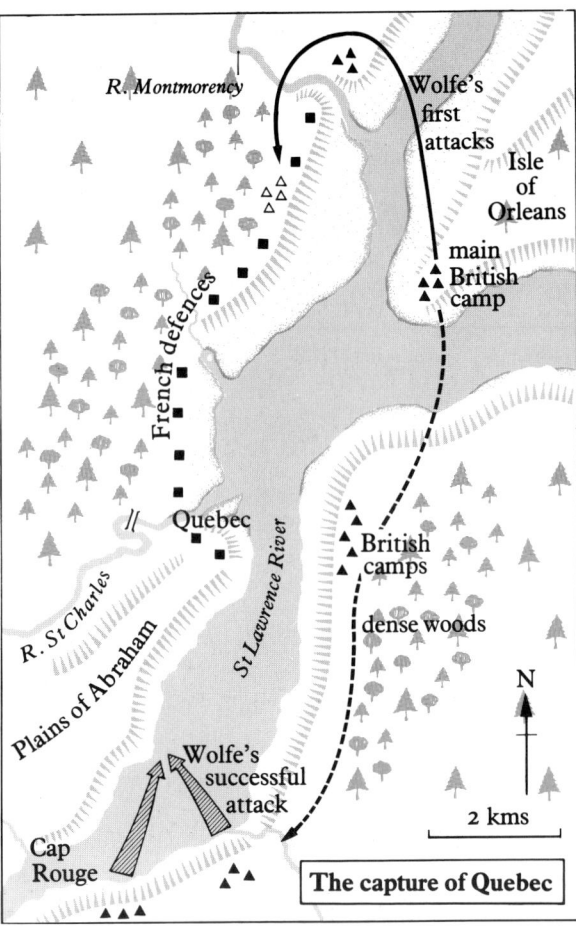

The capture of Quebec

At the same time about 20 000 British regulars were dispatched to strengthen the colonial volunteer forces. This ensured that the French were considerably outnumbered. Then, in 1758, a threefold attack was launched against Louisburg, Fort Duquesne and Fort Ticonderoga. In July, after a seven-week siege, Louisburg fell, opening the route into the St Lawrence. By November Fort Duquesne was in the hands of the British (who renamed it Pittsburgh). In spite of a convincing French victory at Ticonderoga in July the French presence in Canada was restricted at the end of the year to the St Lawrence Valley.

The capture of Quebec, 1759

The British could now strike at the heart of this presence. In June 1759 a British armada of some two hundred transport ships and warships entered the St Lawrence carrying an army of 8500 troops under the command of Major-General James Wolfe. Wolfe's orders were to take Quebec.

Rocks and dangerous currents made the St Lawrence extremely treacherous and in preparation for this expedition a young naval officer called James Cook had been sent to make a thorough survey of the river.

Following the course charted by him the fleet reached the Island of Orleans, just below Quebec, without suffering a single mishap. There the British made their camp.

The capture of Quebec, 13 September, 1759

The task now facing the young Major-General (Wolfe was only thirty-two) was formidable. Quebec was built on a cliff which jutted out into the St Lawrence river. Stretching fourteen or fifteen kilometres to the west were steep cliffs, the summits of which were called the Plains of Abraham. The shore to the east was very strongly defended. The bulk of the French troops were deployed here and a line of batteries extended to the Montmorency river.

The cliffs seemed to rule out the west and so Wolfe's first attacks were to the east. They failed. On 20 August Wolfe, who suffered from continual ill-health, fell sick. He begged his doctor to: 'make me up so that I may be without pain for a few days and able to do my duty, that is all I want'. By now time was running short because the St Lawrence would soon begin to freeze. It was in this situation that Wolfe decided to attempt to scale the cliffs to the west of the city.

Early in September Wolfe moved a large number of his troops upstream and stationed them on the south bank of the St Lawrence.

Marquis de Montcalm
1712–59

During the night of the 12th and 13th about 4500 troops were silently ferried across the river. They were landed at a small cove about three kilometres west of Quebec from where they climbed a steep path which led to the cliff top. By 6 a.m. on the morning of the 13th Wolfe's army was drawn up in battle formation on the Plains of Abraham.

The French were taken completely unawares. Montcalm, the French commanding officer, had expected Wolfe to launch another assault east of Quebec. As soon as he realised what had happened he moved his troops across the St Charles river and positioned them between Wolfe and the city of Quebec. Soon after 10 a.m. he decided to attack without waiting for reinforcements. The British lines held their fire until the French had advanced to within forty metres. Then Wolfe gave the order and two volleys were discharged which destroyed the French lines. The French fled the field with the exultant British in pursuit. The battle, which claimed both Wolfe and Montcalm among its victims, had lasted less than ten minutes.

The British were now able to enter Quebec. The following year they took Montreal and so completed the conquest of Canada. Nor was this all. When peace was made at Paris in 1763 France not only accepted the loss of Canada, she also abandoned her claims to the lands east and west of the Mississippi. With Spain now her only European rival in the area, Britain was clearly the dominant power in North America.

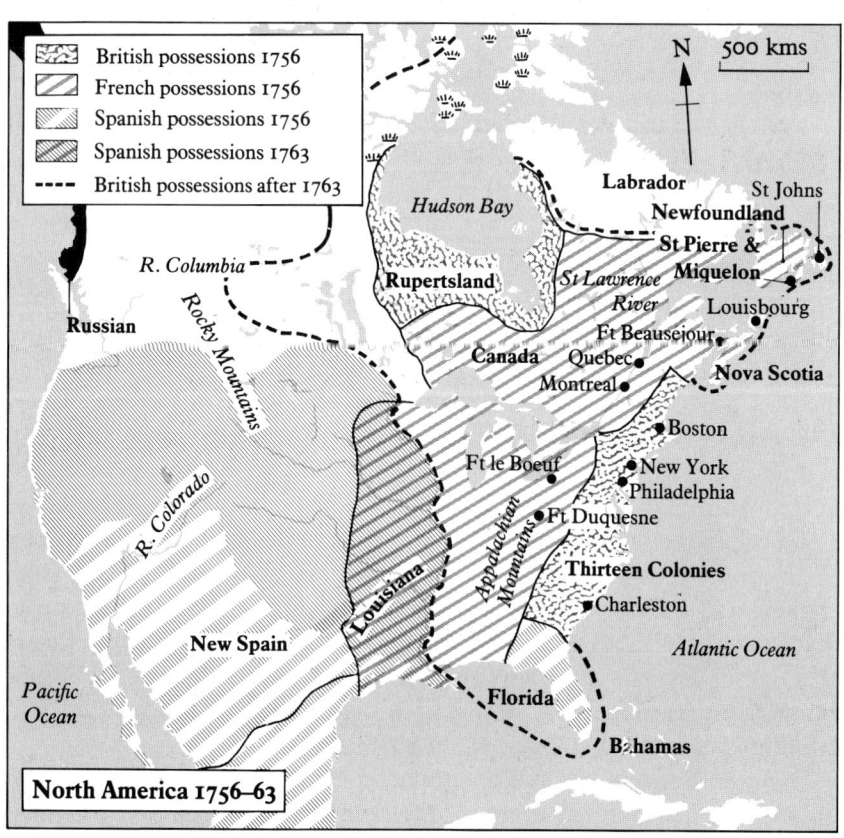

| British possessions 1756 |
| French possessions 1756 |
| Spanish possessions 1756 |
| Spanish possessions 1763 |
| British possessions after 1763 |

North America 1756–63

TO BE SOLD on board the Ship *Bance-Ysland*, on tuefday the 6th of *May* next, at *Afhley-Ferry*; a choice cargo of about 250 fine healthy

NEGROES,

juft arrived from the Windward & Rice Coaft. —The utmoft care has already been taken, and fhall be continued, to keep them free from the leaft danger of being infected with the SMALL-POX, no boat having been on board, and all other communication with people from *Charles-Town* prevented.

Auftin, Laurens, & Appleby.

N. B. Full one Half of the above Negroes have had the SMALL-POX in their own Country.

An eighteenth-century advertisement for a cargo of slaves to be sold in South Carolina

Using the evidence: slavery and the slave trade

Olandah Equiano was born in 1745 in the interior of what is now Nigeria. At the age of ten he was kidnapped by local raiders, taken to the coast and sold to white slave traders bound for the West Indies. After eleven years of slavery in the West Indies and America he purchased his freedom and subsequently described his experiences in a book published in 1789; this was called *The Interesting Narrative of the Life of Olandah Equiano, or Gustavus Vassa, the African.*

Here he describes how he felt when he was first taken on board the slave ship:

(1) The first object which saluted my eyes when I arrived on the coast was the sea, and a slave ship which was then riding at anchor and waiting for its cargo. These filled me with astonishment, which was soon converted into terror when I was carried on board. I was immediately handled and tossed up to see if I were sound by some of the crew, and I was now persuaded that I had gotten into a world of bad spirits and that they were

Slaves planting sugar cane

going to kill me. Their complexions too differing so much from ours, their long hair and the language they spoke (which was very different from any I had ever heard) united to confirm me in this belief. . . . When I looked round the ship too and saw a large furnace or copper boiling and a multitude of black people of every description chained together, every one of their countenances expressing dejection and sorrow, I no longer doubted of my fate; and quite overpowered with horror and anguish, I fell motionless on the deck and fainted.

As a slave Equiano appears to have been relatively fortunate with his masters. He escaped the brutal treatment inflicted on many of his brethren:

(2) It was very common in several of the islands, particularly in St Kitts,

for the slaves to be branded with the initial letters of their master's name, and a load of heavy iron hooks hung about their necks. Indeed on the most trifling occasions they were loaded with chains, and often instruments of torture were added. The iron muzzle, thumbscrews, etc., are so well known as not to need a description, and were sometimes applied for the slightest faults. I have seen a Negro beaten till some of his bones were broken for even letting a pot boil over. . . .

Jamaican slaves being punished in a house of correction

Whether Britain should continue to sanction slavery and the slave trade was one of the great issues of the eighteenth and early nineteenth centuries. Those in favour of slavery stressed the commercial advantages it brought (Document 3) but also frequently emphasised that it benefited the Negro slaves themselves (Document 4 and Illustration 5).

...host approved Judges of the Commercial Interests of these King-
[...]e been of the opinion that our West India and African Trades are
the most nationally beneficial of any we carry on. It is also allowed on all
Hands that the Trade to Africa is the Branch which renders our American
Colonies and Plantations so advantageous to Great Britain; that Traffic
only affording our Planters a constant supply of Negro Servants for the
Culture of their Lands in the Produce of Sugars, Tobacco, Rice, Rum,
Cotton, Fustick [yellow dye], Pimento [Jamaica pepper] and all our other
Plantation Produce....

(4) And now the happy Negro homeward goes,
　　Contented as the honey-laden bee,
　　Because his heart no earthly sorrow knows.
　　Deluded sons of Britain! Would that ye,
　　The proud, the brave, the omnipotent[1], the free,
　　Beheld him seated at his ample meal,
　　With all his children smiling at his knee!
　　Then would ye know the nature of his weal[2],
　　And honestly confirm, the truth of this appeal.

　　　　　　　　　The Jamaica Monthly Magazine (October 1833)

1 all-powerful　　　　　　　　2 lot/situation

Right: inside the boiling house on a sugar plantation

(5) Slavery and freedom – British poverty and West Indian slavery. A cartoon from The Looking Glass *of 1832.*

The opponents of slavery and the slave trade made much of the cruelties of the slave trader and the plantation owner. They also attacked the basic inhumanity of making a man a slave:

(6) It cannot be that either War, or contract, can give any man such a property in another as he has in his sheep and oxen. Much less is it possible, that any child of man should ever be born a slave. Liberty is the right of every human creature, as soon as he breathes the vital air. And no human law can deprive him of that right, which he derives from the law of nature.

John Wesley, *Thoughts upon Slavery* (1775)

People also began to question the assumption that the plantation colonies were essential to Britain's prosperity. Here, for example, Adam Smith points out how expensive it was for Britain to defend these colonies.

(7) The expense of the ordinary peace establishment of the colonies amounted, before the commencement of the present disturbances [i.e. the American War of Independence], to the pay of twenty regiments of foot; . . . to the expense of a very considerable naval force which was constantly kept up, in order to guard, from the smuggling vessels of other nations, the immense coast of North America, and that of our West Indian islands. The

'Am I not a man and a brother?' A medallion produced in 1787.

William Wilberforce
1759–1833

whole expense of this peace establishment was a charge upon the revenue of Great Britain, and was, at the same time, the smallest part of what the dominion of the colonies has cost the mother country. . . . We must add to it, in particular, the whole expense of the late war, and a great part of the war which preceded it [i.e. the Seven Years War and the War of the Spanish Succession].

The Wealth of Nations (1776)

Abolition

Two years before Equiano published his book, William Wilberforce and other abolitionists formed the Society for the Abolition of the Slave Trade. Their well-organised campaign led to Parliament declaring the British slave trade illegal in 1807. Twenty-six years later slavery was abolished in the British Empire.

Questions and further work

1 Write an account of the taking of Quebec from the point of view of a soldier in Wolfe's army.
2 What in Document 1 shows that Equiano was not familiar with white men before his capture? What impression was made on him by his treatment at their hands?
3 Documents 2 and 4 express opposite views on the life of a slave in the West Indies. Document 2 deals with events on St Kitts and Document 4 with life in Jamaica. Find two other differences between the documents. Which of these differences explains best the contradiction between the two documents?
4 Both Equiano and John Wesley (Document 6) condemned slavery but for different reasons. Explain why each man felt so strongly.
5 Explain the link between slavery and British trade, illustrating your answer with a map.
6 Study Illustration 5. What is the cartoonist saying to those who attacked slavery? Does a cartoon have any advantages over the written word as a way of putting over a point of view?
7 Study the documents then copy and complete the following table.

Document	What it says in favour of slavery	Valid/not valid as an argument
3		
4		
5		

Which do you find the strongest argument?
8 Write a letter from a slave trader or a plantation owner justifying the slave trade and slavery. How might an abolitionist have replied?

The eighteenth century

4 Prussia and Frederick the Great

Europe in the eighteenth century

For the majority of people living in Europe in the eighteenth century the boundaries between the different states meant little. What concerned them was the village where they lived and worked and the area round about it. They were likely to spend the whole of their lives in the same village. Because of this, regional differences remained very striking. Depending on where they lived people spoke and dressed in very different ways.

Wherever they lived, however, most people worked on the land. Outside Britain industry made little progress during the eighteenth century and continued to rely upon the domestic worker. Only in Britain, where Manchester's population had reached 75 000 by 1801, was the purely industrial town beginning to emerge. Elsewhere in Europe the only towns of any size, and there were few of them, were the seaports and the capital cities.

The majority of people were peasants who worked enough land to survive on but had little or nothing put by to help them when disaster struck in the form of a bad harvest. In some countries most, if not all, of the peasants were free men. In France for example, serfdom was confined to a few eastern parts of the country. In countries such as Russia, Prussia and Austria many peasants were still legally bound to their lord. In practical terms this meant that they had to work for part of the year on their lord's lands and that in numerous other ways their lives were subject to strict rules and regulations. They were not free, for example, to move or even to marry without their lord's consent.

Throughout Europe small classes of landowners owned much of the land worked by the peasant. Almost everywhere these landowners had special privileges such as being exempt from certain taxes or from what were considered degrading forms of punishment such as hanging. In return for their privileges many landowners served as army officers. Others took government jobs either in the capital or in their own

Carpenters in their workshop. Only the wealthy would be able to afford the fine furniture made by craftsmen like these.

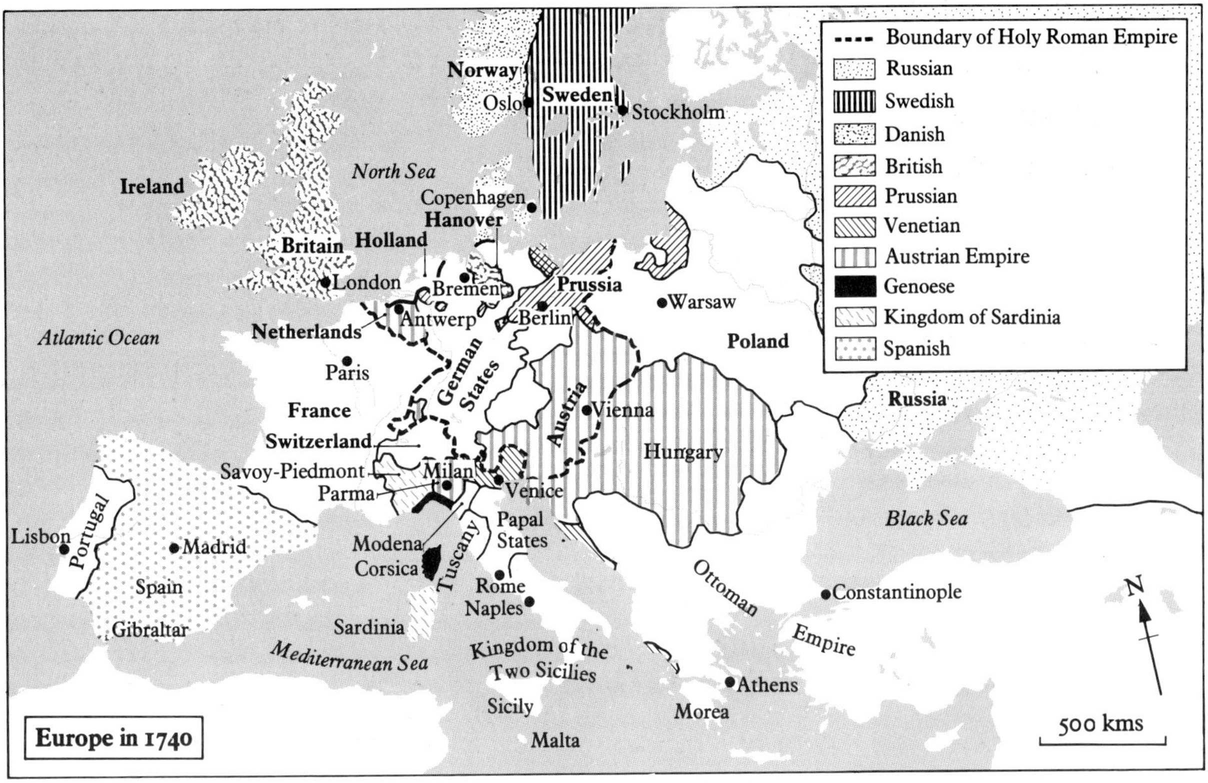

Map

Europe in 1740

Legend:
- ---- Boundary of Holy Roman Empire
- Russian
- Swedish
- Danish
- British
- Prussian
- Venetian
- Austrian Empire
- Genoese
- Kingdom of Sardinia
- Spanish

Labels on map: Norway, Oslo, Sweden, Stockholm, North Sea, Ireland, Copenhagen, Hanover, Britain, Holland, London, Bremen, Antwerp, Prussia, Berlin, Warsaw, Netherlands, Atlantic Ocean, Paris, Poland, France, German States, Russia, Switzerland, Vienna, Savoy-Piedmont, Parma, Milan, Austria, Hungary, Venice, Papal States, Black Sea, Lisbon, Portugal, Madrid, Modena, Corsica, Tuscany, Spain, Rome, Naples, Ottoman Empire, Constantinople, Gibraltar, Sardinia, Mediterranean Sea, Kingdom of the Two Sicilies, Sicily, Morea, Athens, Malta, 500 kms, N

locality. Their services as soldiers or as administrators were vitally important to the different rulers.

Most European countries were ruled by hereditary monarchs. In Britain the monarch's powers were being reduced by the growing influence of Parliament. Elsewhere, except in one or two countries such as Poland and Sweden, the monarchs remained extremely powerful. A Frenchman who lived at the time of Louis XIV, wrote: 'Consider the prince in his cabinet. From there issue the orders which set in motion together the magistrates and the captains, the citizens and the soldiers, the provinces and the armies by sea and land.' One such powerful monarch was Frederick the Great.

Frederick the Great

Frederick the Great ruled Prussia between 1740 and 1786. It was under his leadership that Prussia finally emerged as a country of major importance.

Until he became king at the age of twenty-eight his life was overshadowed by his constant quarrels with his father, Frederick William I, who flew into violent fits of rage whenever anything happened to displease him. As a child Frederick was beaten for wearing gloves in cold weather. Later his interest in all things French aroused his father's anger. Frederick William hated the French so much that when criminals were executed he had them dressed in French clothes so that

Frederick William I, King of Prussia 1713–40

Frederick as a young boy

Frederick William (seated second from the right) enjoying one of his tobacco evenings. Frederick is sitting next to him.

people would have a horror of such fashions. Because of this hatred it was inevitable that he should be angered by his son's passionate interest in French literature and his attempts to copy French customs. On one occasion he suddenly realised that Frederick had grown his hair and was combing it in the French style. Immediately he hauled him off to a barber and ordered that the offending locks be cut off.

In very many ways the two were quite dissimilar. Frederick William loved hunting and went riding every day. Frederick was forced to take part but he found it a very dull pastime. Frederick William liked to while away the evenings smoking and drinking with a few select friends. Frederick preferred to spend his time reading or playing his flute. Frederick William had a mania for cleanliness. Frederick preferrred to remain dirty.

As time went on Frederick William's evil temper, which probably stemmed from his chronic ill-health, grew even worse. Life in the royal court became practically unbearable and in 1730 Frederick tried to escape with an officer friend called Katte. The attempt failed and both men were placed under arrest. On Frederick William's orders Katte was beheaded outside the window of Frederick's cell and for a time it seemed as though Frederick himself might be executed. Pleas for mercy came from all over Germany and eventually Frederick William relented. Frederick was duly released from the fortress at Küstrin but for some time afterwards he was not allowed to move outside the town.

In 1733 Frederick married a German princess, Elizabeth of Brunswick-Bevern. The match was arranged by his father and Frederick made little or no attempt to disguise his dislike for the unfortunate woman. As time went on he spent less and less time with her and for the greater part of their long married life (Elizabeth survived Frederick) the two led completely separate lives.

Frederick William was in many ways a very effective ruler. When he died in 1740 he left an efficiently governed and financially sound country which possessed a well-equipped and well-trained army of 83 000 men. If he had feared that Frederick did not possess the right qualities to be a strong king he need not have worried. Frederick soon showed that he was quite capable of building upon the foundations laid by his father.

A grenadier in the army of Frederick William

The invasion of Silesia

The first thing he did was to seek the enlargement of his kingdom by invading the Austrian province of Silesia. Frederick wanted Silesia for a number of reasons. It was a rich agricultural region and it contained a thriving linen industry. Its transfer to Prussia would, moreover, greatly strengthen that country's defences in the event of an Austrian attack. When the Austrian ruler, Emperor Charles VI, died a few months after Frederick's accession to the Prussian throne the moment for attack seemed to have arrived, particularly as there was no son to inherit the Austrian throne which passed instead to Charles's twenty-three-year-old daughter, Maria Theresa.

The Prussian invasion of Silesia started a conflict with Austria which was to last on and off for the next twenty-three years. During this period Frederick proved himself to be the greatest military commander of the age. During the Seven Years War Prussia faced the combined armies of Austria, Russia and France and on more than one occasion seemed to be on the verge of total defeat. In 1760, for instance, Frederick wrote: 'Everything seems as black as if I were at the bottom of the tomb.' Time and again, however, Frederick's skill enabled the Prussian forces to fend off the advancing armies. At last the situation eased in 1762 when Russia's new ruler, Tsar Peter III, decided to abandon his allies. When

(After 1759, Britain and France took little part in the European war.)

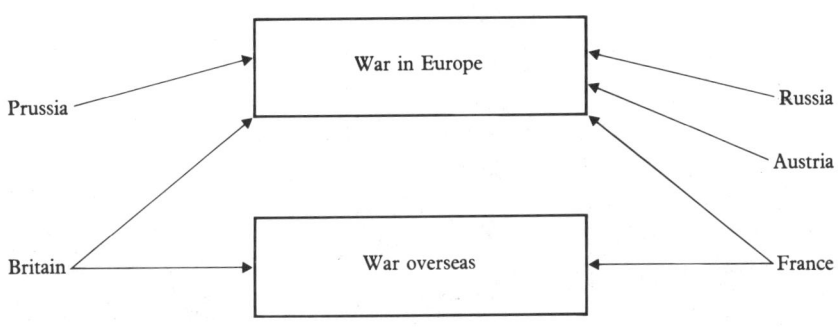

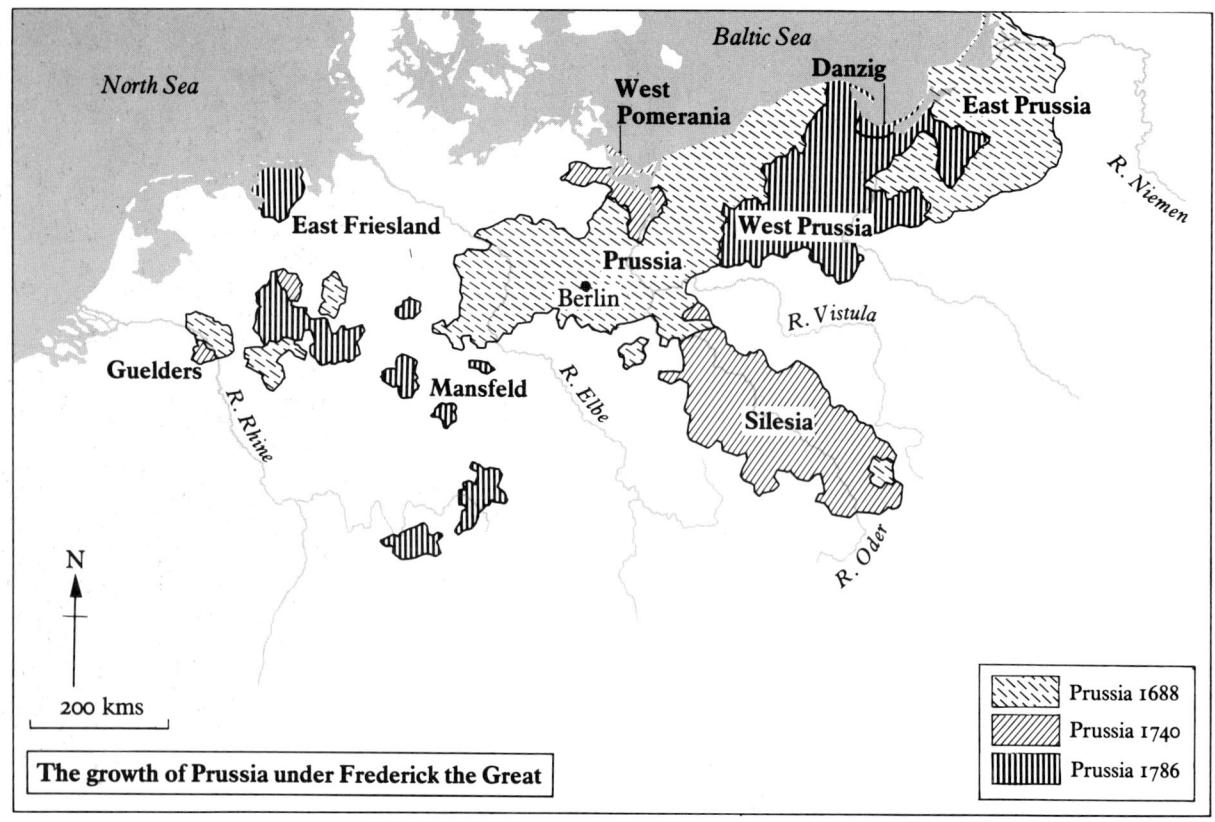

The growth of Prussia under Frederick the Great

Prussia 1688
Prussia 1740
Prussia 1786

peace was made in 1763 not only was Prussia intact but she retained Silesia.

During these years Frederick also showed himself to be utterly ruthless in pursuing Prussian interests. If Prussia needed Silesia then Prussia should take it, according to Frederick, and the fact that it belonged to Austria did not matter. Likewise if it was in Prussia's interests to abandon her allies and make peace with Austria then she should do this. By backing out of the War of the Austrian Succession (1740–48) no less than three times Frederick quickly earned an unrivalled reputation for unscrupulous and untrustworthy behaviour.

Prussia had won Silesia. More than this she was now respected as one of the strongest countries in Europe. Military success, however, had cost Prussia dear. Frederick reckoned that a ninth of the population had been lost and in 1763 much of the country lay devastated by the war.

Nine years later, through clever diplomacy, Frederick obtained a further considerable slice of territory for Prussia in what is known as the First Partition of Poland. After 1763, however, he was not interested in further military conquest and he set about repairing the damage caused by his wars. Peasants were given money and supplies in an effort to speed up the revival of agriculture, and the expansion of trade and industry was encouraged by such measures as imposing import duties on foreign manufactured goods.

Right: 'The Polish Plumcake'. A cartoon about the first Partition of Poland of 1772. Poland was weak in the eighteenth century and between 1772 and 1795 was divided up by Russia, Austria and Prussia. Catherine the Great of Russia, Joseph II of Austria (co-ruler with his mother Maria Theresa after 1765) and Frederick the Great are shown sitting round the table together with, on the left, Louis XV of France. (France in fact received no territory.)

'Now thank we all our God'. Prussian soldiers sing in thanksgiving after defeating the Austrians at Leuthen in 1757.

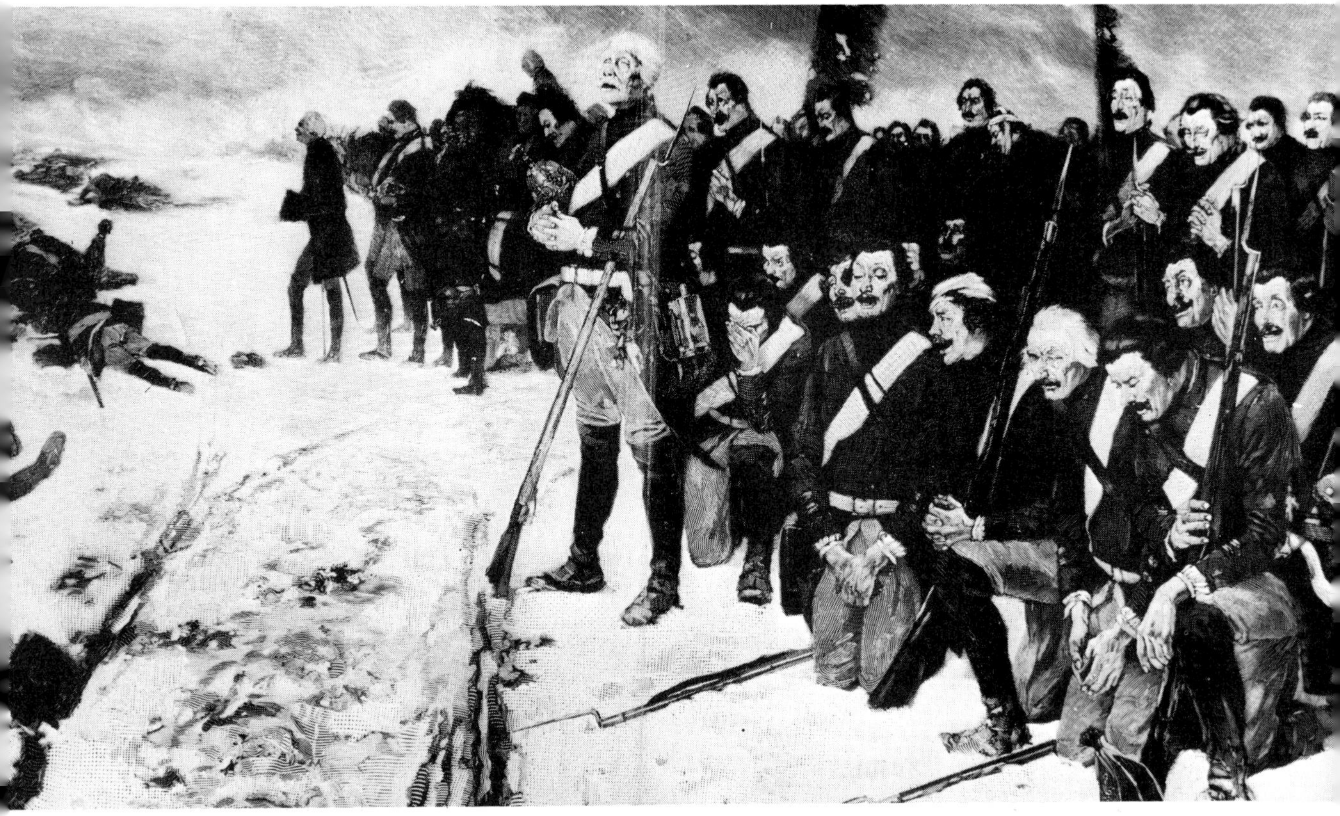

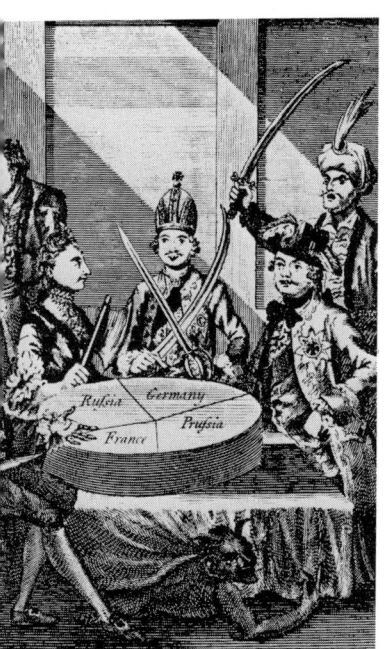

The enlightened despot

At home Frederick ruled firmly. However, he was familiar with the works of Voltaire and the other enlightened writers who argued that a king's job was to increase the happiness of his people by for example, ridding his country of cruelty and unfairness. Frederick is sometimes known as an enlightened despot because he did, to a certain extent, attempt to do this. For instance he abolished torture and retained the death penalty only for the most serious offences. The extensive legal reforms carried out by his Chancellor, Samuel von Cocceji, left Prussia with a fair and efficient system of justice, an achievement of which Frederick was proud: 'One thing is certain. Injustice in the courts has become comparatively rare, the judges are less corrupt, trials shorter and there are fewer cases pending.' Despising religion himself, Frederick was tolerant of all religious faiths. Prussia was a Protestant state but Catholics were allowed to worship freely and indeed were given a magnificent church next door to the royal palace in Berlin.

There were, however, clear and strict limits to Frederick's enlightenment. He would not contemplate any action which might weaken Prussia. He refused for example, to abolish serfdom for fear of offending the nobility. (The nobles or *Junkers* provided officers for the army and made it possible to raise taxes and maintain law and order in the country.) Frederick remained keenly aware of what was practicable.

Sans Souci, Frederick's palace at Potsdam

He also remained a despot, very much in sole command and granting his people no say in the running of their country. To disobey Frederick was to invite imprisonment.

At the same time he did not object to personal criticism. When out riding one day he saw a crowd of people staring at an unflattering picture of himself which had been fastened high up on a wall. Frederick ordered his attendants to lower it. 'They can't see it properly up there,' he said. As he rode away the crowd cheered him.

At the end of his life he seems to have been genuinely popular. He was nicknamed Old Fritz and cheered in the streets as he rode by. A British official in Berlin wrote: 'You have no idea the joy the people express to see the King on horseback . . .'. Not that Frederick was very impressed. He once said: 'Put an old monkey on a horse and they would cheer him the same.'

By now Frederick had become decidedly eccentric. He took little pride in his appearance and always wore the same threadbare blue coat. His palace at Potsdam likewise began to look shabby and neglected. He developed a taste for highly spiced dishes. Only a few weeks before his death he dined on a richly flavoured soup, beef soaked in brandy, eel pie, and cheese spiced with garlic.

After several months of illness Frederick died on 17 August 1786. He was buried next to his father.

Using the evidence: advice to the ruler of Prussia

It was quite common for eighteenth-century rulers to write political documents for the benefit of their successors. In these 'testaments' they would summarise their thoughts on the question of how their country was best governed.

Frederick the Great wrote his in 1752:

(1) *The nobility*
An object of policy of the sovereign of this State is to preserve his noble class; for whatever change may come about, he might perhaps have one which was richer, but never one more brave and more loyal.

A military flogging, a reminder of the strict discipline maintained in Frederick's army

The aged Frederick inspecting his troops

(2) *Foreign policy*

The acquisitions which one makes by the pen are always preferable to those made by the sword. One runs fewer risks, and ruins neither one's purse nor one's army. . . .

If the glory of the State obliges you to draw the sword, see that the thunder and the lightning fall on your enemies at the same time. . . .

It is a grave political fault always to act haughtily, to want to decide everything by force, or, again, always to use softness and suppleness. A man who always follows a uniform conduct is soon penetrated, and one must not be penetrated. If your character is known, your enemies, will say: 'We will do this and that, then he will do that,' and they will not be deceiving themselves, whereas if one changes and varies one's conduct, one misleads them and they deceive themselves on issues which they thought to have foreseen.

(3) *Foreign treaties*

. . . take good care not to place your trust in the number and good faith of your allies; count only on yourself; then you will never deceive yourself, and look on your allies and your treaties only as second strings. A large number of treaties harms more than it helps; conclude few of them, always to the point and of such nature that you have all the advantage from them and involve yourself in the least risks.

(4) *The king's job*

Idleness, self-indulgence, or weakness are the causes which prevent a Prince from working on the noble task of creating the happiness of his peoples. Such sovereigns make themselves so contemptible that they become the butts and laughing-stocks of their contemporaries, and in history books their names are useful only for the dates. They vegetate on thrones that they are unworthy to occupy, absorbed as they are in self-indulgence. A sovereign has not been raised to his high rank, the supreme power has not been conferred on him, to live softly, to grow fat on the substance of the people, to be happy while all others suffer. The sovereign is the first servant of the State. He is well paid, so that he can support the dignity of his quality [dress and behave as a king should]; but it is required of him that he shall work effectively for the good of the State and direct at least the chief affairs with attention.

Questions and further work

1 Find five reasons why Frederick William and Frederick did not get on well with each other.
2 What do you think Frederick meant by his remark 'Put an old monkey on a horse and they would cheer him the same' (see page 52)? What does it reveal about his attitude towards his people?
3 In Document 1 Frederick gives one reason why he is determined to 'preserve his noble class'. What other reasons can you find for him wanting to do this?
4 Read Document 2. What do you think Frederick means by 'The acquisitions which one makes by the pen'? Name one territory he acquired in this way.
5 Explain what Frederick meant by the second paragraph in Document 2. His father had this to say of war:

> I beseech my dear successor in God's name not to start any unjust wars and not to be an aggressor, for God has forbidden unjust wars and one day you will have to give account for every man who has fallen in an unjust war.

How do you think Frederick's father would have regarded the invasion of Silesia in 1740?
6 Read Document 3. What did Frederick mean by 'A large number of treaties harms more than it helps'? How would you advise a ruler considering a treaty with Frederick?
7 Why, according to Document 4, were monarchs not always successful? What does this extract reveal about Frederick's approach to the job of being king?
8 List Frederick's main achievements. Why do you think he became known as Frederick the Great? What criticisms can be made of him?

5 France before the Revolution

Jacques and Marie

The year is 1780. The place is a village somewhere in France. Jacques is now thirty-two years old and he has spent all his life in Petit Moulin. Together with his wife, Marie, and their four children he lives in a small, mud-walled, roughly furnished cottage. He owns a few strips of land in the village's three open fields but the soil is not particularly good and he can't hope to grow enough wheat or rye to support his growing family. For this reason he also works as a part-time labourer for the local *seigneur* or lord of the manor. The family owns one cow. With four children the milk is invaluable and Jacques uses the cow to pull his wooden plough. (Once Jacques had a goat and then he used to hitch the two together.)

Jacques works hard to support his family. So does Marie. She bakes bread and makes soups. She makes clothes for all the family and spins cotton yarn in order to earn a little extra money. She gathers weeds in the nearby wood for their cow and, when she can find the time, helps Jacques in the fields. She has, moreover, been bearing children regularly for the past ten years. (In addition to the four children who have survived one was stillborn and another died in infancy.) The strain of this continuous childbearing is beginning to tell and Marie looks considerably older than her thirty years.

The peasants

Jacques and Marie are imaginary figures. Most French people in the eighteenth century were peasants and many were extremely poor. One reason for this poverty was the heavy burden of taxes.

Village women washing linen

Jacques would for example, pay tithes to the Church, perhaps to the abbot of a local monastery. Such a person was likely to be very wealthy and might have left his monastery to live in the king's palace at Versailles.

Because he owned some land Jacques would also pay taxes to his *seigneur*. As part of these feudal dues Jacques might have to grind his corn in the *seigneur*'s mill while Marie could be obliged to use his oven to bake her bread. Obligations such as these were common in eighteenth-century France and, because the *seigneurs*' charges were high, aroused a lot of bitterness. Matters were made worse when *seigneurs* took to reviving obligations which over the years had been allowed to lapse.

The heaviest taxes of all, however, were those imposed by the government. Jacques might pay half the value of his harvest in direct taxes such as the *taille*. (Direct taxes are paid straight to the government; a present-day example is income tax.) In addition there were taxes on some of the goods such as salt and wine which people had to buy. (These were indirect taxes; a present-day example is VAT.) Nor did the government stop at taking money. Many peasants were forced to spend part of the year repairing local roads. This duty was known as the *corvée* and it was doubly burdensome. It was unpaid and it took the peasants away from their own work.

French peasants spent much of their time working to benefit other people. As a result there was mounting resentment. As one peasant woman put it just before the outbreak of the French Revolution: 'We are being crushed by the taxes and dues.'

How France was governed

The condition of the peasants provides one reason why an explosive situation developed in eighteenth-century France. There are others.

Until the Revolution, France, like most other European countries, was ruled by a monarch. Like Frederick the Great, the French kings ruled despotically. They did not, for instance, consult an elected assembly. The States General, which was roughly equivalent to the British Parliament, had not met since 1614. Unlike Frederick the Great the French kings were in no way 'enlightened despots'. For example, they did not allow their people to speak or write freely. To be outspokenly critical of the way the country was governed was to invite arrest by the secret police and imprisonment without trial. Trials were not held whenever the king issued a special order called a *lettre de cachet*. An Englishman called Arthur Young, who travelled through France on the eve of the Revolution, was shocked by this procedure:

Take the road to Lourde, where is a castle on a rock, garrisoned for the mere purpose of keeping state prisoners, sent hither by *lettres de cachet*. Seven or eight are *known* to be here at present; thirty have been here at a time; and many for life. . . .

It became increasingly common during the course of the eighteenth century for educated Frenchmen to compare their country unfavourably with Britain where laws could only be made with Parliament's consent

The burden of taxation fell most heavily on the peasants. These cartoons appeared in France with the caption: 'It is to be hoped that this game will end soon.'

Versailles, the famous royal palace built by Louis XIV in the seventeenth century

and where every citizen was guaranteed certain basic rights. These included the right to speak or write freely and the right to be brought to trial if arrested. In his novel *L'Ingénu* Voltaire wrote of a North American Indian who landed in Brittany in 1689 and helped the local inhabitants to drive off a British raiding party. Later he was unjustly arrested and imprisoned in the Bastille. There he complained bitterly to his fellow prisoner: '. . . Are there then no laws in this country? They condemn men without a hearing. It is not so in England. Ah! it was not against England that I should have fought.'

This book was first published in 1767. A few years later the American War of Independence and the emergence of a democratic new nation, the United States of America, provided further food for thought. The system of government adopted by the Americans contrasted even more sharply with the despotic ways of the French monarchy. Yet it was French troops who had helped the Americans to win their independence. It is perhaps not surprising that several of the French

Francois Arouet de Voltaire
1694–1778

Madame de Pompadour, mistress of Louis XV

soldiers who fought in America between 1778 and 1783 played leading roles during the early months of the French Revolution.

The approach of bankruptcy

France was not only governed unfairly, it was also governed extremely inefficiently. During the course of the eighteenth century the country's finances got into such a mess that by the summer of 1788 the government was bankrupt. This happened because the government had, for many years, spent more money than it was able to collect in taxes.

So far as spending was concerned it was popularly thought that Louis XVI and his predecessors had spent far too much money on the royal palaces, on lavish entertainments and on gifts to court favourites and royal mistresses. Certainly vast sums of money had been spent in this way. Far more, however, had been spent on wars. France was at war for nearly half of the hundred years between 1688 and the outbreak of the French Revolution:

1688–1697	War of the League of Augsburg
1702–1713	War of the Spanish Succession
1733–1735	War of the Polish Succession
1741–1748	War of the Austrian Succession
1756–1763	The Seven Years War
1778–1783	The American War of Independence.

A fancy dress ball at Versailles

The main enemy was Britain and for her the wars brought triumph and vast new overseas territories. For France the wars brought defeat and financial ruin. Only in one war, the War of American Independence, did France emerge on the winning side and it was this war which finally crippled the country financially.

Because the government was spending a lot of money, taxes were inevitably high. Many people, however, paid less than their fair share. For example, the Church as a whole owned about a tenth of all land in France. This yielded an annual income of around 120 million *livres*. Yet the Church was not compelled to pay any taxes. What the government received from the Church depended on what the clergy were prepared to vote as a 'free gift'. Usually this was in the region of two to three million *livres*. Tax exemptions like this were very numerous in eighteenth-century France and members of the nobility and clergy, in spite of being the most obviously privileged, were not the only ones to benefit. In all the major towns, for example, people with the freedom of the city were more or less exempt from all direct taxation as well as the obligations of the *corvée*.

Louis XVI, King of France 1774–92

Because of these financial privileges the government was compelled to extract as much money as it could from peasants like Jacques.

Under Louis XVI France moved further and further into debt. A full-scale reform of the country's taxation system became an urgent necessity and eventually in 1786 a series of drastic changes were proposed by the king's finance minister, Calonne. These would have reduced the financial privileges of the nobility and clergy. Both groups resolutely opposed the measures and in the face of their opposition Louis XVI backed down and abandoned his belated attempt at reform.

By 1788, therefore, France was bankrupt and without any prospect of financial reform. In desperation Louis XVI agreed to the summoning of the States General. When this met in May 1789 events took a completely unexpected turn. The French Revolution had begun.

Using the evidence: the English traveller abroad

Foreign travel became fashionable for the well-to-do during the course of the eighteenth century and the letters and journals written by visitors to Britain, France, Germany and Italy are a valuable source of information about life in Europe at this time. However, these accounts are not always accurate.

In the eighteenth century, as today, some travellers appear to have disliked virtually everything they found abroad. One such was the novelist Tobias Smollett:

(1) There are three methods of travelling from Paris to Lyons, which, by the shortest road is a journey of about three hundred and sixty miles [580 kilometres]. One is by the *diligence*, or stagecoach, which performs it in five days; ... The inconveniences attending this way of travelling are these. You

are crowded into the carriage, to the number of eight persons, so as to sit very uneasy, and sometimes run the risk of being stifled among very indifferent company. You are hurried out of bed, at four, three, nay often at two o'clock in the morning. You are obliged to eat in the French way, which is very disagreeable to an English palate; and, at Châlons, you must embark upon the Saône in a boat, which conveys you to Lyons, so that the two last days of your journey are by water. All these were insurmountable objections to me, who am in such a bad state of health, troubled with an asthmatic cough, spitting, slow fever, and restlessness, which demands a continual change of place, as well as free air, and room for motion.

Travellers admiring the Pont du Gard, a Roman aqueduct near Nîmes

A model of a basket-work carriage which carried passengers between Paris and Versailles

Travels in France and Italy (1766)

John Douglas, who during 1748 and 1749 travelled through various parts of Europe as tutor to Lord Pulteney, thought many of his fellow countrymen learned little of real value while they were abroad:

(2) However fond they seemed of the French capital, I am sure most of them returned very much in the dark with regard to everything which a traveller ought to learn. The reason is obvious; they are seldom or never in company with the natives of the country; and unless a traveller converses with the people, he may please his eye with sights; but will never improve his understanding with knowledge.... Whether it be owing to a certain shyness in their tempers, or whether it arises from a want of acquaintance with the language of the country, it is certain that Englishmen in foreign countries seem to be most happy in the company of each other, and in conversing in their mother tongue.

Journal of a Tour through Germany, Holland and France

In his novel *Tristram Shandy*, Lawrence Sterne made fun of those travellers who passed through foreign countries at great speed and yet still managed to produce detailed reports of their journeys:

(3) For my own part, as Heaven is my judge, and to which I shall ever make my last appeal – I knew no more of Calais (except the little my barber told me of it as he was whetting his razor) than I do this moment of Grand Cairo; for it was dusky in the evening, when I landed, and as dark as pitch in the morning when I set out; and yet, by merely knowing what is what, and by drawing this from that in one part of the town, and by spelling and putting this and that together in another – I would lay any travelling odds that I this moment write a chapter upon Calais as long as my arm; and with so distinct and satisfactory a detail of every item which is worth a stranger's curiosity in the town – that you would take me for the town clerk of Calais itself. . . .

Sometimes different travellers produced vividly contrasting views of the same place. Here for example, are two views of Paris in 1789.

(4) Suffice to say, that it is the most ill-contrived, ill-built, dirty, stinking Town that can possibly be imagined; as for the inhabitants they are ten times more nasty than the inhabitants of Edinburgh. At the same time there are many Publick buildings, and many parts of the Town which are extremely magnificent.

Letter from Sir Francis Burdett

(5) We have now seen enough of Paris to be convinced that it is not that dirty, ill-built inconvenient place, which our ill-tempered countrymen have described it. There are more magnificent buildings than in London; all the places worth seeing are likewise more accessible than in London, it costs less to be admitted, and many may be seen without paying anything. The people too, are very communicative. I own, I am disposed to think very highly of this people.

Letter from Dr Rigby

Paris: part of the Louvre, a royal palace which was made into a museum in 1793

Paris: the Seine, with Notre Dame in the background

Questions and further work

1 List five reasons why Jacques and Marie were poor.
2 In what ways did the French government spend too much money in the eighteenth century?
3 Why did France's system of taxation need to be reformed? Why were attempts at reform unsuccessful?
4 In Document 1 which parts are statements of opinion by Smollett and which provide factual information about travelling between Paris and Lyons?
5 Can you find any clues as to why Smollett should have liked so little of what he found in France? Could you rely on what he had to say about the country?
6 Documents 2 and 3 each give a reason why some travellers learn little about the countries they visit. What are these reasons? Can you suggest any others?
7 How do the descriptions of Paris in Documents 4 and 5 differ? On what point do they agree? What questions would you ask about the writers and their visits to assess the reliability of the two accounts?
8 Of Documents 1, 4 and 5 which one might have been written by the sort of traveller described by John Douglas in Document 2? Explain your choice.

6 A new nation

The first human inhabitants of North America came from Asia between 25 000 and 40 000 years ago. From them and from those who followed them across the Bering Straits are descended the people we call Red Indians.

At the time of the War of American Independence the Indians were the only people living in much of North America. Depending on where they lived some tribes hunted, some farmed and some did both. Those tribes known collectively as the Plains Indians were hunters.

The Plains Indians

The Plains Indians roamed the bleak grasslands which stretched from the river Mississippi to the foothills of the Rockies. They moved in search of the buffalo which provided them with virtually everything they needed. Bands or villages of several hundred men, women and children wandered together taking their homes and all their belongings with them. Each family possessed a *tipi* or tent which consisted of a framework of long poles around which a cover, made out of buffalo skins, was fitted. It was easily dismantled and when the village was on the move the poles were converted into a simple sledge known as a *travois*. This was pulled by a horse and on to it were piled the *tipi* cover and the rest of the family's possessions and perhaps some of the younger children or an aged relative as well. It was a hard life, especially in the winter when deep snow and ice covered much of the plains.

Originally the Indians had hunted on foot. Now they did so on horseback (the Spanish had brought horses to North America during the sixteenth century) and they rode their mustang steeds with the utmost skill. The artist George Catlin described the Comanches as: 'the most extraordinary horsemen that I have seen yet in all my travels, and I doubt very much whether any people in the world can surpass them'. Their weapon was the short bow, seventy-five to ninety centimetres

A Pawnee Indian

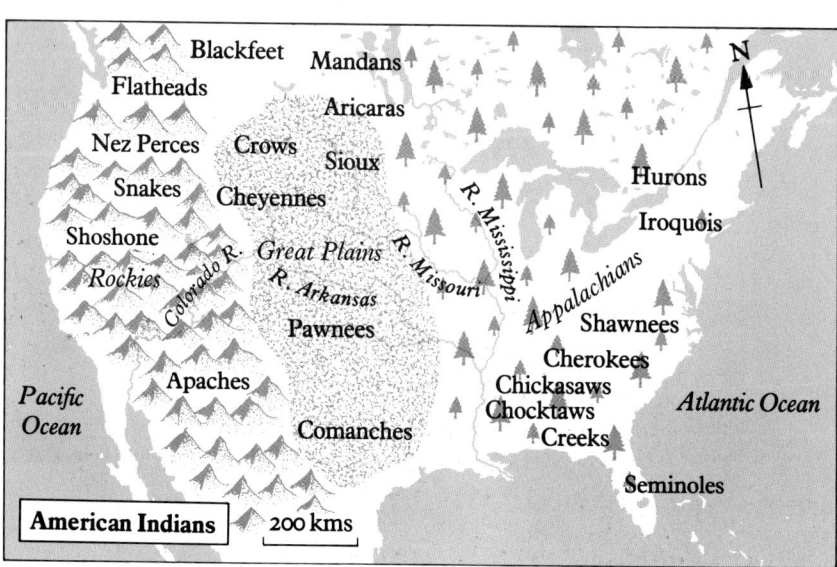

American Indians   200 kms

A horse travois. *Sometimes miniature* travois *were pulled by dogs. Behind are two* tipis.

long, easily used on horseback. With this the Indians were deadly, as soldiers in the United States army later found to their cost. Some visitors to Kansas in 1854 were surprised 'when a young officer ... deliberately asserted that our mounted men, though armed with revolvers, were in general not a match in close combat, for the mounted Indians, with their bows and arrows'. Not surprisingly they were more than a match for the buffalo.

Hunting buffalo. Nearly every part of the buffalo was of use to the Indians. For example, the skin was used for leggings, moccasins and tipi *covers, bones were made into arrow heads and knives and the stomach served as a water bucket.*

Cheyenne mother with her child

However, hunting buffalo was still a dangerous business and the Indians sought help from their gods in numerous religious ceremonies.

Bravery was the virtue prized above all others by the Indian warriors. They hoped to prove themselves fearless in the hunt and in battle. This helped to make them formidable opponents in war. Pain and the risk of death seemed to mean nothing to them.

Tribal wars were an essential part of the Indian tradition. They were bloody affairs and raids into neighbouring territory were not infrequent. Soon, however, an enemy appeared from the East which threatened alike Pawnee and Sioux, Crow and Cheyenne.

The coming of the Europeans

After Christopher Columbus's famous voyage across the Atlantic in 1492 the Spanish began to establish settlements in North America. They were followed by the French, the British and the Dutch.

In 1763 the Peace of Paris left Britain and Spain as the two European countries with claims on North America. These claims were vast but most of North America remained unexplored.

The British settlements were on the eastern seaboard. Here, by 1733, thirteen British colonies had been established.

A Sioux buffalo dance

The Thirteen Colonies

These colonies attracted many settlers. Throughout the seventeenth and eighteenth centuries people from Britain and various parts of continental Europe risked the long and hazardous Atlantic crossing in order to start life afresh in the New World. Some were driven by poverty. Others were attracted by the prospect of being able to worship God in their own way unmolested by intolerant governments. Others again had visions of quick and easy fortunes. All thought that life would be better than in the old world. Some were disappointed and returned. The majority stayed.

By 1760 over 1 500 000 people lived in the Thirteen Colonies. Not all of this number, however, were European in origin. Many Africans had been brought over, mainly to work as slaves on the tobacco and rice plantations of the south (see pages 39–44). In South Carolina blacks outnumbered whites by three to one. Altogether about 230 000 Negroes were living in the Thirteen Colonies at this time.

Some of the white settlers were merchants. Some were fishermen. Some were skilled craftsmen of one kind or another. Perhaps nine-tenths, however, were farmers. A few of these were farmers on a grand scale. Southern planters, like George Washington, owned estates which were often a thousand or more hectares in size. Here is one planter's description of the various buildings to be found upon his estate:

Slaves at work in the cotton fields

Upon the same land is my own dwelling house furnished with all accommodations for a comfortable and genteel living . . . four good cellars, a dairy, dovecote, stable, barn, henhouse, kitchen, and all other conveniencys and all in a manner new. . . .

Most colonists lived rather more modestly in simple huts or log cabins and worked farms which consisted of sixty-hectares of land or less. In the majority of cases the bulk of the work was done by the farmer himself, together with help from his wife and children and perhaps a hired labourer. The work was hard, especially when the land was being cultivated for the first time and had to be cleared of trees and stones. North America was no place for idlers.

For those able and willing to work, however, the land was there. For this reason there was less grinding poverty than in Europe. At the same time the wealthy colonists such as the southern planters or the prosperous merchants of New England were not as rich as the great landowners in, say, France or the powerful merchants of the City of London. Society was less divided than in the old world. A French settler called Crèvecœur described what a visitor to America would see:

If he travels through our rural districts, he views not the hostile castle, and the haughty mansion, contrasted with the clay-built hut and miserable cabin, where cattle and men help to keep each other warm and dwell in meanness, smoke and indigence. A pleasing uniformity of decent competence appears throughout our habitations. . . .

The availability of land was one of the good things about life in North America. Another was that being far from Britain the colonists were in many ways left to their own devices. In each colony local matters were

Settlers on a hunting trip

handled by an assembly elected by every man possessing enough land to meet the voting qualification. (This qualification varied from colony to colony. Overall, perhaps one out of four white men possessed the right to vote.) Decisions had to have the approval of the king's representative, the governor, but since the assembly voted his salary this was not usually too difficult to obtain.

As British possessions the Thirteen Colonies were subject to the many regulations relating to colonial trade and industry made by successive British governments during the seventeenth and eighteenth centuries. By law, the American colonists were not free to make what they liked, sell where they liked or ship how they liked but they do not appear to have greatly resented this. In practice they were able to evade many of the restrictions placed upon them and in any case the mercantile system did bring them certain benefits. For example, Britain might insist that certain goods such as Virginian tobacco or the timber, pitch and turpentine she needed for shipbuilding could be exported only to her but she did provide the colonists with a secure market for these products. Like all British subjects the colonists did, moreover, enjoy the protection of the British army and the British navy.

When the Seven Years War ended in 1763 most people living in the Thirteen Colonies were happy to remain under British rule. Only twelve years later, however, the first shots were fired in the war which was to end that rule.

THE FOLLY OF ENGLAND
AND THE RUIN OF AMERICA

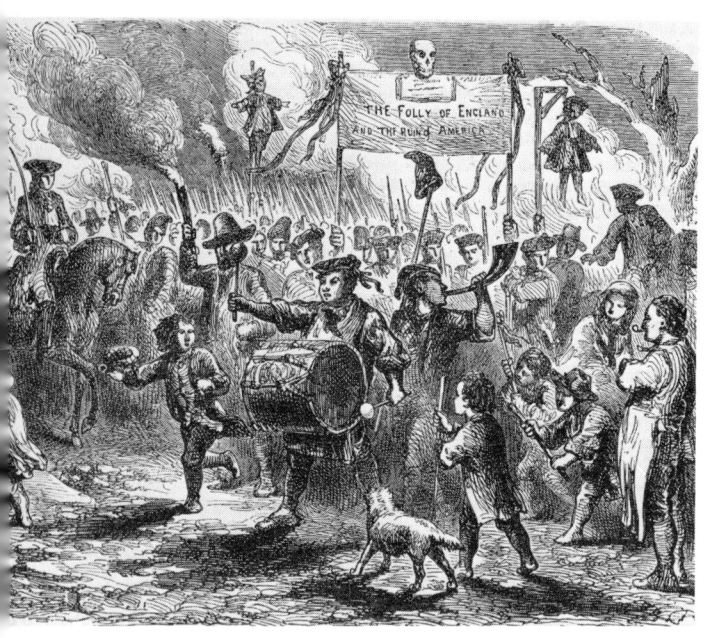

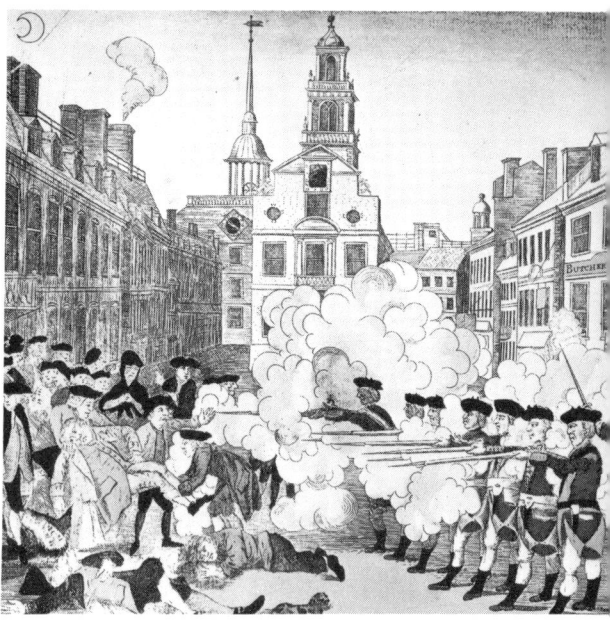

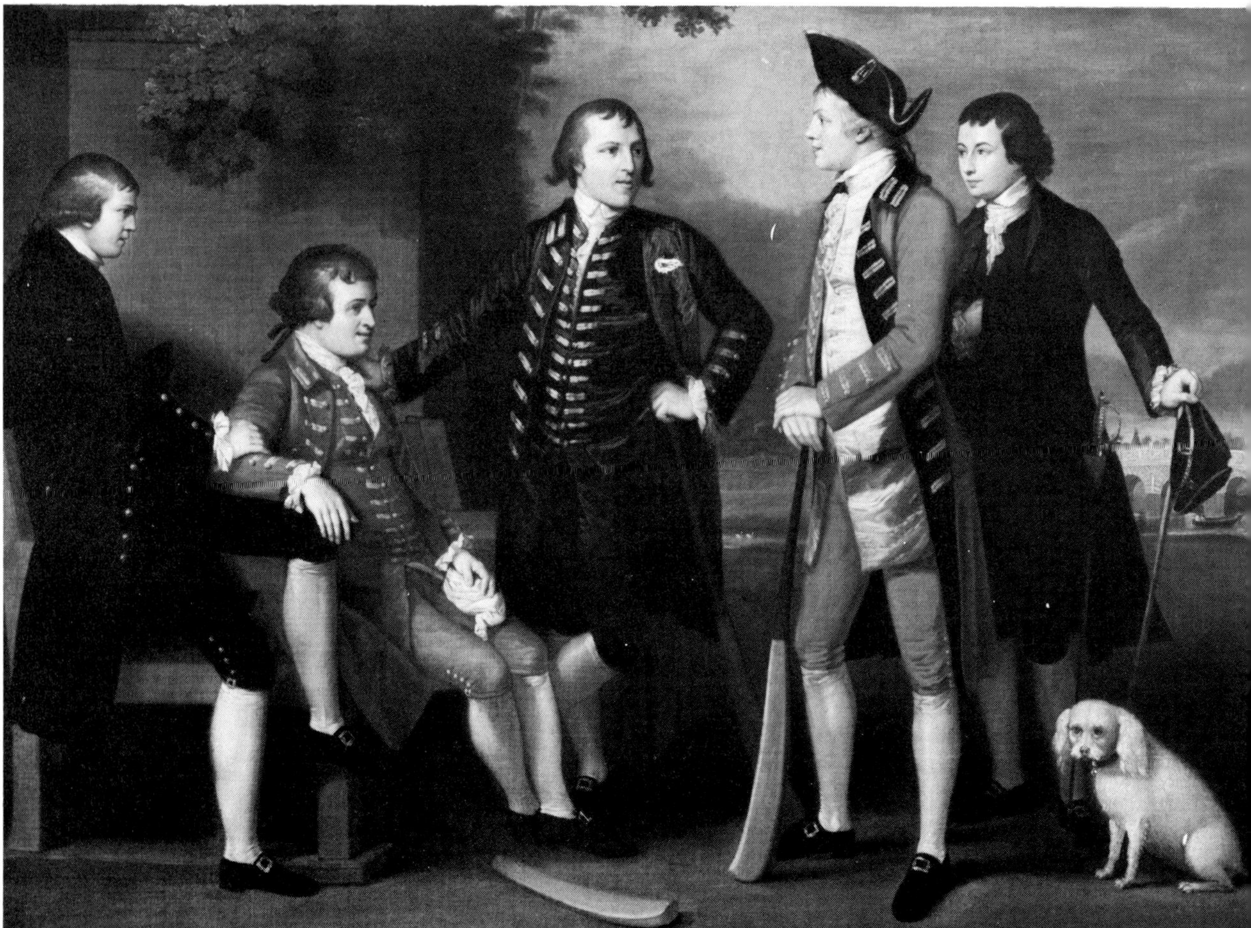

Stamp Act riots in Boston. The conflict between the American colonists and the British government centred on the question of whether Britain had the right to tax the colonists. The British government introduced several measures designed to make the colonists contribute towards the cost of the Seven Years War and the upkeep of British troops stationed in North America. The colonists argued that they should not be taxed since they were not represented at the Westminster Parliament. 'No taxation without representation' was the cry. The Stamp Act of 1765 was Britain's first attempt to tax the colonists. It taxed legal documents and newspapers. Following widespread opposition in the colonies the Act was repealed in 1766.

The 'Boston Massacre' of 1770 increased the tension between Britain and the colonists. Because of this popular print by Paul Revere it was seen by many in America as an act of brutality by British troops. In fact the redcoats did not line up and fire as shown. An angry mob attacked a handful of soldiers. As the crowd pressed closer the soldiers opened fire and killed five people.

'The Cricketers'. Not all Americans supported the war against Britain. Perhaps one-fifth were loyal to King George III in 1775. The war divided friends. Of the five young Americans painted in this picture three were to support the British government and two the colonists.

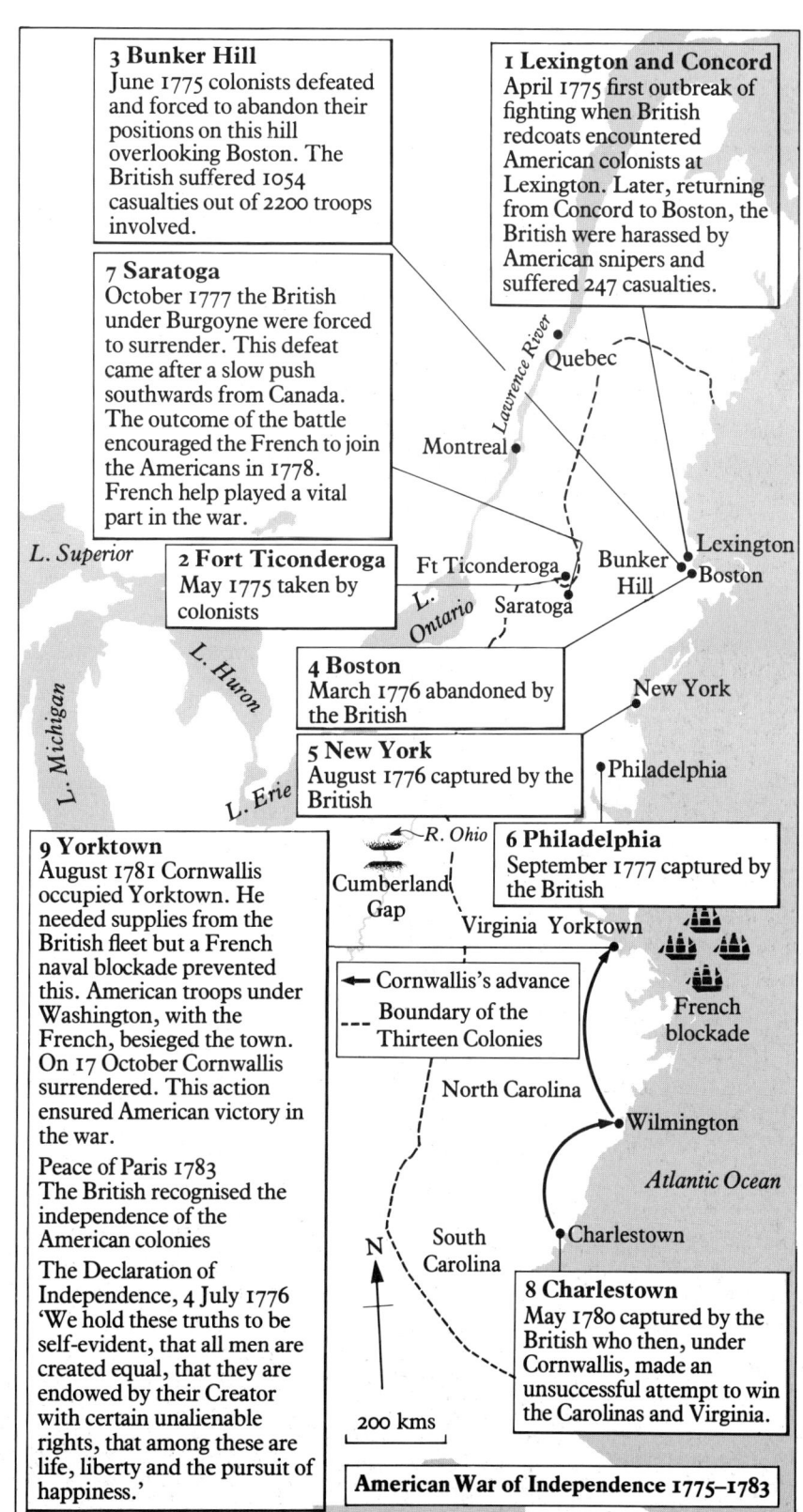

3 Bunker Hill
June 1775 colonists defeated and forced to abandon their positions on this hill overlooking Boston. The British suffered 1054 casualties out of 2200 troops involved.

7 Saratoga
October 1777 the British under Burgoyne were forced to surrender. This defeat came after a slow push southwards from Canada. The outcome of the battle encouraged the French to join the Americans in 1778. French help played a vital part in the war.

1 Lexington and Concord
April 1775 first outbreak of fighting when British redcoats encountered American colonists at Lexington. Later, returning from Concord to Boston, the British were harassed by American snipers and suffered 247 casualties.

Laurence River

Quebec

Montreal

L. Superior

2 Fort Ticonderoga
May 1775 taken by colonists

Ft Ticonderoga

Bunker Hill

Lexington
Boston

L. Ontario

Saratoga

L. Huron

4 Boston
March 1776 abandoned by the British

New York

L. Michigan

5 New York
August 1776 captured by the British

Philadelphia

L. Erie

R. Ohio

9 Yorktown
August 1781 Cornwallis occupied Yorktown. He needed supplies from the British fleet but a French naval blockade prevented this. American troops under Washington, with the French, besieged the town. On 17 October Cornwallis surrendered. This action ensured American victory in the war.

Peace of Paris 1783
The British recognised the independence of the American colonies

The Declaration of Independence, 4 July 1776
'We hold these truths to be self-evident, that all men are created equal, that they are endowed by their Creator with certain unalienable rights, that among these are life, liberty and the pursuit of happiness.'

Cumberland Gap

6 Philadelphia
September 1777 captured by the British

Virginia Yorktown

French blockade

→ Cornwallis's advance
--- Boundary of the Thirteen Colonies

North Carolina

Wilmington

Atlantic Ocean

N

South Carolina

Charlestown

8 Charlestown
May 1780 captured by the British who then, under Cornwallis, made an unsuccessful attempt to win the Carolinas and Virginia.

200 kms

American War of Independence 1775–1783

Using the evidence: the Boston Tea Party

Most of the documents used in this book date from the time of the people and events they describe. They are known as primary sources. The documents used in this section, which all describe the events leading up to the Boston Tea Party, are of a different kind. They are extracts from history books published at various dates between 1956 and 1971, well after the events they describe. They are known as secondary sources.

(1) They [i.e. the colonists] disliked the taxes which the British Government imposed on them, particularly those which were put on tea, paper, glass, lead, sugar and coffee. They objected to paying a duty for stamps to make many documents legal. They wanted to decide their own taxes.

After much quarrelling, in 1773 a group of colonists dressed up as Red Indians boarded some ships in Boston harbour and threw the cargoes of tea into the sea, as a protest against the taxes.

Donald Turnbull, *The Shape of History*, Book 2 (1962)

(2) In 1773, ships of the East India Company loaded with tea tied up in the port [i.e. Boston]. A small duty was still payable on tea, and this remained a sore point with the colonists. In other ports, the Americans just refused to touch the tea. In Boston, hundreds of young men boarded the ships and threw a cargo of tea worth eighteen thousand pounds into the sea.

P. J. Larkin, *Britain's Heritage*, Book 3 (1960)

(3) In May 1773 Lord North had tried to help the East India Company by the Tea Act, by allowing the Company's ships to trade direct with America in order to avoid British customs duties. The colonists felt they were being offered cheap tea to make them pay the Townshend duty at American ports. North also allowed the Company to sell exclusively to certain American merchants. An increased boycott of tea by the colonists was the result. On 26th December, 1773, men dressed as Mohawk Indians and organized by Sam Adams, boarded three vessels in Boston harbor and jettisoned tea worth over £9000 ($45 000).

Roger Parkinson, *The American Revolution* (1971)

*Three different versions of the
Boston Tea Party*

(4) The crisis came in 1773 over the Tea Act. Parliament passed the measure, not to discipline the colonies but to help the floundering British East India Company sell the seventeen million pounds [seven and three-quarter million kilograms] of tea in its warehouses. The Tea Act authorized its sale in the colonies at bargain prices. The colonists had continued to boycott British tea in protest against the threepence a pound Townshend duty. Now Parliament kept the Townshend duty but omitted the tax paid in England on tea shipped to the colonies. By their act, East India tea was not only cheaper in the colonies than in London, but cheaper than the smuggled Dutch tea. Colonial merchants holding considerable stocks of Dutch tea faced ruin. In addition, the East India Company would sell its tea directly in the colonies, eliminating the merchants. If parliament could grant one such monopoly, it might grant others to drive the merchants out of other lines of trade.

Merchants had economic reason to object to the East India Company tea. The great mass of Americans angrily protested as a matter of principle. Mass demonstrations in Philadelphia and New York forced the East India ships back to London with their cargoes; in Charlestown the tea was locked in a warehouse..

The Boston protest was more spectacular . . . a number of colonists, dressed as Indians, boarded the three vessels at Griffin's Wharf and dumped into the harbor their cargoes of tea.

Frank Freidel and Henry N. Drewry, *America:
A Modern History of the United States* (1970)

(5) A new ogre entered the picture in 1773. The powerful British East India Company, overburdened with 17 000 000 pounds of unsold tea, was facing bankruptcy. If it collapsed, the London Government would lose heavily in tax revenue. The ministry therefore decided to assist the company by giving it a complete monopoly of the American tea business. The terms thus granted would enable the giant corporation to sell the leaves more cheaply then ever before, even with the three-pence tax added. But to many American consumers, principle was more important than price.

Violence was inevitable, for the new tea monopoly had many aspects that were hateful to the colonials. Above all, it seemed like a shabby attempt to trick the Americans, with the bait of cheaper tea, into acceptance of the detested tax. Once more the colonials rose in their wrath. Not a single one of the several

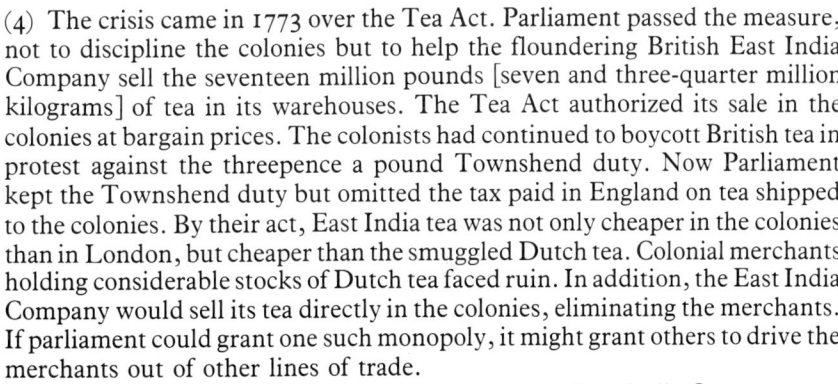

thousand chests of tea shipped by the company was landed in the hands of the consignees. At Annapolis, the Marylanders burned both the cargo and the vessel. At Boston, which was host to the most famous tea party of all, a band of white townsfolk, disguised as Indians, boarded the three ships on December 16, 1773. They smashed open 342 chests and dumped the 'cursed weed' into the harbor, while a silent crowd watched approvingly from the wharves.

T. A. Bailey, *The American Pageant* (1956)

Questions and further work

1 Copy and complete the following table to compare what the different accounts say about the points listed below.

Document	1	2	3	4	5
(a) When was the Boston Tea Party?					
(b) How many men took part in it?					
(c) How were they disguised?					
(d) How much tea was destroyed?					
(e) What was it worth?					
(f) Where else in the colonies was there unrest at this time?					

2 These documents are all taken from secondary sources yet they do not all agree. Write out one point on which they:
   (a) agree
   (b) disagree
   (c) give different but not necessarily conflicting information.
3 The Stamp Act was passed in 1765 and repealed in 1766. The Townshend duties on such things as tea, paper and glass were imposed in 1767 and, except for the duty on tea, were abolished in 1770. Using this information, how convincing do you find the reasons given in Documents 1 and 2 for the Boston Tea Party taking place?
4 Documents 3, 4 and 5 all say the Tea Party was caused by the Tea Act passed by the British Parliament in 1773. What were the terms of this Act?
5 Why, according to Documents 3 and 4, did (a) American merchants and (b) American colonists generally object to the Tea Act?
6 To what is the writer of Document 5 referring when he says; 'A new ogre entered the picture in 1773'? Judging from this sentence would you say that the writer's sympathies are with the British or the Americans?
7 Document 5 does not mention the reaction of the American tea merchants to the Tea Act. Why might this be?

Developing Britain

7 The Agricultural Revolution

The Agricultural Revolution took place during the eighteenth and early nineteenth centuries when farmers had to produce more food to feed Britain's growing population. They did this by improving the way they farmed and by cultivating more land.

The most important change in farming during the Agricultural Revolution was the enclosure of the open fields, which in 1700 still accounted for something like half the arable land in England and Wales. When a village was enclosed each farmer's land was consolidated into a single holding. This process had been going on for centuries but in the eighteenth century the enclosure movement accelerated rapidly.

The enclosure of Low Wold

What follows is the story of the enclosure of an imaginary village somewhere in England.

One cold wintry evening early in the year 1780 all owners of land in the village of Low Wold were crowded into their local inn, The Bull. Squire Middleton, a young man who had only recently inherited his father's lands, was there. So was the rector, Parson Ward. Like all rectors of

A village after enclosure. Compare the diagram on page 15.

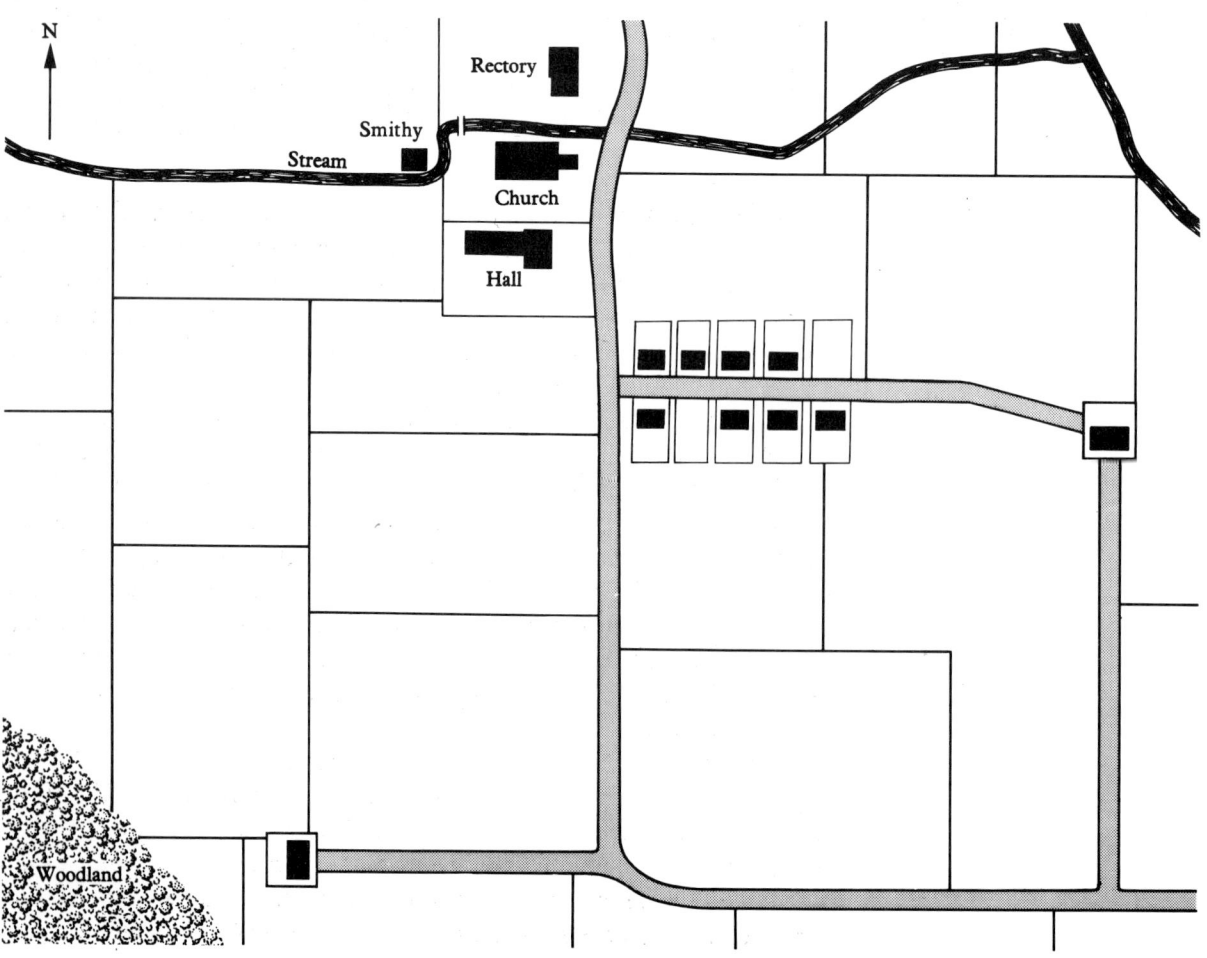

Low Wold as far back as anybody could remember, he had the right to farm fifty strips in the open fields. A fire was blazing and all the men were drinking. However, they were not there just to drink. They were discussing a proposal put forward by Squire Middleton and supported by the rector and several of the more substantial landowners that the village lands should be enclosed.

Enclosure, Squire Middleton said, could bring many benefits. Only recently he had spoken to some farmers from the neighbouring village of High Wold, which had been enclosed years before. They had told him how they preferred the new arrangement because it left them free to farm as they wished, free for example, to try new and very successful crop rotations. They were still amazed at the time they saved now that their holdings were no longer scattered all around the village. They had also pointed out that should cattle plague break out there was more chance of containing it now that all the village cattle were no longer grazed together.

Some of the farmers were nodding wisely over their pots of beer as Squire Middleton recounted all this. Not everybody in The Bull, however, was in agreement. Old John Gospel didn't like the sound of enclosure one little bit. What was good enough for his father, he said, and his father before him was good enough for him now. Sam Hugill, who owned fifteen strips, had a cousin who used to farm a similar

amount of land in High Wold. This cousin had found his share of the enclosure costs too high, had therefore sold his land and now worked as a labourer. Would the same thing not happen in Low Wold, asked Sam. Squire Middleton had to admit the costs were high. When High Wold was enclosed the commissioners' fees alone had come to £750 and that was only one of a number of expensive items. But not all the small farmers in High Wold had had to sell out and people should remember, Squire Middleton added, that there would be more land available for cultivation. Not only the common but the waste land to the north of the village would be shared out.

Eventually it was decided that a petition should be sent to Parliament as soon as possible requesting that an Act of Enclosure be passed for all the lands in Low Wold. All the bigger landowners were in favour because enclosed farms were more profitable than open-field ones; they knew they could expect to charge their tenant farmers more rent. In High Wold rents were said to have doubled. Old John, of course, refused to sign the petition and so did Sam and several of the other smaller owners.

The meeting drew to a close. Squire Middleton ordered extra beer for everyone and then departed. Some of the others drifted away while the remainder settled down to discuss the evening's events until the early hours of the next morning.

By law the whole village had to be informed of the intention to petition Parliament to enclose the village lands and so a notice telling of the petition was displayed for three weeks on the church door. The news caused a great stir although it was not unexpected, because a rumour had been going round the village for some months that Squire Middleton wished to enclose.

It was not welcome news for the labourers and cottagers of the village and their families. They were worried by the prospect of no longer having access to the common and the village waste. Take Peter Wainwright for example, who worked as a labourer for Squire Middleton. He kept a cow on the common. Where would he graze her if the common went, he wanted to know, and nobody could tell him. If the waste went he and his family would no longer be able to collect the berries which grew there in abundance, nor would they be able to collect firewood from the wood which marked the boundary between Low Wold and High Wold. All in all Peter stood to lose a great deal but at least he wasn't living on the waste. Some families, the so-called squatters, had built themselves shacks on the edge of the wood.

The petition was sent off and for over three months nothing more was heard about the proposed enclosure. Peter's wife, Martha, was beginning to have secret hopes that perhaps the petition had been turned down. Then, in the middle of April, the news came that the petition had been successful and that an Act of Enclosure had been passed. Three men had been appointed to organise the enclosure and they were expected to announce soon when they intended to start work. Rumour had it that each of these commissioners, as they were known, was to be paid £2.2s (£2.10) for each day they worked on the enclosure. Old John had a thing or two to say when Sam told him about that in The Bull, and added that he supposed it would all soon be over now.

In fact it was not. Certainly a notice appeared on the church door a few days later listing the commissioners' names and stating that they intended to hold their first meeting in The Bull next 1 May. But it was another two and a half years before their work was finished.

During this period the commissioners held many meetings in The Bull. They questioned every landowner and recorded how much land each owned in the open fields. This was to ensure that when the land was divided into enclosed holdings each man received the amount of land to which he was entitled. The commissioners were also interested in who used the common. Those villagers who had the right to do so would be given some land to compensate for the common disappearing. Peter became more hopeful about keeping his cow when he heard of this. However, when it was his turn to speak to the commissioners they asked him if he had anything in writing about having access to the common. When Peter said he did not the commissioners told him that legally he had no right to use the common and therefore was not entitled to any compensation. Peter protested for over half an hour about this but the commissioners insisted that there was nothing they could do.

Armed with all this information and a detailed plan of the whole village which a surveyor had drawn up for them, the commissioners were ready to begin the job of replanning the village lands. Each landowner was to be given a compact unit of land to replace his strips in the open fields. The common and the village waste were to be shared out. Because of all the boundary changes new roads had to be planned. All this took time but eventually in the middle of October 1782 a notice

Surveyors at work at Henlow in Bedfordshire

Thomas Coke (1750–1842) inspecting sheep on his Holkham estates. Coke was a landowner who did much to popularise the Norfolk system of crop rotation and other improved methods of cultivation.

appeared on the church door announcing that the commissioners would hold their final meeting in The Bull on the last day of the month. At this meeting the commissioners signed the enclosure award. This was a leather-bound volume containing twenty skins of parchment on which was listed every single change made by the commissioners. It also included a map showing all the new boundaries and roads. At matins the following Sunday the award was handed over to the rector whose job it was to keep it safe. All that remained was for the landowners to fence their new holdings and then the enclosure of Low Wold was complete.

The results of enclosure

Below: A Dishley ram, so called after Dishley in Leicestershire where Robert Bakewell (1725–95) farmed. This animal, like the Berkshire hog, would have a lot of saleable flesh.

Enclosures led to many improvements in farming. For example, they accelerated the spread of new farming methods. One of the most important was the development of new crop rotations to replace the traditional system whereby one field was left fallow each year. Farmers in Norfolk were among the first to discover that fallowing was unnecessary if proper use was made of crops like turnips and clover. These were fodder crops which enabled farmers to keep more livestock. More animals meant more manure to enrich the soil. Because of this, and because turnips and clover and other similar crops actually increased the fertility of the soil, fallowing could be avoided if they were regularly alternated with the grain crops. The Norfolk system, or some variation of it, was well established in East Anglia, the home counties and much of southern England by 1700. During the eighteenth and early nineteenth centuries the new rotations became increasingly popular.

A Berkshire hog

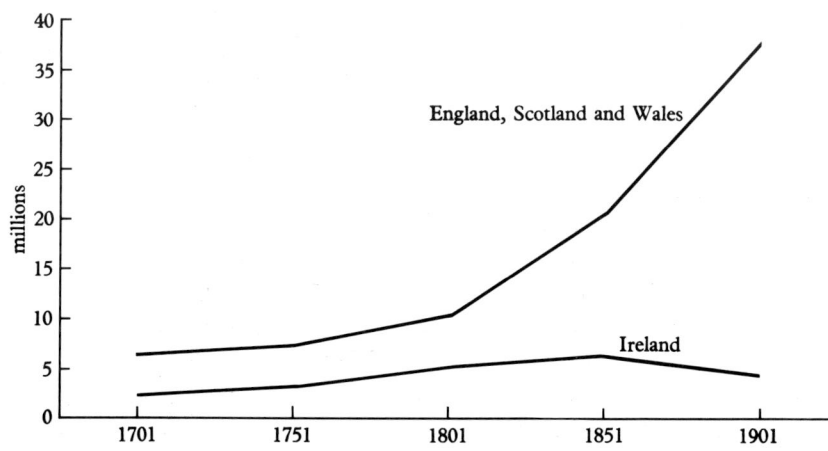

Population growth 1701–1901

Because they kept more animals, farmers were able to experiment with selective breeding. Robert Bakewell was the most famous of a number of men who, by careful breeding, managed to produce much heavier livestock.

Enclosure did not, however, automatically lead to improvement. Some soils were unsuitable for growing turnips and clover and some farmers were reluctant to change their ways. It is unlikely that enclosure would alter the way Old John farmed.

The enclosure movement also extended the area under cultivation. In deciding to enclose the village common and the village waste, the landowners of Low Wold were typical of many. Between 1760 and the end of the century at least two million acres of waste land were brought into cultivation in England and Wales. Perhaps this more than anything else explains why, during the period of the Industrial Revolution, Britain was able to support a much larger population without buying large quantities of food from abroad.

The cost of enclosure

On the other hand enclosure was expensive. Landowners did not have to petition Parliament to pass an Act of Enclosure. They could simply agree to enclose. After 1750, however, most landowners enclosed by Act. For one thing an Act of Parliament was a way of forcing the hand of owners like Old John and Sam who would never agree to the change. Parliamentary costs, however, were high and then there were all the other expenses like the cost of fencing and the cost of building new roads, quite apart from those commissioners' fees which so upset Sam. Towards the end of the eighteenth century the Board of Agriculture estimated that the cost of enclosure by Act of Parliament was about twenty-eight shillings (£1.40) per acre (0·4 hectare). Some small owners like Sam's cousin in High Wold, found this too much and had to sell out. Most, however, seem to have survived. They were helped by the fact that enclosure increased the value of their land which enabled them to meet their share of the costs by mortgaging it or by selling a few acres.

Less fortunate were people like Peter. They felt the loss of the commons and wastes and, as Peter found to his cost, only those legally entitled to use the common were automatically given land in compensation. This came at a time when the increase in population was beginning to make it difficult for some labourers to find work. By moving fifty kilometres some found work in the expanding industrial towns and villages. Those who did not live in areas where industries were developing had to seek help from the parish authorities (see pages 17–20).

The changing landscape

One of the most striking results of the enclosure movement was the altered appearance of the countryside. The huge open fields were replaced by a chessboard pattern of small enclosed fields. In stone country these were divided by dry walling, elsewhere by fences until the seedling hedges grew. The thousands of kilometres of new fences reduced considerably the number of trees. The poet John Clare wrote:

> Ye banish'd trees, ye make me deeply sigh –
> Inclosure came, and all your glories fell.

In place of the narrow winding roads so characteristic of unenclosed country there appeared the wider, straighter roads planned by the commissioners. These are still very much in evidence as are the isolated farmhouses which increased in number during the nineteenth century. After enclosure many farmers owned holdings a long way from their village homes. They found this inconvenient and in time a good number of them built new farmhouses in the middle of their land.

These were big changes. People who lived through them would probably feel they hardly knew their own village. Doubtless Old John had much to say about the disappearance of the Low Wold he had known all his life.

Using the evidence: rural life

Old photographs enable us to see what people and places looked like in the past. Here are three examples:

![A mowing team at Wenham Grange, Suffolk, in 1880]

(1)

A mowing team at Wenham Grange, Suffolk, in 1880

(2)

The rector of West Hellerton, Yorkshire, together with his family and other helpers, stacking hay in 1892

(3)

This photograph was taken in the village of Barston, Warwickshire in 1890

In her book *Lark Rise to Candleford*, Flora Thompson describes in considerable detail Oxfordshire village life during the latter part of the nineteenth century. Here she writes of harvest time:

(4) In the fields where the harvest had begun all was bustle and activity. At that time the mechanical reaper with long, red revolving arms like windmill sails had already appeared in the locality; but it was looked upon by the men as an auxiliary, a farmer's toy; the scythe still did most of the work and they did not dream it would ever be superseded. So while the red sails revolved in one field and the youth on the driver's seat of the machine called cheerily to his horses and the women followed behind to bind the corn into sheaves, in the next field a band of men would be whetting their scythes and mowing by hand as their fathers had done before them.

With no idea that they were at the end of a long tradition, they still kept up the old country custom of choosing as their leader the tallest and most highly skilled man amongst them, who was then called King of the Mowers. For several harvests in the eighties they were led by the man known as Boamer. He had served in the Army and was still a fine, well-set-up young fellow with flashing white teeth and a skin darkened by fiercer than English suns.

With a wreath of poppies and green bindweed trails around his wide, rush-plaited hat, he led the band down the swathes [paths through the corn made by the mowers] as they mowed and decreed when and for how long they should halt for a 'breather' and what drinks should be had from the yellow stone jar they kept under the hedge in a shady corner of the field. They did not rest often or long; for every morning they set themselves to accomplish an amount of work in the day that they knew would tax all their powers till long after sunset. 'Set yourself more than you can do and you'll do it' was one of their maxims, and some of their feats in the harvest field astonished themselves as well as the onlooker.

Questions and further work

1 Explain briefly the attitudes towards enclosure of each of the following inhabitants of Low Wold: (a) Squire Middleton (b) John Gospel (c) Sam Hugill (d) Peter Wainwright.
2 Using the information on pages 78 to 84 list the advantages and disadvantages of enclosure.
3 Study Illustrations 1, 2 and 3. Choose one photograph and describe it as accurately as you can.
4 What information about village life in the nineteenth century can be gained from the photographs? Use this information to complete the following table.

Photograph	Date	Subject	Points of special interest
1			
2			
3			

5 How useful would the photographs be without captions? Write a new caption for each photograph which would alter the meaning of the picture. Why is it important to have accurate captions?

6 Photography began in the 1820s. How useful are photographs to the historian compared to paintings and drawings as a means of finding out about the past?

7 Look again at Illustration 1 then read Document 4. Compare what they tell you about the following aspects of harvesting at the time:
   (a) the parts played by the men, women and children
   (b) tools and machinery
   (c) farmworkers' clothes
   (d) harvest customs.

8 Are there any ways in which an old photograph is a much more useful source of information about the past than a written account? What kinds of subjects are old photographs especially useful for? Are there any dangers of using this kind of evidence without written accounts? (Look at your answer to question 5.)

Threshing by machine at Harlington, Middlesex in 1868. It was the introduction of the threshing machine which provoked the 'Swing' rising of 1830 (see pages 114–17).

8 The coming of the factories

Richard Arkwright

Richard Arkwright

Richard Arkwright, who is sometimes known as 'the father of the factory system', was born in Preston in 1732. As his parents were poor he received little education but he trained as a barber and wig-maker and eventually in 1760 established his own business in Bolton. The following year he married.

To begin with he devoted himself to his trade and became particularly skilled in dyeing hair. Before long, however, he began to develop an interest in making machines, much to his wife's annoyance. She thought he was wasting his time and, following an incident in which she smashed up some of his experimental models, the two separated.

In 1767 Arkwright decided to devote himself entirely to the task of producing a machine which would speed up the spinning of cotton. Such a machine was badly needed and was likely to attract many buyers. He abandoned his barber's business and moved first to Preston and then to Nottingham.

At this stage Arkwright was very poor. While he was in Preston his appearance was so shabby that when an election was held a number of friends clubbed together to provide him with a decent set of clothes in which to appear at the polling room. For his work Arkwright needed money and so he went into partnership with three men, John Smalley, Samuel Need and Jedediah Strutt, who could supply him with the necessary funds.

He was not to be poor for very much longer. By 1768 his spinning machine, which worked best when powered by water and so became known as the water-frame, was ready. It is now thought that in developing this machine Arkwright made considerable use of other people's ideas. But in applying for a patent in 1769 he acknowledged no such debt, stating that he had, 'by great study and long application invented a new piece of machinery, never before found out, practised or used, for the making of weft or yarn from cotton, flax and wool'.

Unlike previous spinning machines the water-frame was too large either to fit into a worker's cottage or to be driven by hand. From the start it was a factory machine and Arkwright now embarked on a new career as a factory-owner. In 1771 he and his partners built a large factory at Cromford in Derbyshire which was soon employing about 600 workers. Before long Arkwright was part-owner not only of this and other factories in Derbyshire but also of factories in Lancashire and Scotland. By 1782 he was reckoned to be employing about 5000 workers.

There is no doubting Arkwright's energy and skill as a factory-owner. His working day lasted from 5 a.m. until 9 p.m. Hating to waste a single moment he dashed on horseback from one factory to another. In his factories he encouraged hard work by offering prizes and distinguishing clothes to the best workers. His rewards were fame and a substantial fortune. He died in 1792, six years after being knighted.

Why factories?

Arkwright's factories and others like them transformed Britain's cotton industry. When he invented the water-frame in 1768, cotton was still relatively unimportant compared with the much older woollen cloth industry. After 1770, however, cotton rapidly became the most advanced and the most important industry in the country. By 1830 cotton exports formed over half of Britain's total exports.

This dramatic development marks the first stage of the Industrial Revolution. Why did it take place?

Expanding cotton sales

With the domestic system the employer avoided the expenses of building a factory. However, he could face difficulties if he wished to produce a great deal more of his product. He could only cast his net more widely in his search for domestic workers and he might already be operating over considerable distances. In the second half of the eighteenth century the cotton clothiers of Lancashire faced precisely this problem. They wished to produce more cotton in order to satisfy an ever-increasing number of customers at home and abroad. The domestic workers, and more particularly the domestic spinners, simply could not produce enough so there was a need for labour-saving machinery such as Arkwright's frame. Manufacturers, for their part, were willing to spend money on machines and factories because they were confident that they could sell the finished product.

At work with a spinning wheel, 1808

Improved communications

In other ways the situation after 1750 favoured the building of factories. As the population increased and greater quantities of food and fuel had to be moved into the expanding towns, communications were improved. Roads were repaired and canals were built. As a result the factory owners were able to move goods around the country more quickly, more cheaply and with greater safety, than would have been possible fifty years earlier.

Roads were improved through the setting-up of turnpikes. A group of landowners and merchants might wish to improve a particular stretch of road. They would obtain Parliament's permission to set up turnpikes or toll-gates at each end of the road and would then charge people for travelling on it. The money collected from the tolls could then be used to improve the road. For example, a professional road engineer might be employed. One of the first such men to achieve fame was John ('Blind Jack') Metcalf of Knaresborough. He was followed by Thomas Telford and John Loudon Macadam.

Apart from wood, which was already scarce in many parts of the country, Britain's only fuel was coal. This was bulky and heavy and difficult to transport by road even when the road engineers had been at work. It was far easier to use the sea and the rivers:

Six or eight men by the help of water carriage can carry and bring back in the same time the same quantity of goods between London and Edinburgh as fifty broad-wheeled wagons attended by a hundred men and drawn by 400 horses.

Roadmenders at work

The turnpike keeper awakened by a post boy

As the towns grew they required more coal than could easily be transported on the existing river network. In 1759 the Duke of Bridgewater started building a canal which would connect his colliery at Worsley with the expanding town of Manchester. The canal proved a great success and soon a canal network began to develop. The canal barge was an ideal way of moving heavy goods. A fifty-tonne load could be pulled by one horse walking along the canal towpath. (Compare this with the pack-horse's average load of about one-eighth of a tonne.) The factory owners had to move large quantities of bulky goods and needed the canals. As factories were built, more canals were constructed and the system was more or less completed in the 1790s in the excitement of 'canal mania'.

Other reasons

Improved communications helped to ensure that Britain was ready for the Industrial Revolution. Likewise, the revival of the iron industry which took place in the eighteenth century meant that when factory owners discovered that steam engines shook wooden machines to pieces they could have them built of metal instead. The large profits earned by merchants in the eighteenth century were to prove useful to a number of would-be manufacturers who did not themselves have enough cash to set up a factory. The mushroom growth of country banks which began in the 1780s ensured that banking facilities were not confined to the

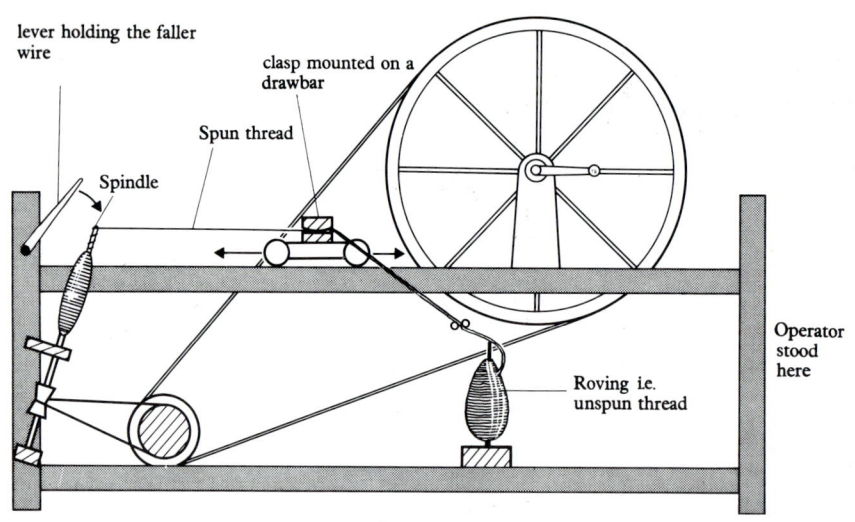

lever holding the faller wire

clasp mounted on a drawbar

Spun thread

Spindle

Operator stood here

Roving i.e. unspun thread

How the spinning jenny worked. (Remember that there would be at least eight spindles.) (a) The operator pulled the drawbar towards him. At first the clasp was open to allow the roving to pass through it. Then the clasp was closed which meant that more roving was pulled loose. (b) The wheel was turned. This revolved the spindles which in turn twisted the thread. (c) The faller wire was brought down. This guided the threads on to the spindles as the spindles were slowly turned. As this happened the drawbar was slowly pushed forward.

capital. The increase in population meant that when factories were built there were plenty of people to work in them.

But however well prepared Britain might be for the industrial changes which lay ahead, factories were not going to be built until there were suitable machines to go in them. It was the invention of these which sparked off the Industrial Revolution.

The Age of Cotton

Before James Hargreaves invented the spinning-jenny a bottleneck was developing in the cotton industry. The spinners could not supply the weavers with enough yarn. Before the weavers began to adopt John Kay's flying shuttle in the 1750s it had taken three or four spinners to supply one weaver. Kay's invention, which considerably improved the loom, meant that even more spinners were needed. The spinning-jenny was an improved version of the traditional spinning-wheel. Instead of spinning just one thread of yarn at a time it could spin several. The earliest jennies spun eight threads, by 1784 they were spinning eighty and by the end of the century some models were spinning 120 threads at the same time. Such a machine was precisely what the spinners needed and the jenny was soon in widespread use.

The jenny eased the bottleneck in the cotton industry without destroying the domestic system, for smaller jennies easily fitted into the workers' cottages. It was the invention of the water-frame which led to the setting up of factories.

Samuel Crompton's mule, although designed for the domestic spinner, was quickly adapted for the factory. Like the water-frame it was powered by water, and the early spinning factories, whether they housed water-frames or mules, were situated in the countryside along-side millstreams. There were plenty of suitable sites in Lancashire, the traditional centre of the industry.

Factories were built elsewhere and a very significant cotton industry

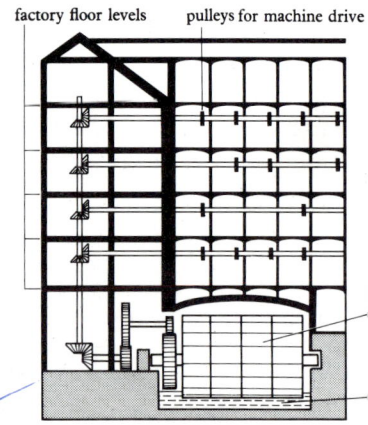

factory floor levels   pulleys for machine drive

A water-powered factory

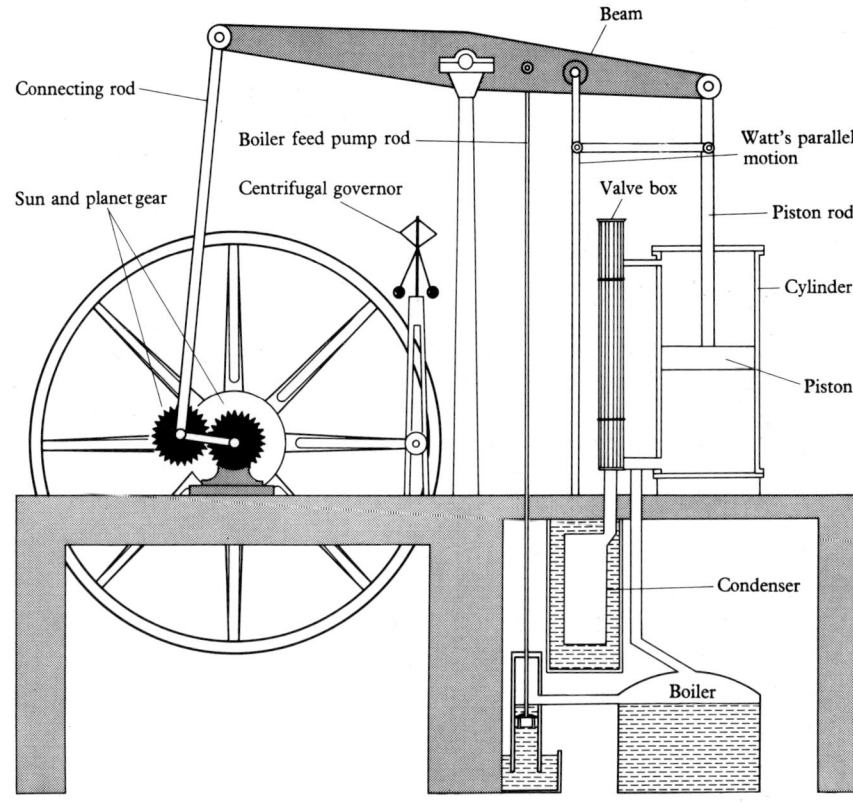

Beam

Connecting rod

Boiler feed pump rod

Watt's parallel motion

Sun and planet gear

Centrifugal governor

Valve box

Piston rod

Cylinder

Piston

Condenser

Boiler

James Watt's rotative steam engine

began to develop in the south-west of Scotland which, like Lancashire, was damp and had plenty of hills. (Both areas were rich in coal and so had plenty of fuel for the steam engines when they came into use.)

If the factories could be built in the towns the employers would have a large work force near to hand. For this to happen an alternative source of power was needed. The steam engine seemed the answer but to drive machinery it would need to turn a wheel and this it could not do. In the early 1780s James Watt set to work to devise an engine with a rotative motion. His partner, Matthew Boulton, urged him on, realising that many manufacturers would buy such a machine. He wrote to Watt in 1781: 'The people in London, Manchester, and Birmingham are *steam mill mad.*' Boulton's optimism proved justified. Following the successful installation of a rotative steam engine in a spinning mill in 1785 (the year Arkwright's patent expired) the firm of Boulton and Watt supplied eighty-four such engines to cotton mills before 1800. Powered by these machines, factories were built in ever-increasing numbers in the towns of Lancashire and in Glasgow. In 1782 there had only been two cotton mills in the Manchester area; by 1802 there were fifty-two.

These factories brought about a phenomenal increase in the amount of yarn produced. Between 1780 and 1800 there was an eightfold increase in the amount of raw cotton imported for the industry's use. Not only was there more yarn but it was of a higher quality. The

Above: Crompton's mule

Below: the weaver at his loom

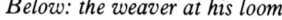

weavers did not have to mix yarn spun on frames or mules with linen in order to strengthen it and so, for the first time in this country, a pure cotton cloth was being produced. Mule yarn was not only strong, it was smooth as well and the mule became the most widely used spinning machine.

Until about 1815 the success of the cotton industry was based on the spinning factory and the domestic weaver. Because of technical problems, weaving took longer than spinning to become a factory process. Consequently the domestic weavers found themselves flooded with work as the factories turned out the yarn. Their numbers increased so that by 1820 there were 240,000 domestic cotton weavers. At times some manufacturers had difficulty getting all their yarn woven. One wrote: 'We employed every person in cotton weaving who could be induced to learn the trade, but want of population, want of hands, and want of looms, set us fast.' Because they were needed so badly, the weavers found their wages increasing. The weavers of Bolton were seen swaggering about with five-pound notes stuck in their hatbands.

But such prosperous times were not to last. As their numbers increased so the weavers lost their scarcity value and after 1805 wages began to fall. Then came the power-loom. This was invented in 1784 by a Leicestershire clergyman called Edmund Cartwright. Like the frame it was designed as a factory machine. It needed many improvements before it could be used effectively, but by the 1820s weaving factories,

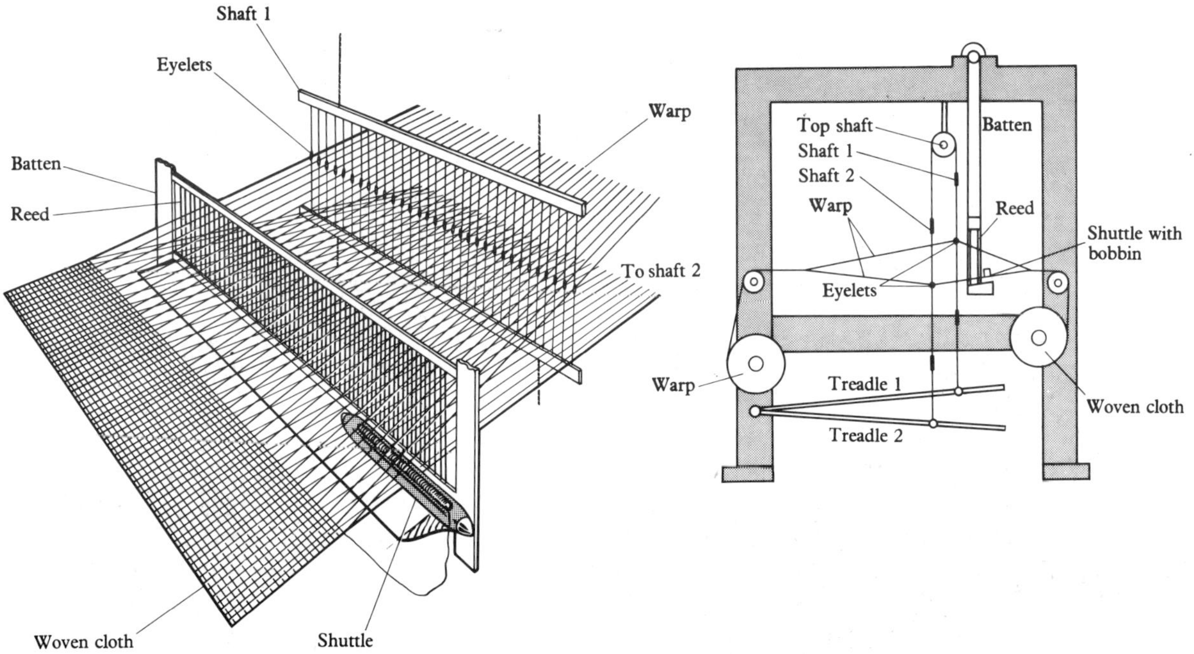
Shaft 1
Eyelets
Warp
Batten
Reed
To shaft 2
Woven cloth
Shuttle
Top shaft
Shaft 1
Shaft 2
Warp
Batten
Reed
Shuttle with bobbin
Eyelets
Warp
Treadle 1
Treadle 2
Woven cloth

How cloth was woven on a hand-loom. (a) Warp threads were passed through the eyelets of the two shafts. (b) One of the treadles was pressed down. This created a gap between the threads connected to shaft 1 and those connected to shaft 2. (c) The shuttle containing the weft thread was thrown through this gap from one side of the loom to the other. (d) The other treadle was pressed down and the procedure repeated.

often built alongside existing spinning factories, were becoming increasingly common. As this happened, the domestic weavers found themselves in a rapidly worsening position. Their wages slumped and they were thrown out of work. One anonymous weaver expressed his feelings in verse:

> Aw'm a poor cotton wayver as many a one knows.
> Aw've nowt t'eat in the house, an aw've wore out me clo'es.
> Me clogs are both brokken an stockins aw've none.
> Ye'd hardly gie tuppence for all aw've got on. . . .

There were outbreaks of violence as the weavers tried to draw attention to their plight by attacking the factories. The hard fact was that a loom factory was a more efficient way of weaving cloth than putting work out to hundreds and perhaps thousands of domestic weavers. By 1850 the number of domestic cotton weavers had dropped to 43 000. In 1862 the figure was 3000.

People were astounded by the rapid growth of the cotton industry. Manchester, which grew from 1700 inhabitants in 1760 to 180 000 in 1830, was a new kind of town, a town dominated by factories. One visitor wrote of it: '. . . we observe hundreds of five- and six-storeyed factories, each with a towering chimney by its side, which exhales black coal vapour . . .'. People saw in this dynamic town a sign of things to come and in this they were right.

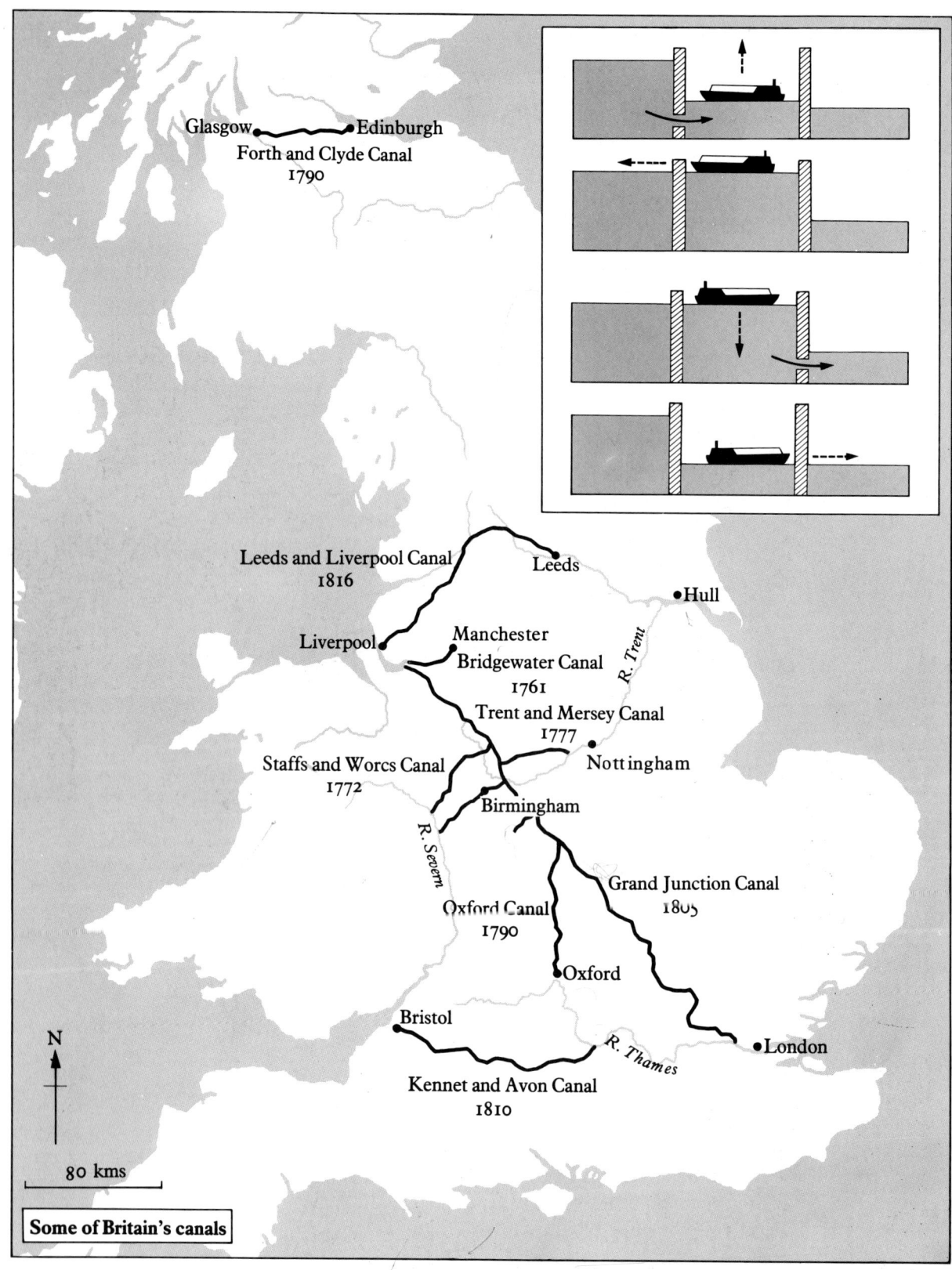

Glasgow ● Edinburgh
Forth and Clyde Canal
1790

Leeds and Liverpool Canal
1816

● Leeds

● Hull

Liverpool ●

Manchester
Bridgewater Canal
1761

R. Trent

Trent and Mersey Canal
1777

Staffs and Worcs Canal
1772

● Nottingham

Birmingham

R. Severn

Grand Junction Canal
1805

Oxford Canal
1790

● Oxford

Bristol ●

R. Thames

● London

Kennet and Avon Canal
1810

N

80 kms

Some of Britain's canals

Using the evidence: the narrow boats

Narrow boats were used throughout the Midland canal network. They measured about twenty-one metres by two metres and carried a load of about twenty tonnes. The cabin was always aft and, because there was no room to walk along the sides of the boat, a removable running plank, about twenty centimetres wide fitted above the hold. This was supported at one end by the cabin, at the other by the deck cratch (which served to stop water splashing into the hold) and in between by a number of removable stands. If necessary the whole of the cargo area could be covered with tarpaulins.

The cabin was small. It was about three metres long by two metres wide and was likely to be less than two metres high. In time as the railways began to make life difficult for the canal companies and the boatman found his wages going down, he and his family were forced to live on board and to make the cabin their permanent home. They soon learned to make good use of what little space there was:

(1) *A narrow boat christening around 1900. The clothes worn by the women were traditional among canal folk.*

(2) Close to the hatchway is the usual fat little stove in full glow; opposite this is a 'bunk' or locker which serves as wardrobe and sofa on which three men might sit; at the end of the cabin is another bunk, about three feet [one metre] wide, the sleeping place on which the family bed – now boxed up in a cupboard at the end of the bunk – is laid. By the side of the stove is the cupboard that serves as a larder and the door of which forms the dining table. It is fastened up with a wooden button and when let down it makes a board about a foot and a half long by one foot wide, on which all meals are eaten. Small cupboards, pigeon-holes and shelves are contrived everywhere, and the kitchen and cooking utensils hang gracefully on hooks behind the stove. Every inch of space is utilised.

George Smith, *Our Canal Population* (1875)

To ease the congestion a tiny second cabin was often added to the fore part of the boat. This served as a bedroom for some of the children.

The boatman and his family took great pride in the appearance of their cabin and when they did the result was very distinctive.

(3)

The same care was often lavished on the exterior of the boat. The following drawing shows one colour scheme in detail:

(4)

Painting the boats was a highly skilled job. Very often it was done by the boat-builder when the boat was taken in for repair. In his book *Narrow Boat*, which was first published in 1944, L. T. C. Rolt described a visit to Tooley's dockyard in Bambury:

A well maintained narrow boat

(5) When the heavier jobs on the hull have been completed, the boat-builder's next task is the redecoration, and I was lucky enough to see this work carried out on the boat *Florence*, which was on the dock at the time of my arrival. Each member of the family played his special part. George began in his spare time from the factory; he was the lettering expert, and painted the owner's name and port of origin in elaborate cream lettering, shaded with blue, on the large vermilion [bright red] centre panel of the cabin side. Then it was the old man's turn to embellish his son's work with little garlands of bright flowers in the four corners and between the lettering. Finally it was left to Herbert, the younger son, to paint his castles on the four small side panels. Apart from striking a line with a chalked string to keep the lettering level, they did no preliminary sketching or spacing out whatever, but worked straight out of their heads with wonderful rapidity and skill.

However well-painted the boat, the fact remained that the boatman and his family lived in extremely cramped conditions. Through his book *Our Canal Population* George Smith did much to make people aware of this. He also showed that not all boats were well looked after. Here he describes the boats which carried ironstone:

(6) These were in very many instances scarcely fit to be used; old and worn out, leaky, and therefore, very damp, never painted or well cleaned for years (beyond an occasional fumigation) and consequently filthy beyond description. . . . The state of the cabins in these boats occasionally becomes so unendurable from vermin that the inmates are literally compelled to resort to a process of fumigation technically termed 'smoking them out' or 'bug-driving', which consists of taking out the bedding and cooking utensils, stopping up the chimney with a large turf, and all other cracks and openings with soft clay, and then burning brimstone inside until the number of their unpleasant companions is reduced by suffocation.

Something else which began to attract attention was the canal children's lack of education. Here is an extract from an NSPCC report published in 1910:

(7) On the ninety-six boats observed by the Inspector, he found 167 children – 83 boys and 84 girls. . . . There were 99 children of school age. Of these 35 were *not attending school at all*.

Others were said to be attending school when it was possible; but this must

Narrow boats on the Grand Union Canal, 1896

be very seldom. The Inspector's means of questioning the children were very poor; but he discovered 18 who could not read.

56 children were found to be working. . . .

One boy of thirteen driving the horse was going to work all through the night. One of twelve had been four years on the boat driving the horse.

Life aboard the narrow boats had its attractions and its disadvantages. Here is L. T. C. Rolt's final assessment in his book *Inland Waterways*.

(8) It is a hard, tough life particularly in winter when there is little shelter from the rain until the boats stop, or when frost stiffens the wet ropes and makes decks and lock sides treacherous with ice. But it is also an independent life, in fresh air and constantly changing surroundings, so that the boatman does not envy those who spend their days shut up in factories even though they may make more money.

Questions and further work

1 Give four reasons for the building of factories and the decline of the domestic system.

2 Copy the following table and fill in the details to explain the importance of the four inventions to the cotton industry.

Invention	Inventor	Date	Importance
spinning-jenny			
water-frame			
mule			
power-loom			
rotative steam engine			

3 Using Document 2 and Illustration 3 draw a plan of the inside of a narrow boat cabin. Why was it necessary to use 'every inch of space'?

4 Copy the narrow boat in Illustration 4 and colour it according to the information provided. Why do you think so many narrow boats were decorated in this way?

5 What in Document 5 makes it clear that the Tooley family were not perhaps as busy as they had been in former times? List as many reasons as you can find why in the twentieth century many canals have ceased to carry any traffic.

6 What information does Document 7 contain which helps to explain why canal boat children did not attend school regularly? Can you suggest any other reason?

7 Using the documents and illustrations in this section draw up a list of the advantages and disadvantages of life aboard a narrow boat.

9 Life in the factory towns

John Mears

John Mears lived in Wigan during the early part of the nineteenth century. His father was a soldier and for much of the time his mother was left struggling to support a family of seven young children. For this reason John started working in a local cotton factory when he was only five years old. There he had to work hard. If he did not there was the encouragement of the stick or the strap. The strain was too much for him and by the time he was eleven his knees and ankles were beginning to go out of joint. After working like this for several years he visited a doctor who told him there was nothing he could do for him, but that he should try to eat as much good food as possible. This was easier said than done. At this particular time all the family except for John and his mother were ill and so the family income was much reduced. John found it increasingly difficult to walk and to add to his troubles he was injured at work by some falling machinery. His reward for years of hard work in the factory was to be made a cripple for life.

The factories

John Mears was one of the casualties of the Industrial Revolution. There were plenty of others. Factories provided employers like Richard Arkwright with an effective means of producing a lot of goods. For the men, women and children who spent fourteen or so hours of each working day in them, however, the factories were places of relentless drudgery. In 1832 Samuel Coulson, a factory worker, told how in the 'brisk time' (which lasted for about six weeks) his own children worked from 3 a.m. to 10 p.m. One reason why the cotton industry expanded so rapidly was that employers could demand so much work. The first effective Factory Act was not passed until 1833 and as late as the 1860s the only industries regulated by Act of Parliament were the textile industries and coal mining.

The 1833 Factory Act limited the hours which children could work in certain textile industries, including cotton. It reflected a growing concern with the lives many children were leading in Manchester and other industrial towns. There was nothing new in child labour. Children had worked and continued to work in domestic industries. What was new was the regularity of factory work. Under the domestic system families alternated between periods of very hard work and periods of idleness. In the factories children, like everybody else, were expected to work excessively long hours all the time. Moreover, the factories disrupted family life. Children had to work for a strange employer and spent very little time at home. Richard Oastler, one of the men who fought hard to improve the lives of child factory workers, commented on this with reference to the villages around Leeds and Huddersfield:

It is almost the general system for the little children in these manufacturing villages to know nothing of their parents at all excepting that in the morning very early, at 5 o'clock, very often before 4, they are awaked by a human being that they are told is their father, and are pulled out of bed (I have heard many a

THE POOR MAN'S ADVOCATE,
And People's Library.

"Open thy mouth, judge righteously, and plead the cause of the poor and needy."—Prov. xxxi. 9.

No. 22.   MANCHESTER, SATURDAY, JUNE 16, 1832.   Price 1d.

"FOR TRUTH, THE POOR, AND JUSTICE."

his limbs gave way. His knees and ancles grew crooked. This unfortunate man has suffered more from this inhuman system than nine-tenths of the transported felons have endured in their entire punishment. JOHN MEARS has not only been doomed to hard toil for many years in a cotton factory, but he has been made a cripple for life, and rendered incapable of procuring a livelihood by any other laborious occupation. He was

John Mears

Unemployed factory workers at the time of the great Lancashire Cotton Famine. The outbreak of the American Civil War in 1861 meant that Lancashire could not obtain its normal supplies of raw cotton. As a result many factories had to close or go on to short time.

score of them give an account of it) when they are almost asleep . . . and they see no more of their parents, generally speaking, till they go home at night, and are sent to bed.

The textile industries made great use of child labour. Many hands were needed in the factories and children could easily be trained to perform some of the tasks. Elizabeth Bentley for example, told how she began work at the age of six as a doffer in a flax mill. This involved removing full bobbins from the frames and replacing them with empty ones. By making use of child labour in this way an employer reduced his wage bill since children were paid less than adults. In the cotton industry some forty to fifty per cent of the workforce was under eighteen, the youngest workers being nine or ten years old. The silk industry, with about seventy per cent of its workforce under eighteen, was particularly dependent on child labour. Here children started working at the ages of six or seven.

Calico printing

As with children, so with their mothers. Very often they too worked in the factories. They needed the money. This meant, of course, that they were removed from their homes for most of the week and so had little time to spend on household duties. They had the additional burden of childbearing. Women were frequently seen at work in the last stages of pregnancy and they often returned to the factory as soon as their child was born.

The factories were grim in appearance and inside they were likely to be hot, stuffy and full of dust. By the 1830s the average Manchester factory housed about 400 workers and there were several firms in the area which employed over a thousand. These employees worked extremely long hours. Having bought machinery, employers were anxious to make as much use of it as possible. Sunday was the one rest day and in some factories the children had to turn up for work even then in order to clean machinery. Some employers cheated their workers by

Left: a Manchester cotton factory in the 1820s

Right: child labour at a brickworks

Far right: labourers at work. Compare this picture with the others in this chapter. Notice how strong and healthy the labourers are and what a happy scene it is. Do you think the painter, Ford Madox Brown, was being true to life?

tampering with the factory clock. A worker from Dundee commented on this: 'The clocks at the factories were often put forward in the morning and back at night...'. As another factory hand reported, workers were discouraged from carrying their own watches: 'There was one man who had a watch.... It was taken from him and given into the master's custody because he had told the men the time of day...'. Workers found the regularity of factory hours irksome. A hosier commented:

I found the utmost distaste on the part of the men, to any regular hours or regular habits.... The men themselves were considerably dissatisfied, because they could not go in and out as they pleased, and have what holidays they pleased, and go on just as they had been used to do....

The tradition of 'Saint Monday' died hard (see page 16). As late as 1800 spinners were missing from factories on Mondays and even Tuesdays. By some means or other the employers had to persuade their workers to attend regularly and promptly and, once at the factory, to work hard throughout the long day. Various methods were tried. Children were beaten. Adults were dismissed or threatened with dismissal. Fines were deducted from the weekly wage. An alternative approach was to encourage rather than to punish. Payment by results was widely adopted. Some employers offered prizes or cash bonuses to hard-working factory hands. In Robert Owen's factory at New Lanark a piece of wood with each side painted a different colour (black, blue, yellow and white) was fastened to every worker's machine. This 'silent monitor' could be turned round and the colour showing on the outside represented the superintendent's assessment of the worker's previous day's work. Black was the lowest assessment, white the highest.

At work in a weaving mill. Notice how the power looms are driven.

The long hours of hard work in an unhealthy atmosphere took their toll. Children suffered particularly. Some became deformed like John Mears or Elizabeth Bentley. By the time Elizabeth was thirteen her shoulders were beginning to go out of joint as a result of pulling heavy loads around the factory: '... it was a great basket that stood higher than this table a good deal. It was a very large one, that was full of weights up-heaped ...'. Deformities apart, children grew up with their general health impaired. In addition they, like everybody else, ran the risk of being mutilated by some piece of machinery. The machines were unguarded and a loose garment or a woman's long hair could easily get caught up in them. Fingers were vulnerable. Samuel Coulson told of an accident involving his eldest daughter: '... the cog caught her forefinger nail and screwed it off below the knuckle, and she was five weeks in Leeds infirmary.'

The factory towns

The factory towns were built in a hurry. Houses were needed quickly for the rapidly increasing numbers of people working in the factories.

The growing population of the factory towns		
	1801	1851
Glasgow	77 000 persons	345 000
Leeds	53 000	172 000
Manchester	75 000	303 000

The jerry-builders put up houses at a rate which astonished observers but even so they could not keep pace with demand. Houses, therefore, were subdivided and whole families were crowded into single rooms. Sometimes they had to share even this meagre accommodation. In Lancashire the problem was made more acute by the large numbers of Irish who came in search of work. In Manchester, for example, many families were compelled to live in cellars. As late as 1840 Dr Robertson, a Manchester surgeon, could write: 'The number of cellar residences is very great in all quarters of the town . . .'.

Living conditions were squalid and in addition to being over-crowded, rooms were frequently damp and dark. Cellars were particularly bad. Dr Robertson protested about them: '. . . how can a hole underneath of from twelve to fifteen feet [less than five metres] square admit of ventilation so as to fit it for a human habitation?' Houses crowded in on one another whether they were built back to back or round a courtyard as many were, for instance, in Glasgow. Streets were often unmade and until proper drains were laid sewage flowed along open channels. Water was obtained from the communal tap at the end of the street or in the courtyard. This meant that in conditions which made washing essential there was a serious shortage of water. As a result people resorted to using water from stagnant pools. Small wonder that the 1830s and 1840s witnessed serious outbreaks of cholera (caused by drinking unclean water).

Inside a Manchester slum. Why do you think the room is so bare?

The builders not only built how they wished, they built where they wished. Dr Robertson commented:

Manchester has no public park or other ground where the population can walk and breathe the fresh air. Now streets are rapidly extending in every direction, and so great already is the expanse of the town, that those who live in the more populous quarters can seldom hope to see the green face of nature....

There was little that workers could do in their spare time except drink.

These problems were not confined to the factory towns. Birmingham, which contained hundreds of small workshops producing between them metal goods of all kinds from guns to cooking pots; Liverpool, which prospered as Lancashire's link with the outside world, and London, which remained the country's chief port, all grew rapidly during this period. Future generations were left with the job of improving these towns as well as towns such as Manchester, Leeds and Glasgow. It was a daunting task and generally speaking it was not until the 1870s that significant progress was made.

A street tap in London 1863. The houses in this street would not have running water. Instead all the families who lived there would have to come to a single tap which was only turned on for a certain length of time each day.

Using the evidence: factory reform

We have seen that most factory owners cared little about their workers. Robert Owen was one who did. A bad environment, he argued, had a bad effect upon the people living in that environment. A good environment had a good effect. When he took over the cotton factory at New Lanark in Scotland in 1800 he decided to show that factory owners could improve their workers' lives and still make money.

The factory together with the workers' houses and other buildings such as the schools formed a complete village a large part of which was built by Owen's predecessor and father-in-law, David Dale.

(1) New Lanark

Robert Owen, 1771–1858

Owen described his work at New Lanark in a book entitled *The Life of Robert Owen by Himself:*

(2) The retail shops, in all of which spirits were sold, were great nuisances. All the articles sold were bought on credit at high prices, to cover great risks. The qualities were most inferior, and they were retailed out to the work people at extravagant rates. I arranged superior stores and shops, from which to supply every article of food, clothing, etc., which they required. I bought everything with money in the first markets, and contracted for fuel, milk, etc., on a large scale, and had the whole of these articles of the best qualities supplied to the people at the cost price. The result of this change was to save them in their expenses full twenty-five per cent, besides giving them the best qualities in everything, instead of the most inferior articles, with which alone they had previously been supplied.

The effects soon became visible in their improved health and superior dress, and in the general comfort of their houses.

Owen was particularly concerned about the children in the village. Here he is giving evidence to a Parliamentary Select Committee which had been set up to inquire into the problem of child labour:

(3) **Questioner.** At what age do you take these children into your mills?

Owen. At 10 and upwards.

Quest. What are your regular hours of labour per day, exclusive of meal times?

Owen. $10\frac{3}{4}$ hours.

Quest. What time do you allow for meals?

Owen. $\frac{3}{4}$ hour for dinner and $\frac{1}{2}$ hour for breakfast.

Quest. Then your full time of work per day is 12 hours?

Owen. Yes.

Quest. Why do you not employ children at an earlier age?

Owen. Because I consider it would be injurious to the children and not beneficial to the proprietors. . . . I found there [i.e. at New Lanark] 500 children, who had been taken from poor houses, chiefly in Edinburgh, and these children were generally from the age of 5 and 6, to 7 and 8. . . . The hours of work at that time were 13, inclusive of mealtimes, and an hour and a half was allowed for meals. I very soon discovered that, although these children were extremely well fed, well clothed, well lodged and very great care taken of them when out of the mills, their growth and their minds were materially injured by being employed at those ages within the cotton mills for $11\frac{1}{2}$ hours per day. . . .

Quest. Do you give instruction to any part of your population?

Owen. Yes . . . to the children from 3 years old, upwards; and to every part of the population which chooses to receive it. . . . There is a preparatory school, into which all the children, from the age of 3 to 6 are admitted at the option of their parents, there is a second school in which all the children of the population, from 6 to 10 are admitted; and if any of the parents, from being more easy in their circumstances, and setting a higher value upon instruction, wish to continue their children at school for one, two, three or four years longer, they are at liberty to do so; they are never asked to take their children from the school to the works. . . .

This extract forms part of the Committee's *Report* which was published in 1816.

(4) Owen built two schools. Here is a view of one of them.

The village of New Lanark

In many other ways Owen tried to improve the lives of those who lived in New Lanark. The workers' houses were enlarged and the village streets were paved. The mills were made lighter and airier. Weekly deductions from the workers' wages were used to establish a special fund for the benefit of the sick and the aged. To reduce and, if possible, eliminate drunkenness public houses were banned from the vicinity of the village.

Visitors came from far and wide to see what Owen was doing. Their impressions confirm the success of the New Lanark experiment. Here, for example, is the verdict of a deputation from Leeds:

(5) Mr Owen's establishment at Lanark is essentially a manufacturing establishment, conducted in a manner superior to any other the deputation ever witnessed, and dispensing more happiness than perhaps any other institution in the kingdom where so many poor persons are employed; ...

In the education of the children the thing that is most remarkable is the general spirit of kindness and affection, which is shown towards them, and the entire absence of everything that is likely to give them bad habits – with the presence of whatever is calculated to inspire them with good ones; the consequence is, that they appear like one well-regulated family, united together by the ties of the strongest affection.

In the adult inhabitants of New Lanark we saw much to commend. In general they appeared clean, healthy and sober. Intoxication, the parent of so many vices and so much misery, is indeed almost unknown here. The consequence is that they are well clad, and well fed, and their dwellings are inviting. ...

Owen hoped that other factory owners would follow his example. Few did. For this reason it became necessary for Parliament to act to improve conditions in the factories:

1833 Act Children under nine were not to be employed.
Children under thirteen were not to work more than nine hours a day and they were to have at least two hours of schooling a day.
Young persons between the ages of thirteen and eighteen were not to work more than twelve hours a day.
This law was to be enforced by factory inspectors.

1844 Act Women were to work no more than twelve hours a day.
Children under thirteen were to work no more than six and a half hours a day.
Dangerous machinery was to be guarded.

1847 Act Women and young persons between the ages of thirteen and eighteen were to work no more than ten hours a day. (In practice men also came to work a ten-hour day.)

These regulations applied to textile factories other than those making lace and silk. Gradually they were extended to cover all factories and workshops.

Questions and further work

1 What would a domestic worker find difficult about working in a factory?
2 Owen's 'silent monitor' proved to be a very good way of encouraging hard work. Why do you think this was so?
3 Look carefully at Illustration 1. In what ways do you think the location of the New Lanark factory helped Owen in his efforts to improve the lives of his workers?
4 In Document 2 Owen makes the following claim about the results of his changes on the lives of his workers: 'The effects soon became visible in their improved health and superior dress, and in the general comfort of their houses.' Can you find any evidence elsewhere in this section to support this statement?
5 Documents 2, 3 and 5 all give a favourable picture of Owen's work at New Lanark. Which do you find the most convincing? Give reasons for your answer.
6 What does Illustration 4 tell us about the schooling provided by Owen? Why did Owen feel it was so important that the children had an opportunity to go to school?
7 Read through the chapter and the section on Owen's work then draw up a chart to compare life in a typical factory town with life in New Lanark:

Conditions	Typical factory town	New Lanark
The factory itself		
Hours of work		
Workers' homes		
Shops		
Sale of drink		
Children's lives		

8 Why do you think so few employers followed Owen's example?

10 Protest

The Peterloo Massacre

1819 was a bad year for foreign trade. As a result, in Manchester and elsewhere, wages were reduced and people were thrown out of work. Manchester, like other industrial towns such as Birmingham and Leeds, had no MP and the suffering caused by the trade slump led to a big increase in popular support for those who argued that the town needed somebody to represent its interests in Parliament. On 16 August some 50 000 to 60 000 people assembled in an open space known as St Peter's Field to listen to a well-known campaigner for parliamentary reform, Henry Hunt. The crowd met in an orderly way under the eyes of the magistrates, who were occupying a nearby house together with a number of special constables. Banners were held aloft, bugles sounded and when Hunt arrived, complete with his famous white top hat, he was given an enthusiastic reception. As Hunt began to speak the magistrates decided that the meeting could not be allowed to continue and summoned a detachment of yeomanry cavalry who were standing by. Ordered to arrest Hunt, the soldiers rode into the crowd but were unable to force their way through. They drew their sabres and began to hack about them. More soldiers arrived and the crowd panicked:

The people began running in all directions; and from this moment the yeomanry lost all control of temper: numbers were trampled under the feet of men and horses: many, both men and women, were cut down by sabres. . . .

The Peterloo massacre

For ten minutes the soldiers attacked the crowd in furious fashion. At the end of that time the more or less deserted field presented a grim spectacle: 'Several mounds of human beings still remained where they had fallen, crushed down, and smothered. Some of these still groaning – others with staring eyes, were gasping for breath, and others would never breathe more.' Eleven people had been killed and some four hundred wounded.

The Prince Regent congratulated the magistrates on their 'prompt, decisive and efficient measures'. The government, fearing that the country might be on the verge of revolution, responded by placing restrictions on the holding of public meetings. In the country at large the common reaction was one of horror that an orderly crowd should have been cut down in this way. Four years earlier the British army had been applauded for its part in the Battle of Waterloo. Now, in a cynical play upon words, people spoke of the 'massacre of Peterloo'.

The Prince Regent, later George IV

Years of distress

The first half of the nineteenth century was a particularly grim time for the working classes of Britain. The growth of the factory system caused hardship not only for those who lived and worked in the new factory towns, but also for the many domestic workers who found work increasingly difficult to come by. The widespread unemployment caused periodically by a decrease in foreign trade made things even worse, especially if bread prices happened to be high following a harvest failure.

There seemed to be little that the working classes could do to improve their situation. An effective trade union movement did not yet exist and with no vote and very often no MP, workers could not bring influence to bear on Parliament. Not surprisingly, therefore, these were years of agitation and unrest.

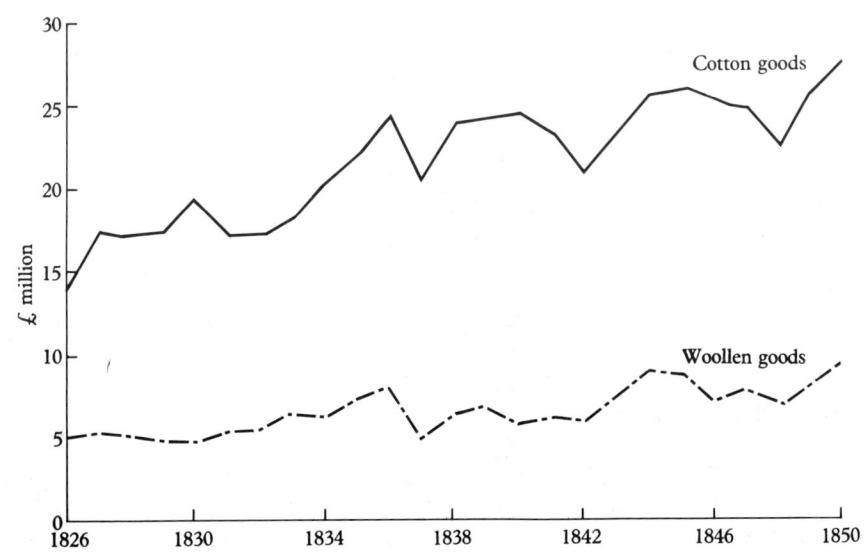

Fluctuations in Britain's exports 1826–50. Throughout the nineteenth century there were periodic dips in trade, which put people out of work at home.

The machine-breakers

Men like Henry Hunt believed that a thorough reform of the parliamentary system would lead to improvements in the condition of the working classes. If working people were represented in Parliament then something would be done about the way they lived and worked. This idea was to be taken up by the Chartists in the 1830s. But sometimes workers felt the need for immediate action. The machine-breakers were such men.

Machine-breaking was not new. In the 1740s, for instance, miners in the Northumberland coalfield had burnt pithead machinery in an attempt to win wage increases. Between 1811 and 1812, however, there was a particularly serious wave of machine-breaking.

Ned Lud

The disturbances started in Nottinghamshire where the framework knitters, like workers elsewhere, were suffering because of a fall in foreign trade. The knitters, who claimed to be led by someone called Ned Lud and so were known as Luddites, blamed their troubles on the inferior stockings which some hosiers were ordering them to make. The frame-smashing which began in March 1811 was primarily a protest against this and the violence did win some concessions from the hosiers.

From Nottinghamshire the Luddite movement spread to Yorkshire and Lancashire. In Yorkshire the croppers were protesting about the introduction of the gig and the shearing-frame which they rightly saw as a threat to their jobs: '. . . if they [i.e. the gigs and shearing-frames] are allowed to go on many hundreds of us will be out of bread.' By smashing the machines which they feared, the croppers were attempting to halt the progress of the Industrial Revolution. As a result of their actions some of the new machines were withdrawn but in the long run the croppers were fighting a losing battle. So too were the hand-loom weavers of Lancashire whose wages had been declining for some years because of the large number of workers in the industry. By attacking those factories where power-looms were already installed the weavers hoped to jolt their employers and the government into doing something about their deteriorating position. Nothing was done and the weavers' wages continued to fall.

The government responded to these disturbances with a heavy hand. Troops were used and machine-breaking was made punishable by death. By the end of 1812 peace had been restored.

This was not, however, the end of machine-breaking. In 1826 a considerable number of power-looms were destroyed by the Lancashire hand-loom weavers and in 1830 perhaps the most serious outburst of all flared up throughout the southern and eastern counties.

Captain Swing

The object of attack in this case was the threshing machine which was increasing the number of farm labourers out of work during the

Above left: celebrations on Blackfriars Bridge as the Albion flour mills burn down. The mills were destroyed in 1791. Arson was suspected as the mills were popularly thought to raise the price of bread.

Right: a meeting of trade unionists, London 1834. In the late twenties and early thirties there were several unsuccessful attempts to establish large national unions of workers. The government did not welcome these unions and in 1834 magistrates at Dorchester sentenced six men from Tolpuddle to transportation for their trade union activities. The meeting in this picture was organised to protest against the treatment of the 'Tolpuddle martyrs'.

A Luddite riot

Above: a 'Swing' letter

Below: the House of Commons, 1833

winter months when threshing was done. The farm labourer's life was hard enough as it was. Ever since the end of the French Wars in 1815 when 400000 soldiers and sailors had been demobilised, too many men had been seeking work on the land. The results were unemployment and low wages for those who did find work. William Cobbett saw the conditions in which labourers in Leicestershire were living:

Look at these hovels, made of mud and of straw; bits of glass, or of old cast-off windows, without frames or hinges frequently, but merely stuck in the mud wall. Enter them, and look at the bits of chairs or stools; the wretched boards tacked together to serve for a table; the floor of pebble, broken brick, and of the bare ground. . . .

The violence which erupted in 1830 had, then, been building up for some years. The disturbances started in Kent and quickly spread as far west as Dorset and as far north as Northamptonshire and East Anglia. An imaginary leader, Captain Swing, was invented and under his 'orders' farm labourers destroyed nearly four hundred threshing machines.

The Swing rising did not last long. Magistrates dealt sternly with any rioters. Six were hanged, over four hundred transported and about the same number imprisoned at home. In this way order was restored by the end of the year.

The rising did delay the spread of threshing machines. The problem of low wages remained, however, and increasing numbers of labourers decided to seek their fortunes in the towns.

The Chartists

Machine-breaking was an act of desperation by men who saw no other way of making their voice heard. The Chartists believed that the working classes needed to be given a voice in Parliament. This would lead, they argued, to a proper settlement of their grievances. As things were, even after the Reform Act of 1832, five out of six men were without the vote and the industrial areas were still under-represented in the House of Commons. The Chartists sought to change this situation by petitioning Parliament to accept the six points listed in the People's Charter:

1 Every man should have the vote.
2 Voting should be in secret.
3 All constituencies should have the same number of voters.
4 A general election should be held every year.
5 The property qualifications for Members of Parliament should be abolished.
6 Members of Parliament should be paid.

The Charter was first published in May 1838. Its adoption by a crowd of 200 000 people at a meeting in Birmingham three months later marked the launching of the Chartist movement. The size of the crowd is an indication of the support the movement was already attracting and this support was geographically widespread. The meeting was attended by working men from London, Yorkshire, Lancashire and Scotland. Corn prices were rising and 50 000 workers in the Manchester area alone were either out of work or on short time by the middle of 1837. Things got worse between 1839 and 1842 and it was during this period that Chartism flourished. As one man bluntly put it: 'The people are discontented because they want food.' Some supporters, like the handloom weavers, were starving before the collapse of foreign trade in 1837. But without that collapse Chartism would not have had the vitally important support of unemployed workers from the manufacturing districts.

The Chartist petition of 1848 being presented to the prime minister Lord John Russell. A cartoon from Punch.

In the north of England support for Chartism was bound up with opposition to the Poor Law Amendment Act of 1834. The idea of having to enter the workhouse whenever a fall in trade threw them out of work was bitterly opposed by factory workers. What happened to Assistant Commissioner Power when he sought to apply the Act in Bradford was not unusual: 'On leaving the courthouse I was violently assaulted. The first blow I received was upon my head from a tin can. Umbrellas, stones and mud were applied very freely...'.

The man chiefly responsible for turning opposition to the New Poor

Feargus O'Connor, 1794–1855

Law into support for the Charter was Feargus O'Connor. O'Connor was an Irishman of striking appearance with a forceful personality. After founding a newspaper called *Northern Star* in Leeds in 1837 to promote opposition to the New Poor Law, O'Connor decided to throw his weight behind the Chartist programme. Until Parliament was reformed it seemed unlikely that the hated 1834 Act would be repealed. O'Connor quickly became the dominant Chartist figure in the north. Indeed, his weekly letter in the *Northern Star* and his endless speeches at mass meetings soon made him the outstanding personality of the entire movement. O'Connor warned his followers that they might have to defend themselves against attack: 'Let everyone who has not arms procure them – let him keep them clean and bright and ready for use when wanted ...'. Many Chartists did this and in the evenings men turned out to drill by torchlight on the hillsides of Lancashire and Yorkshire and in the Welsh valleys. The movement was beginning to appear menacing.

But not for long. The first petition in support of the Charter was presented, complete with one and a quarter million signatures, to the House of Commons in 1839. It was rejected by 235 votes to forty-six. Faced with this rebuff the Chartists could not agree on what to do next. In the event, John Frost, a prominent Welsh Chartist, led a futile attack in 1840 on the town of Newport which prompted the arrest and imprisonment of leading Chartists all over the country. The Chartist wave ebbed and never, in fact, regained its force of the years 1839–40.

Until 1842, however, the movement continued to attract consider-

The Newport riots, 1840

able support. In that year a second petition was presented to the House of Commons and its rejection was followed by a number of disturbances. Thereafter support began to dwindle as industry revived and a run of good harvests (starting with that of 1842) reduced the price of corn. A brief revival of interest followed the economic collapse of 1847 and a third petition was organised in 1848 but this was the movement's final flourish. Support evaporated after the rejection of the petition and the prosperity of the 1850s ensured that there was no revival. The last time that Chartists turned out in any great number was for O'Connor's funeral in 1855, which was attended by a crowd of over 50 000.

Not one of the Charter's aims had been realised. Chartism had drawn people's attention to the condition of the working classes but apart from this the movement had failed.

The second Chartist petition is carried to the House of Commons, 1842

Using the evidence: a Luddite trial

In January 1813 numerous Yorkshire Luddites were brought to trial in York. Three cloth-dressers, George Mellor, William Thorpe and Thomas Smith, stood accused of murder. Together with Benjamin Walker, who had taken advantage of an Act passed in 1812 which granted a free pardon to those who turned King's evidence, they were said to have murdered William Horsfall, a Yorkshire mill owner who had made no secret of his contempt for the Luddites. All three accused, none of whom was older than twenty-three, pleaded not guilty. The case aroused great interest and when the trial opened the courtroom was packed. Here are some extracts from an account of the trial:

The Prosecution

(1) Mr Park (Counsel for the Crown) addressed the Jury:

... Mr Horsfall, into whose death we are now to inquire, was about forty years of age; he was a married man; had a family of children, and was a manufacturer to a considerable extent, in the West Riding. It is well-known to you all, that for a considerable period, dreadful disturbances have taken place in this county.... About 11 April a very violent attack was made on the mill of Mr Cartwright, in which, by the gallant and successful defence that was made, a number of assailants were wounded, and two killed. ... It will be proved that this defence gave rise to the most gross abuse and threats against the proprietors of such machinery, and more particularly against Mr Horsfall, who had an extensive establishment of this kind; who employed a great number of workmen, by whom he is represented to me to have been greatly beloved. But inasmuch as he employed this obnoxious machinery, and had expressed himself with a manly warmth against the delusions under which the manufacturing classes laboured, ... he became the object of the most barbarous revenge, and was marked out for destruction....

It was known that he [Mr Horsfall] was in the constant habit of attending the Huddersfield market. He left Huddersfield between five and six in the afternoon, on 28 April, ... on his return to Marsden, a distance of seven miles. When he had rode as far as the Warrener House, a public house ... kept by Joseph Armitage, he stopped to get some refreshment, but without alighting from his horse, having got a glass of rum and water ... he proceeded homewards: when he had got as far as the corner of a plantation, belonging to Mr Radcliffe, a distance of about three hundred yards from the Warrener House, at the corner of this plantation Mr Horsfall was shot....

Gentlemen, I shall call before you an accomplice, one of the four men, who perpetrated the deed ... but I shall not ask you to convict the prisoners on his testimony only, I shall confirm it by a chain of strong and well-connected circumstances, all tending to establish the guilt of the prisoners....

The accomplice ... will state to you that when the proposal was first made he rather objected to go, but at length was prevailed to be one of the party. The proposal was made first about four o'clock and it was settled they should be in the plantation of Mr Radcliffe about half past five o'clock. Smith and witness went together and arrived at the spot before Mellor and Thorpe, each provided with a pistol. On the road Walker proposed to Smith to turn back and not to go,

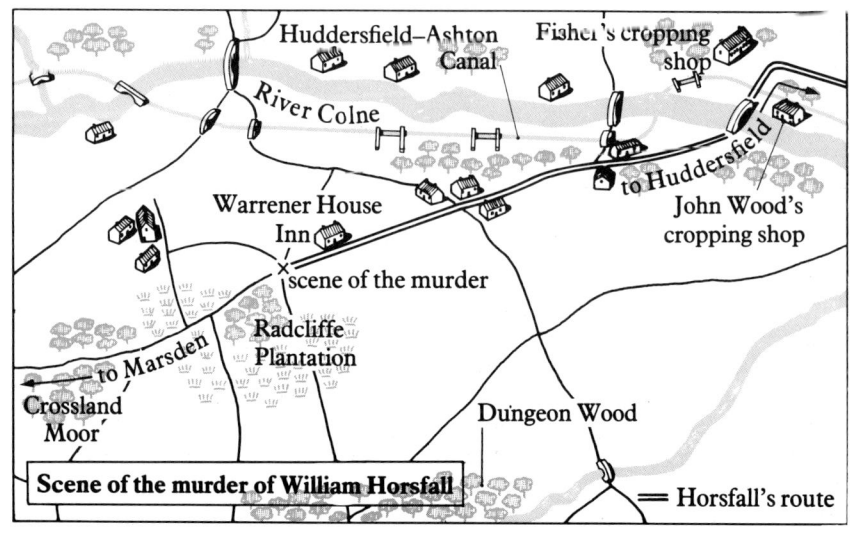

Scene of the murder of William Horsfall

Rawfolds Mill

but Smith said, 'Nay, let us go to the place and try to persuade them not to do it, for if we do not go we shall be shot.' Mellor and Thorpe were to stand at the corner of the plantation where they could command the road, and Walker and Smith at about twenty yards [18 metres] distance. When Mellor and Thorpe had taken their place, Smith went to them . . . to persuade them not to do it, but he returned and said, if they went away they would be shot, and that Mellor and Thorpe would fire first, and if they missed, Walker and himself were to fire. They stooped down that they might not be seen from the road; they had not remained long before the word was given that Mr Horsfall was coming. Mellor and Thorpe almost immediately fired, and ran to Walker and Smith and called them flats, a term of reproach, for not firing. . . . They all four ran over some fields to Dungeon Wood, and Mellor and Thorpe said they must separate, which they did. . . .

Mellor and Thorpe went to Dungeon Wood bottom, to a relation, Joseph Mellor, where they deposited the pistols, concealing them among some flocks, they left their great coats there. . . .

(2) *Henry Parr examined by Mr Holdroyd (Counsel for the Crown) said:*
I was going home from Huddersfield to Marsden on Tuesday, 28 April; I cannot say what time it was when I left Huddersfield; when I came near the Warrener House, I heard the report of firearms, it was a very large crack, and seemed to come out of the nearest corner of Mr Radcliffe's plantation, from which I was about one hundred and fifty yards [140 metres]. I did not know the persons, but they were all dressed in dark coloured clothes; after the report, the horse of a person riding before turned round, and the rider, whom I afterwards found to be Mr Horsfall fell with his face upon the horse's chine; he raised himself up by the mane and called out 'Murder,' . . . I then rode up to Mr Horsfall at a gallop as hard as I could . . . the blood gushed out of his side several inches . . . he then fell off the horse. . . .

(3) *Rowland Houghton, of Huddersfield, surgeon, said:*
I was called in about seven o'clock, and went to the Warrener House as soon as possible. I got to the Warrener House between eight and nine, and found Mr Horsfall lying on a bed . . . he was sick, pale, and much exhausted, and his pulse could scarcely be felt it was so weak and tremulous. . . . One ball had been extracted from the right thigh and I extracted one musket ball from the outside of the right thigh, near the hip joint. . . . [Horsfall died two days later on Thursday 30 April.]

The shooting of William Horsfall. How does this picture differ from the account of Horsfall's murder presented by the prosecution?

(4) *Benjamin Walker, the accomplice, a cropper by trade said:*
I worked at John Wood's near two years, at Longroyd-bridge, about a quarter of a mile [half a kilometre] from Huddersfield; Mellor and Smith worked also at Wood's in April last. Thorpe worked at Mr Fisher's, a shop about two or three hundred yards [200 metres] from Mr Wood's – I was not acquainted with Thorpe; I remember the report respecting the attack on Mr Cartwright's mill; it happened before the shooting of Mr Horsfall, and was conversed about in the works of Wood; when they conversed about it, Thorpe was one of the party, and the men killed at Cartwright's were talked about by them. They said it was a hard matter. Mellor said, 'The method of breaking the shears must be given up, and instead of it, the masters must be shot.' That was the most I heard said; they said they had lost two men, and they must kill the masters. I do not remember what day Horsfall was shot, but I was that day at Wood's . . . I remember being with Mellor between four and five in the afternoon, and there was William Hall and my father William Walker. He asked me if I would go with him to shoot Mr Horsfall? . . . [Walker's evidence continued along the lines indicated in Mr Park's address to the Jury.]

(5) *Joseph Sowden, a cloth-dresser, examined by Mr Richardson (Counsel for the Crown) said:*
. . . I saw Mellor, the evening of the murder, about half-past seven. I had then heard what had happened to Mr Horsfall. The day following, the three prisoners, and Benjamin Walker jointly and separately represented to me the circumstances of the murder, substantially the same as that you have heard today.

The Defence

The defence case was that the accused were nowhere near the scene of the murder at the time Horsfall was said to have been shot. Several witnesses were called to support this case and what follows is the evidence of two of them.

(6) *John Womersley, a clock and watch-maker*, saw Mellor on the evening Mr Horsfall was shot, at a quarter after six in Huddersfield, at the corner of the Cloth-Hall street, had a note in his pocket for him, he owing him seven shillings for business done, went with him to Mr Tavernor's, the White Hart near the Cloth Hall and stopped in the house about twenty minutes, where he drank with the prisoner Mellor, and left him there with one William Battersby. Witness went then to the Brown Cow, another public house, and had no sooner got in than the news arrived that Mr Horsfall was shot, and the soldiers were going.

(7) *William Battersby, the next witness*, lived then at Taylor-Hill, was at Huddersfield on 28 April; and recollects that evening being at Tavernor's, saw George Mellor and Jonathan Womersley, and drank with them; they had two pints of ale, and Jonathan Womersley left him in company with George Mellor, they were at this inn half an hour. At the end of that time they heard of Mr Horsfall being shot for the first time. They came out and he parted with Mellor at the door.

Questions and further work

1 Explain briefly why each of the following groups resorted to machine-breaking between 1811 and 1832: (a) framework knitters (b) croppers (c) hand-loom weavers (d) agricultural labourers.
2 Summarise the prosecution's version of the story of William Horsfall's murder by answering the following questions:
   (a) What prompted Mellor and his associates to kill mill owners instead of smashing their machines?
   (b) Why did they select Horsfall as a victim?
   (c) When and where did they lie in wait for him?
   (d) How many shots were fired?
   (e) What did Mellor and his associates do after the shooting?
   (f) Whom did they tell of the murder?
3 Using the information in Documents 1, 4 and 5, what kind of a character do you think Mellor was?
4 What was Mellor's alibi?
5 Which presented the stronger case, the prosecution or the defence? As a class what is your verdict? (You will find the actual verdict on page 224.)
6 Are there any points on which you would have liked to have more evidence?
7 *Either* Act out this trial scene, adding any other parts you consider necessary (e.g. the Judge, Mr Justice le Blanc): or Write a short play based on the prosecution's version of the events leading up to Horsfall's murder then act it out.

11 The Railway Age

Richard Trevithick

Richard Trevithick invented the locomotive steam engine. However, this achievement did not bring him fame and when he died in 1833 he was a forgotten man. He was a Cornish mining engineer who turned his attention to building steam road vehicles. These worked but were extremely noisy and so were particularly unsuitable if there were horses .around. Instead Trevithick began to build steam locomotives which would run along rails. He built four altogether, his most famous being the engine made for the Pen-y-Darron Ironworks in South Wales. This was the first successful locomotive. In 1804 it hauled a load of ten tonnes of iron over a distance of fourteen and a half kilometres at a speed of eight kilometres per hour. Doubtless this was much to the satisfaction of the owner of the works who had laid a wager of 500 guineas [£525] with a neighbour that the engine would perform better than a horse. However, it was discovered later that the rails snapped if the load was too heavy and so the engine was limited in what it could do. It failed to arouse the interest that Trevithick had justifiably hoped for.

In 1808 he tried to capture the public's imagination by setting up a circular track near the site of the present Euston Station. On this, his latest engine, *Catch-Me-Who-Can*, pulled a carriage in which people could ride for the price of two shillings (10p). Unfortunately, the venture brought him no orders for locomotives and, disillusioned, he

A stationary steam engine in use at an eighteenth-century coal mine

built no more. Later he sought his fortune in South America, and when Robert Stephenson met him in Colombia in 1827, Trevithick, now known as Don Ricardo, was engineer to a shaky copper-mining company. He returned, penniless, to England and when he died in Dartford in 1833 was buried in a pauper's grave.

Horse-drawn coal wagons at Denby Colliery in Derbyshire about 1900

The early railways

Trevithick was one of several engineers who, in the early years of the nineteenth century, were trying to produce a successful steam engine which could drive itself along rails. Coal wagons had been hauled along rails by horses or men since the seventeenth century. These were the earliest railways and they were found to be a good way of moving coal away from the pits. A locomotive steam engine would be able to pull much heavier loads and it was no accident that most of the early locomotive engineers worked at collieries. John Blenkinsop and Matthew Murray built their tooth-wheeled engine in 1812 for the Middleton Colliery near Leeds. William Hedley, who demonstrated with his *Puffing Billy* that a smooth-wheeled engine could work, was employed by the Wylam Colliery near Newcastle. A few kilometres away, at the Killingworth Colliery, George Stephenson built his first locomotive, the *Blücher*, in 1814.

Stephenson seems to have had an instinctive understanding of engineering problems. Born at Wylam in 1781, he had no proper

George Stephenson talking to his navvies

The opening of the Stockton and Darlington Railway

schooling and to the end of his days had difficulty in writing. He spent his early years working as a colliery engineer. This involved looking after the steam engines which pumped water out of the mines. He became interested in locomotive steam engines and after building the *Blücher* supplied a number of collieries with locomotives. His fame spread and in 1821 the directors of the newly-formed Stockton and Darlington Railway decided that he should supervise the building of their line. This was not to be a private colliery line but was to be open to the public. Rather than use only horses or stationary steam engines to pull wagons, Stephenson was anxious that locomotives should be employed on the line. The directors accepted his arguments. The track was made level enough for locomotives to be used over most of the distance and in 1825 the line was successfully opened with Stephenson driving *Locomotion No. 1*.

Stephenson was now established as the country's leading railway engineer but some people still had their doubts about locomotives. In 1824 he had been appointed engineer to the Liverpool and Manchester Railways and the directors of this line were not convinced that locomotives should be used. Before abandoning the idea of stationary steam engines they insisted on holding a series of test trials for locomotives at Rainhill. These took place in October 1829. Large crowds lined the three kilometre track and saw Stephenson's *Rocket* win easily at an average speed of twenty-two and a half kilometres per hour. The performance of the *Rocket* convinced the directors that locomotives

Constructing a tunnel at Edgehill on the Liverpool and Manchester Railway

should supply the power on their railway. The tremendous success of the line after it was opened in 1830 showed how right that decision was. The future of the locomotive was assured.

Railway mania

The opening of the Liverpool and Manchester Railway was a turning point in the history of railways in this country. The Stockton and Darlington Railway was important for the use it made of locomotives. But stationary steam engines and horses were still used on that line and many of the coaches and coal wagons were privately owned. These could be used whenever the owners wished, on payment of a toll. The Liverpool and Manchester Railway provided a much more efficient service. The line was suggested by a group of Liverpool businessmen frustrated by the delays and cost involved in transporting goods between Liverpool and Manchester by river or canal.

The 'Rocket'

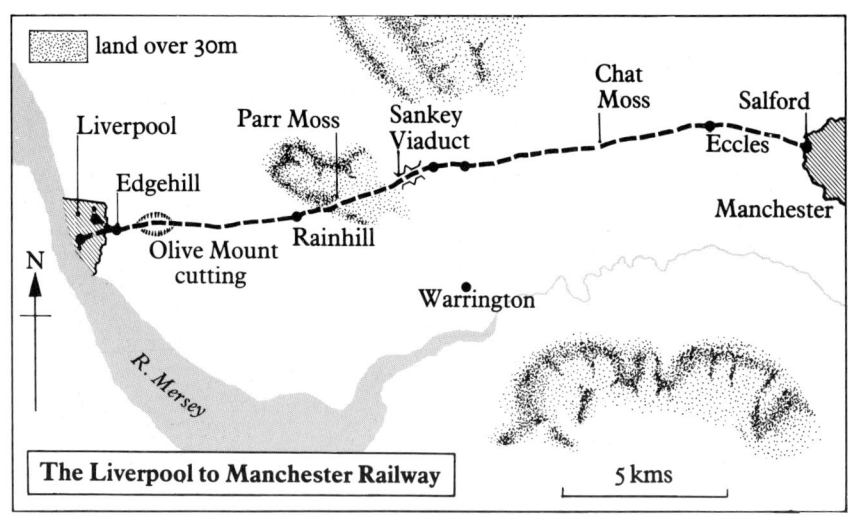

The Liverpool to Manchester Railway

It was a difficult line to build. The country was by turns hilly and marshy and the successful construction of the fifty-one kilometres of double track showed convincingly that Stephenson's skills were by no means confined to locomotive engineering. The most formidable obstacle was the notorious Chat Moss, an enormous peat bog over which the line had to be floated on a mattress of heather and brushwood. After many uneasy moments this was successfully accomplished and the line was opened in 1830. The occasion was marred by a fatal accident to William Huskisson, MP for Liverpool and a member of the Government. He fell into the path of the *Rocket* which 'went over his leg and thigh and fractured them in a most dreadful manner'. In spite of being rushed by locomotive to a doctor, he died a few hours later. After this unfortunate start the line was an unqualified success. The engines soon reached speeds of forty-eight kilometres per hour and traffic flowed between the two towns. The great surprise, however, was the amount of passenger traffic. The Liverpool and Manchester Railway, like the Stockton and Darlington, had been built primarily with freight in mind. Yet not until 1852 did freight traffic earn more than passenger traffic.

Now began a period of intense interest in the railways which reached its peak in two spells of railway mania. The first of these came in the years 1836–7 when some 2400 kilometres of railways were agreed to by Parliament. The second and more feverish came in the years 1845–8 when about 13 750 kilometres of track were authorised. Building a railway was an expensive business. Apart from the cost of construction there were considerable legal expenses and of course a great deal of land had to be bought. It was estimated in 1866 that the cost of the railways in England and Wales worked out at £25 000 per kilometre. Fortunately for the promoters of railways the profits earned by the early companies were vast. Railway shares, therefore, were eagerly sought and bought. To deal with the rush of business the London Stock Exchange had to

'Hyde Park as it will be'. This cartoon was prompted by the frantic railway building of the 1840s.

employ more clerks and provincial towns, starting with Liverpool and Manchester, opened their own stock exchanges for the first time. Newspapers started publishing lists of railway share prices and a magazine called *Railway Times* was launched in 1837 to deal with all matters relating to railway investment. Taking advantage of this situation, George Hudson, the sharp-practising railway promoter from York, built up a railway empire which at its height consisted of 2400 kilometres of track and earned for himself the nickname, 'The Railway King'.

Not all the railways authorised in this period were built. Nevertheless over 10 500 kilometres of railway had been constructed by 1850. There were still areas which had not been penetrated, noticeably the interior of Wales and the Highlands of Scotland. The system was not uniform as it contained broad gauge as well as narrow gauge lines. But the basic framework of the railway system was complete.

A London and North Western Railway goods train, 1899. Throughout the second half of the nineteenth century the railways remained the most efficient means of transporting freight.

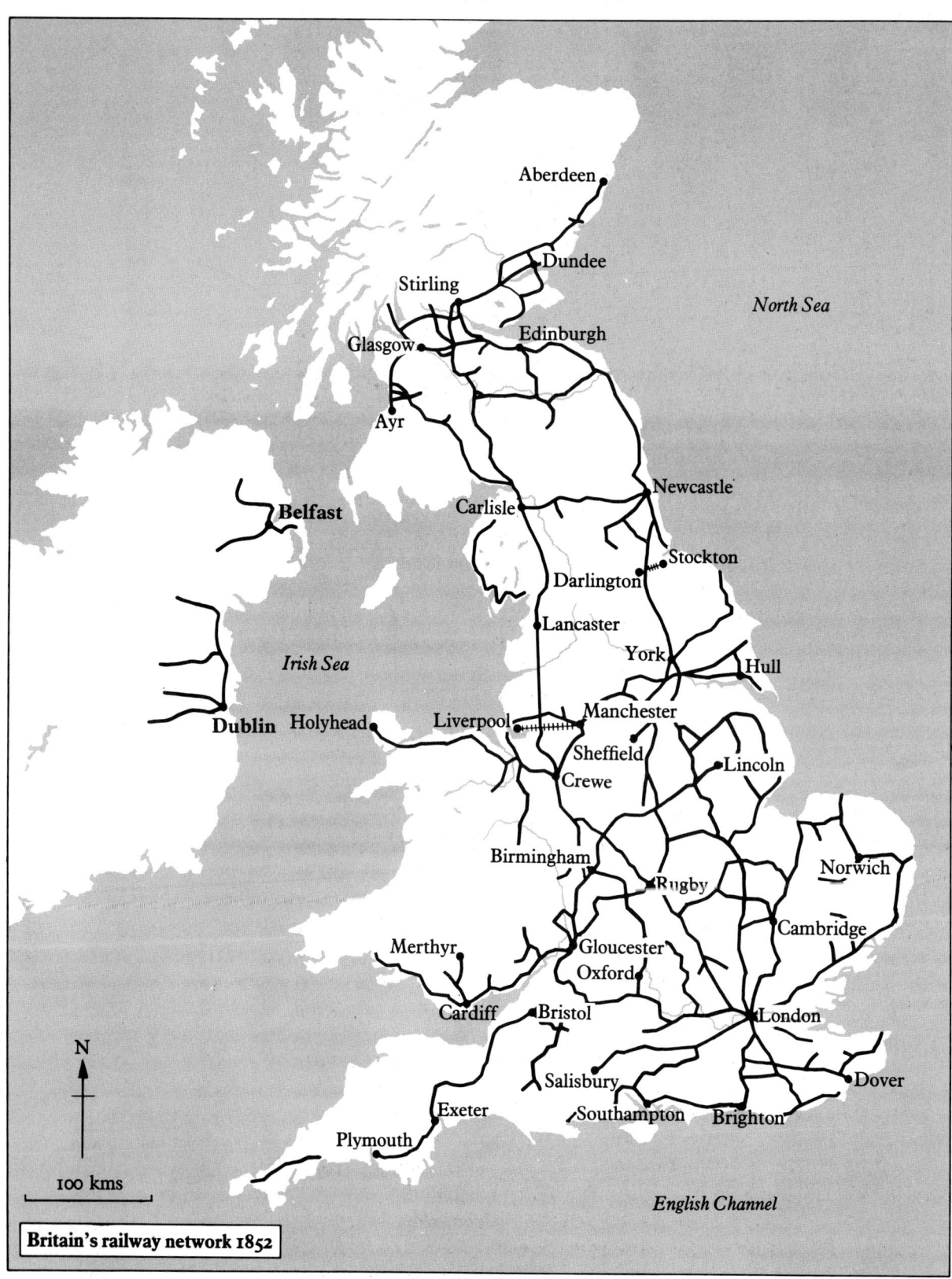

North Sea

Aberdeen

Dundee

Stirling

Glasgow

Edinburgh

Ayr

Belfast

Newcastle

Carlisle

Stockton

Irish Sea

Darlington

Lancaster

Dublin

Holyhead

York

Hull

Liverpool

Manchester

Sheffield

Lincoln

Crewe

Birmingham

Norwich

Rugby

Cambridge

Merthyr

Gloucester

Oxford

Cardiff

Bristol

London

Salisbury

Dover

N

Southampton

Brighton

100 kms

Exeter

Plymouth

English Channel

Britain's railway network 1852

The Sankey Viaduct on the Liverpool to Manchester line

Building the lines

An Act of Parliament was needed to set up a railway company. Building a railway line involved the compulsory purchase of land and Parliament's permission was needed for this. To obtain an Act of Parliament the people who wished to form a railway company had to present a detailed prospectus. This would give details of the route which the engineer proposed to follow and a list of all the landowners affected. These might well protest, like Captain Butler who objected to the route proposed in 1835 by the Sheffield and Rotherham Railway:

... if an Old Sailor may be allowed to speak in his own language he would implore the House not to turn him adrift, when he had fondly hoped that, like an old hulk, he was laid up in a quiet harbour for the remainder of his days.

Some landowners succeeded in changing the route, like Robert Raikes who managed to divert the Hull and Selby Railway past his Welton estate. Others did not and had to be content with the compensation provided.

Once the Act was passed, work could begin. Until the 1850s and 1860s, when more powerful locomotives were developed which could tackle steeper gradients, the engineer had to make his line as level as possible. This involved filling in hollows with embankments or building viaducts across them, cutting through rising ground and driving tunnels through hills. Bridges, some of considerable height and length, were needed. Marshy ground might have to be crossed. All this was difficult work and required great skill on the part of the supervising engineer. The companies were fortunate in the quality of the men they could employ in this position. Three were outstanding: George Stephenson, his son Robert and Isambard Brunel.

But the engineers in turn required men to dig and build for them. At one stage in 1847 there were 300 000 navvies working up and down the country building railway lines. Their predecessors, the navigators, had

'Navvy in heavy marching order'.
This drawing appeared in Punch.

built the canals. Now, armed with pick and shovel, dressed in moleskin trousers, hobnail boots and rainbow waistcoats, they won for themselves an unrivalled reputation for hard work and riotous living. They came mainly from Ireland, Scotland and the north of England. They went wherever they were needed, living in shanty towns thrown together near the works. They consumed huge quantities of food and drink. On one line it was estimated that in one year nearly one and a half million litres of beer and over twenty thousand litres of spirits had been drunk. During a full day's work they might shift in the region of twenty tonnes of earth. The work was often dangerous, especially where gunpowder was used, and the navvies increased the risks through their own recklessness. Three navvies were killed on the London and Birmingham Railway trying to leap over the mouth of a shaft in a game of follow-my-leader. But their skills were required overseas as well as in Great Britain and in the course of the nineteenth century they built railways all over the world.

The effects of the railways

The railways transformed the way people lived. Sydney Smith wrote in 1842: 'Everything is near, everything is immediate, time, distance and

ONDON, CHATHAM & DOVER
RAILWAY.
eap Excursion to Crystal Palace & London.

REAT CRICKET MATCH
AT THE
RYSTAL PALACE
AUSTRALIANS v. PLAYERS.

MONDAY, SEPTEMBER 27th, 1880.

A CHEAP EXCURSION TRAIN		FARES THERE & BACK:—	
WILL LEAVE		To LONDON.	To PENGE (inclu-ding admis-sion to the Crystal Palace).
		THIRD CLASS.	THIRD CLASS.
er Harbour ... ... at 9. 0 a.m.			
er Priory ... ... ,, 9. 2 ,,	5/0	5/0	
eril's Well ... ... ,, 9.16 ,,			
sbourne ... ... ,, 9.31 ,,			
terbury ... ... ,, 9.38 ,,			
asgate ... ... ,, 8.55 ,,			
lstairs ... ... ,, 9. 0 ,,			
gate ... ... ,, 9. 7 ,,			
ington-on-Sea... ... ,, 9.17 ,,			
c Bay ... ... ,, 9.34 ,,	} 4/6	4/6	
stable ... ... ,, 9.43 ,,			
g ... ... ,, 9.53 ,,			
ersham ... ... ,, 10. 0 ,,	4/0	4/6	
ham ... ... ,, 10.14 ,,	3/6	4/0	

ing at PENGE (within Five Minutes' Walk of the Garden Entrance to the
'STAL PALACE) about 11.35 a.m., and VICTORIA STATION,
LONDON, about 12.0 noon.
rning the same day from VICTORIA STATION at 7.20 p.m., and PENGE
at 7.40 p.m.

he Tickets are available to return on the day of issue only, and by the Train named.
No Luggage allowed. Children under Twelve half-price.
eptember 15th, 1880. (BY ORDER.)

TORIA STATION is close to the Royal Aquarium at Westminster.
Trains every few minutes from Victoria (District Railway) to
all parts of London.
—133.—80. Printed at the Company's Works, Victoria Station, Pimlico.

*The workmen's 'Penny Train'
arriving at Victoria Station, 1865*

delay are abolished.' At their swiftest the coaches averaged seventeen kilometres per hour. By 1850 speeds of fifty to sixty kilometres per hour were commonplace on the main railway routes. Moreover, it was cheaper by rail. Railways cut out the hidden costs of coach travel such as the tips to the coachman and guard and the expensive meals at the coaching inns along the road. In 1844 Gladstone's Cheap Trains Act ensured that each company provided at least one train a day on which the charge would be no more than 1d ($\frac{1}{2}$p) a mile. By 1850 the long-distance coaches had disappeared and people were travelling far more than they had ever done before. *The Times* commented: 'Thirty years ago not one countryman in one hundred had seen the metropolis. There is now scarcely one in the same number who has not spent the day there.' Excursion trains were introduced and seaside resorts began to flourish. Suburbs developed as people were able to live farther away from their place of work. From Queen Victoria downwards the railways quickly won acceptance.

The railways brought change in numerous ways. They speeded up the distribution of mail and by 1850 'newspaper expresses' were leaving Euston and Paddington. The need to keep to railway timetables caused Greenwich Time to be adopted throughout the country. (Until then 'local time' had varied from place to place.) The engineering works provided new, and often pleasing, features in the landscape. Cities were transformed by the intrusion of approach lines, stations and marshalling yards.

In addition to all this the railways encouraged industry to expand. Goods traffic moved more quickly and could grow at a rate which would not have been possible had it still been confined to the 6500 kilometres of navigable waterways. The railways also gave particular encouragement to the iron, steel and coal industries. Iron was needed to build the lines and the locomotives and largely because of this the iron industry doubled its output in the 1830s and 1840s. (Later steel was used instead of iron.) Coal was needed to fire the locomotives and by 1850 over a million tonnes a year were being used in this way. As industry grew, more people were needed in the towns and here again the railways helped. They made it easier for agricultural workers to move to the towns in search of higher wages.

Finally it should be remembered that the railways in Britain were themselves a major industry. By 1850, quite apart from the navvies, 60 000 people were employed in running the railways. They ranged from clerks to engine drivers, from porters to carriage builders. Some of them lived in the new towns, like Crewe, which emerged to house the carriage and locomotive works required by the railway companies. Others lived in old towns, like York, which were given fresh life by virtue of being important railway junctions. But the railways, unlike any other industry, employed people throughout the country. Wherever a railway station was opened, station staff were needed and a station master to supervise them.

Using the evidence: the navvies

The navvies who built Britain's railways had no mechanical diggers to help them. Illustrations 1 and 2, from a book published in 1852 *Our Iron Roads* show two methods used to move earth:

(1)

The picture above shows how an embankment was made. A light railway was built on top of the embankment. A train load of trucks, filled with earth would be brought to within fifty metres of the edge of the embankment. Then the first truck was detached from the train and fastened to a horse. The horse, which would walk to one side of the rails, pulled it farther along the track. It was made to gallop and as it approached the edge was detached from the truck. The horse and the

(2) Excavating a cutting

man leading it leaped to one side and the truck ran along the rails until it hit a piece of wood placed across them at the end of the track. This caused the truck to tip up and empty its contents over the edge.

Accidents were commonplace at railway works. In spite of this, however, medical care would seem to have been woefully inadequate. In the following extract Mr Pomfret, a surgeon who attended many of the accidents which occurred in the notorious Woodhead Tunnel on the Sheffield and Manchester line, is giving evidence to a House of Commons Select Committee:

(3) **Questioner.** Did you look upon yourself at all in the relation of being employed by the contractors, or solely as being employed by the men?
Pomfret. I know that the money was paid by the men entirely; though, of course, the money came through the contractors' hands to me. . . .
Quest. Did you give yourself up entirely to that duty?
Pomfret. No.
Quest. What other duty?
Pomfret. I was a surgeon in private practice.
Quest. When some of these accidents happened, did it not sometimes occur that you were away some distance?
Pomfret. I lived eight miles [thirteen kilometres] from the tunnel, and had always to be sent for in severe cases; two hours nearly always elapsed before I got there.

*

Questioner. Was any provision made by the company for the accommodation of the sick?
Pomfret. No.
Quest. They were taken to the huts which they occupied on the tunnel?
Pomfret. Yes.
Quest. The men, I believe, were all lodged in temporary huts?
Pomfret. They were chiefly temporary huts.
Quest. Did you exercise any superintendence over these huts with regard to their cleanliness or healthiness?
Pomfret. I had not the least control.

Navvies were notoriously riotous. The Select Committee heard this account of an episode involving Irish and Scottish labourers:

(4) It was upon the evening of a pay night. Some of the police on the railway had apprehended two Irish labourers upon a trivial charge, the suspicion of stealing a watch, and they were lodged in a temporary lock-up house near the line; their companions immediately proceeded to the huts in the neighbourhood where a great body of labourers were, and having obtained their assistance, they returned to the prison where those two labourers who had been apprehended were confined. They broke it open and overpowered the policemen, who were defending it, and rescued their companions. After they had done so, and within a very short distance of this lock-up house, they met two other policemen coming towards the lock-up house, not aware of what had taken place; they attacked them, and killed one of them, and hurt the other. This outrage was committed almost entirely, I may say, by Irish labourers. It happened on a Saturday night, upon the the last day of February, and upon the Monday the Scotch labourers assembled in a large body and, under the pretext of avenging the death of this policeman, who was a Scotchman, they proceeded to the huts of the Irish people, which they burned, drove the Irish away, and committed various other acts of outrage.

An early photograph of navvies

Undoubtedly the navvies often rioted simply because they were drunk. In this case, however, the witness who recounted the incident thought something else was at least partly to blame:

(5) I have already stated that the men are only paid monthly; they are generally ignorant and illiterate people, who are not able to keep any account to compare with the account against them kept at the store, and therefore when they go to receive their wages, they generally find that they have much less to receive than they expected. . . .

He was referring to the truck system. Navvies who ran out of cash between pay days were forced to live on tickets handed out by the contractor in charge of the works. These could be exchanged for goods, but only at the local truck shop (which the contractor might well own) where the navvies were offered inferior goods at high prices. The day of reckoning for those who resorted in this way to living on truck was pay day. Then the value of all the tickets they had received was taken out of their wages.

The navvies were very much a race apart. As if to emphasise this they adopted special nicknames and developed their own slang. To illustrate this here are two extracts from Terry Coleman's *The Railway Navvies* first published in 1965:

(6) The colour of a man's whiskers could get him called Streaky Dick, Ginger Bill, or Black and Tan. But perhaps the most common sort of nickname was that which revealed where a man had come from. There were Bristol Jacks, Brummagem Joes, Devon Bills, and Yankee Toms. Navvies who came from Lancashire or Yorkshire were called Lanks or Yorkeys. Bacca Lank smoked hugely, and Contrairy was the most famous of the Yorkeys.

(7) ... the navvies also had a talent for slang, some of it very like the rhyming slang of Cockney tradition. 'Now, Jack,' says one navvy to another, 'I'm going to get a tiddly wink of a pig's ear, so keep your mince pies on the Billy Gorman' – meaning he is going to get a drink of beer and wants Jack to keep an eye on the foreman. If he had wanted something stronger than beer he might have spoken of 'Bryan O'Lin', or 'Tommy get out and let your father in', meaning gin.

Questions and further work

1 Examine Illustration 2 carefully. How was the earth moved from the bottom of the cutting? How does this picture help to explain why the navvies had such a reputation for hard work?
2 List five kinds of engineering feature which were generally needed to carry the railway line through different kinds of country. Explain why each might be necessary.
3 What criticism could be made of the navvies' employers on the basis of the information given in Document 3?
4 Explain the truck system. In what ways did it work unfairly for the navvies? In the light of your answer do you think Document 5 explains fully why the navvies might feel resentful when they received their wages?
5 When the navvies came to an area the inhabitants often viewed their arrival with alarm. Were their fears justified? (Illustrate your answer with examples from the text and the documents.)
6 Try to work out the meaning of the following examples of navvy slang: (a) Johnny Randle (b) Charley Friskey (c) Charley Prescott (d) Jimmy Skinner (e) penneth o' bread (f) weeping willow (g) bo-peep (h) Lord Lovel (i) sugar and honey (j) elephant's trunk.
   You will find the answers in Terry Coleman's *The Railway Navvies*.
7 Imagine that you have been a spectator at the opening of one of the early railway lines. Write a letter describing the scene to a friend who has never seen a railway. To help, you could try to find a description of the opening of a local railway in the newspapers of the time. Ask about this at your local library.

12 Coal, iron and steel

Abraham Darby, born in 1678, was the son of John Darby who farmed near Dudley in Worcestershire. Like many other farmers in the area John also worked in the iron trade, in his case as a nailer and locksmith. The forge, therefore, was a familiar sight to the young Abraham, who was later sent to Birmingham and apprenticed to Jonathan Freeth, a maker of malt mills and small machinery. Here he learned the skills of working in iron and steel. He also became acquainted with the possibilities of coke as a fuel since coke had been used to heat malting kilns since the middle of the seventeenth century. After marrying in 1699, he set up in business in Bristol as a maker of malt mills and then in 1702 formed the Bristol Brass Wire Company. He now became interested in the manufacture of metal pots, for which there was a growing demand. Together with his apprentice, John Thomas, he devised a new way of casting iron pots. After working in such secrecy that they blocked the keyhole in the door, Abraham was granted a patent for their method in 1707. He then decided to produce his own iron and in 1708 he took over a derelict iron works in Coalbrookdale. Here in 1709 he successfully smelted iron using coke, and soon was producing 150 pots and kettles a week. There were always plenty of customers and the business prospered. At Abraham's death in 1717 the Coalbrookdale works was valued at £4200, and during the eighteenth century it was to become the most famous centre of iron-making in the country.

View of Coalbrookdale, 1758

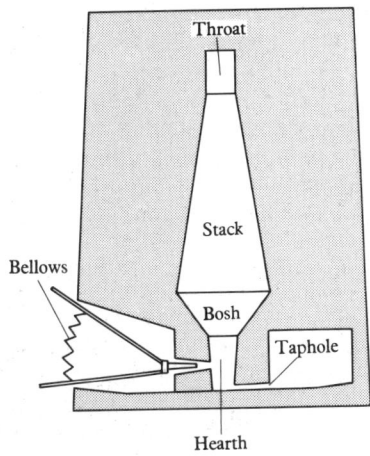

1737

Iron

Abraham Darby's method of smelting iron, using coke, began the process of freeing the iron industry from its dependence upon charcoal. This dependence was causing the industry to stagnate, because charcoal was becoming more and more difficult to obtain as forest after forest was exhausted. The use of coke, however, spread very slowly. One reason was that it could only be used to produce cast iron. Another problem was that because coke did not burn as easily as charcoal, a stronger blast was needed in the furnace.

Until 1775 when Boulton and Watt started building their steam engines the iron masters relied on water to supply the power for their blast furnaces. Abraham Darby used the Coalbrook, a stream which ran into the river Severn. As developed by Boulton and Watt, the steam engine provided the iron masters with the more powerful blast they needed when they were using coke and they were quick to realise its value. The first engine built by Boulton and Watt in their Soho works in Birmingham was supplied to perhaps the most famous of eighteenth-century iron masters, John Wilkinson.

The introduction of the steam engine enabled the iron industry to expand. Whereas in 1760 there were only seventeen coke furnaces in Britain, by 1790 there were eighty-one. Twenty-four of these were in Shropshire which was the most important iron-producing area in the country. Industrial expansion of this region meant that an increasing

Casting cannon balls.

A blast furnace. The iron ore and charcoal (or coke) were poured in from the top. The bellows supplied the continuous blast of air needed to keep the charcoal (or coke) burning. This smelting process got rid of the oxygen in the iron ore. The molten iron which remained was run off through the taphole.

The first iron bridge

number of heavy cargoes had to be ferried across the river Severn. This was time-consuming and, when the river was in flood, dangerous. It was decided, therefore, to build a bridge at Coalbrookdale. The result was the world's first iron bridge.

One of the promoters of the bridge was John Wilkinson who owned an iron works in nearby Willey. Iron-mad Wilkinson, as he was known, also owned works in Staffordshire and North Wales. For many years he supplied Boulton and Watt with the cylinders and pistons they required for their steam engines. He built the world's first iron boat. When he built a chapel for his work-people at Bilston in Staffordshire he used iron for the door and window frames and for the pulpit. He even had a cast-iron coffin made for himself, although by the time he died in 1808 he had grown too fat to be fitted into it.

The steam engine provides one reason why the iron industry was expanding during the last decades of the eighteenth century. The puddling and rolling process provides another. Until Henry Cort

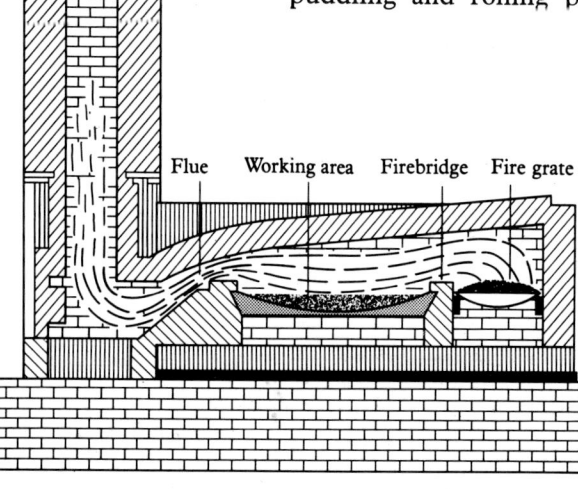

Chimney

Flue Working area Firebridge Fire grate

A puddling furnace. Henry Cort devised this furnace in which the coal was kept separate from the iron and so prevented from contaminating it. In this way a good quality wrought iron could be produced using coal.

patented this process in 1783 and 1784, charcoal was still required for the manufacture of wrought iron which had, consequently, lagged far behind that of cast iron. Wrought iron is pliable and so can withstand more strain than cast iron, which is brittle. This makes it more suitable for nails and tools and any other object which is going to be put under stress. To help supply Britain's needs, wrought iron was imported from Sweden. The use of coke or coal in the manufacture of wrought iron was delayed because they introduced impurities which made the iron unreliable. Cort, who worked a small forge in Fontley in Hampshire, solved this problem by using a furnace which kept the coal and iron separated. The widespread adoption of this process when Cort's patent expired in 1789 meant that both branches of the iron industry were free from fuel shortages.

As a result of these technical developments, the iron industry was in a position to expand. It was fortunate that this was so because this industry had a vital role to play in the Industrial Revolution. Iron was needed, for example, to make the machines which transformed industry. It was needed for the 10 500 kilometres of railway track which were laid in this country between 1830 and 1850 and for the locomotives which ran upon them. Moreover as other countries began to industrialise they required machinery, rails and locomotives and Britain was able to supply their needs. By 1840, for example, Robert Stephenson's factory at Newcastle had supplied locomotives to most European countries and to the United States of America.

Inside view of the Crystal Palace

Nineteenth-century examples of the use of iron in the home

Britain's iron output in tonnes		Britain's steel output in tonnes	
1788	68 000	1850	60 000
1801	258 000	1873	653 000
1851	2 500 000	1900	4 900 000

This table shows how Britain's iron production increased. Not all of the iron, however, was used to construct machinery or to build railways. Joseph Paxton's Crystal Palace, built to house the Great Exhibition of 1851, was made of iron and glass. Increasingly iron was used in buildings whether they were factories, railway stations or houses. When Queen Victoria and Prince Albert had Osborne House built on the Isle of Wight their architect recommended the

The Bessemer converter was designed to rotate. First it was tilted to receive the molten pig iron (drawing A). Then it was rotated into an upright position and air blasts were turned on. These drove out the impurities in the metal (B). Finally the converter was tilted again. Carbon was added to convert the iron into steel and the molten steel was then poured into a ladle (C).

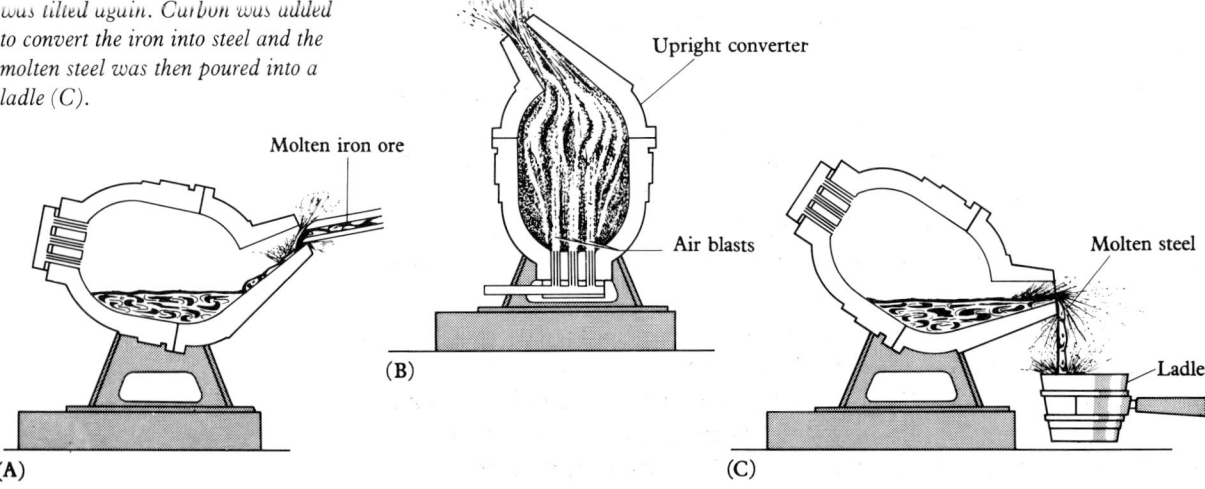

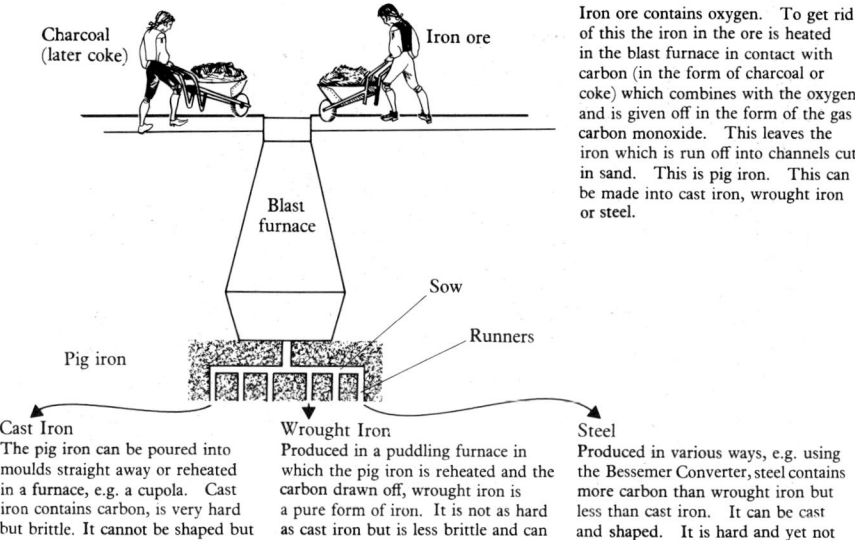

Charcoal (later coke)

Iron ore

Iron ore contains oxygen. To get rid of this the iron in the ore is heated in the blast furnace in contact with carbon (in the form of charcoal or coke) which combines with the oxygen and is given off in the form of the gas carbon monoxide. This leaves the iron which is run off into channels cut in sand. This is pig iron. This can be made into cast iron, wrought iron or steel.

Blast furnace

Sow

Runners

Pig iron

Cast Iron
The pig iron can be poured into moulds straight away or reheated in a furnace, e.g. a cupola. Cast iron contains carbon, is very hard but brittle. It cannot be shaped but has to be poured into moulds when in a molten state.

Wrought Iron
Produced in a puddling furnace in which the pig iron is reheated and the carbon drawn off, wrought iron is a pure form of iron. It is not as hard as cast iron but is less brittle and can easily be shaped. It cannot be **cast**.

Steel
Produced in various ways, e.g. using the Bessemer Converter, steel contains more carbon than wrought iron but less than cast iron. It can be cast and shaped. It is hard and yet not brittle.

Processing iron ore

use of cast iron beams throughout, as this would help to make the building fireproof. Iron railings outside houses became very common. Inside, iron was used for fireplaces and gas pipes, doorstops and umbrella stands, and for that centrepiece of the Victorian kitchen – the range.

Steel

But iron was soon to be challenged by another material. When the first skyscraper was built in Chicago in 1888 wrought iron was used for the framework in the lower floors. In the upper floors steel was used.

Steel was not new and swordsmiths had been aware of the superior qualities of steel for centuries. Yet in 1850 Britain produced only 60 000 tonnes of steel. The problem was that it was about ten times as expensive as wrought iron. Consequently it was only used for such things as weapons, high-quality tools and precision instruments. Steel was produced by the crucible method developed by the Sheffield clockmaker, Benjamin Huntsman, in the 1740s. A swifter and cheaper method was needed. In 1856 a solution was offered by Henry Bessemer. Bessemer was a professional inventor who had devised an artillery shell which required a very long and strong gun. At current prices such a gun made of steel was far too expensive. Bessemer, therefore, set about devising a new way of producing steel.

Once the price of steel was brought down the arguments in favour of using it instead of iron were overwhelming. Wrought iron was too soft and cast iron too brittle for many purposes, and so steel production soared. By the 1870s steel was used for building railways and between 1883 and 1890 the first all-steel bridge was built across the Firth of Forth, in Scotland. By 1890 more ships were being built of steel than of iron. Today, while Britain produces large quantities of cast iron and steel, the manufacture of wrought iron has practically ceased.

A coal face worker about 1900

Coal

The expansion of the iron and steel industries was one reason why coal mining developed so much from the late eighteenth century onwards. There were others. Coal provided the fuel for any factory powered by steam. Railway locomotive boilers were fired by coal as were those of the steamships when they came into use. By 1823 no less than fifty-two English towns were gas-lit; this gas was produced from coal. As the population increased so did the use of coal in the home. In addition to domestic requirements there was an increasing overseas demand for coal as other countries industrialised. To meet this demand more and more coal was sent abroad. (Just as the railways eased the movement of coal around the country so the steel speeded up its export overseas.)

All this meant that a lot more coal had to be mined:

Britain's coal output in tonnes

1700	2·5 million
1800	11 million
1900	225 million

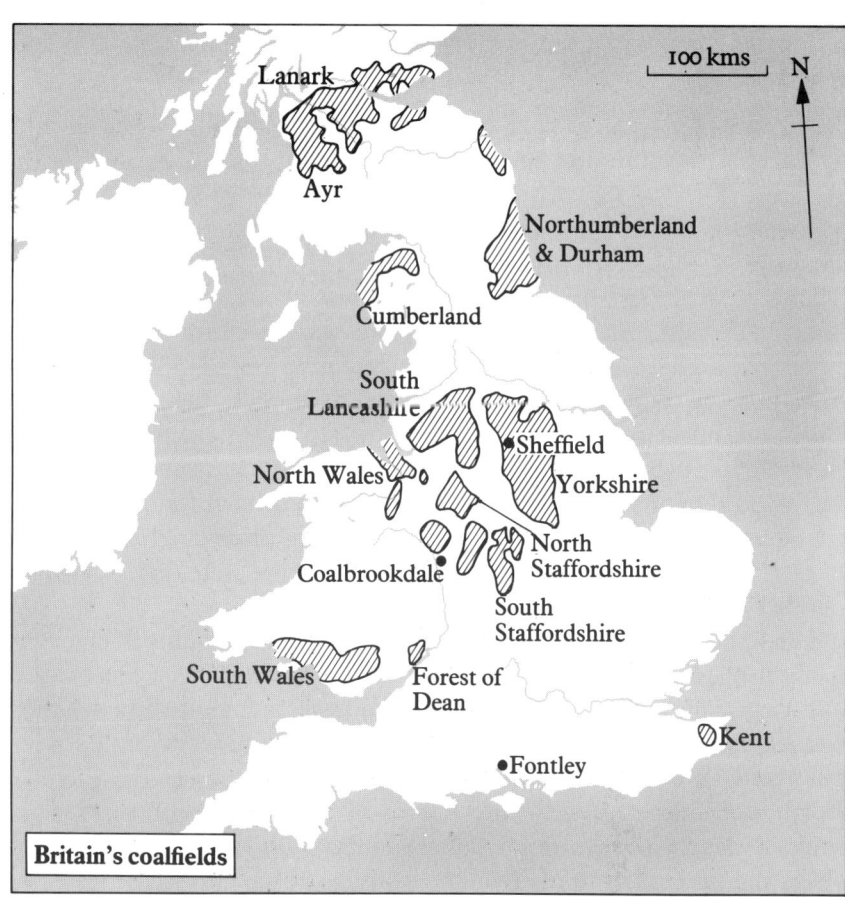

Britain's coalfields

In 1800 the Northumberland and Durham coalfield, which for centuries had supplied London with coal, was by far the most important of Britain's seven major coalfields. Only here were deep workings typical. This situation changed during the nineteenth century as the other coalfields were developed. In 1900, for example, the Yorkshire and Lancashire coalfields produced between them more coal than the Northumberland and Durham one.

In the search for coal, pits were sunk deeper and deeper. By the 1830s one pit, the Apedale Pit near Newcastle-under-Lyme, had reached a depth of over 600 metres. The networks of underground galleries became more and more intricate. These developments increased the dangers involved in working underground. Moreover, because the collieries were employing more workers than in the past (a colliery employing more than fifty or sixty workers was the exception rather than the rule in the eighteenth century) casualties were likely to be higher when accidents occurred. In the eighteenth century accidents rarely claimed more than ten victims. In 1866, 334 people died in the Ardsley Oaks disaster.

YORKSHIRE POST AND LEEDS

—Return of tenth week of he 11th day of corresponding , at a cost of ar, at a cost of oor poor, 402 ;

FRIGHTFUL EXPLOSION
AT THE OAKS COLLIERY,
NEAR BARNSLEY.

ABOUT THREE HUNDRED AND FIFTY
LIVES LOST.

(From our Local Correspondent.)

fternoon, a . .mate of an i. . g his in maki.. g his inder, and . .e- It is sup-

—Yesterday the subject of , between the West Riding

Ye..erday afternoon, about half-past one o'clock, an explosion, which it is feared will result in the loss of at least 300 lives, occurred at the Ardsley Oaks Colliery,

large exhal. become i; terrible ef pit ; and which the loosening o mine, where a stop to an the misfortu of utilising for some tw this part of ment, and s be, that it w under very accident con

One long-standing cause of mining accidents was the gas known as fire-damp. The introduction of the Davy Lamp in 1815 and the development of improved methods of ventilation made fire-damp explosions less likely but there were still plenty of other hazards. Roof falls accounted for many deaths as did accidents in the shafts and the use of dynamite introduced the danger of coal-dust explosions.

Nor were accidents the only cause of death. Miners' lungs were ruined by years of breathing in coal dust: '. . . my guid man died nine years since with bad breath; he lingered some years and was entirely off work eleven years before he died'. This case was typical of many. In 1844 the life-expectancy of miners was about forty-nine years.

A mine tramway at the end of the nineteenth century. Pit ponies such as this one were widely used to haul coal tubs to the foot of the shaft.

A 'bearer' at work. This was one of the drawings which accompanied the 1842 Report.

Public interest in working conditions in the mines was first aroused by the publication in 1842 of the *First Report of the Children's Employment Commission*. This drew attention to one particularly tragic consequence of the increased demand for coal, namely the widespread use of women and children in the mines. Some worked as bearers carrying heavy loads of coal upon their backs. Some, like Patience Kershaw, were hurryers and pushed coal trucks along rails: '. . . the bald place upon my head is made by thrusting the corves; I hurry the corves a mile [two kilometres] and more under ground and back; they weigh three cwt [fifty kilograms]. I hurry eleven a day.' Some were employed as drawers which involved being harnessed to a truck and dragging it along the galleries. A Lancashire drawer, Betty Harris, told the Commissioners how this work exhausted her: 'I am very tired when I get home at night; I fall asleep sometimes before I get washed. I am not so strong as I was, and cannot stand my work so well as I used to.' Like other women she continued with this work even when pregnant: '. . . the belt and chain is worse when we are in the family way'.

Young children (and the commissioners discovered children of four and five years of age working underground) were employed as trappers opening and shutting the ventilation trapdoors as the bearers, hurryers or drawers passed by. Except for these people, the trappers were alone, sitting in the dark by their door throughout the working day. An eight-year-old trapper, Sarah Gooder, described to the commissioners

Another of the pictures published with the 1842 Report

how she felt about her work: 'It does not tire me, but I have to trap without a light, and I'm scared. Sometimes I sing when I have a light, but not in the dark; I dare not sing then. I don't like being in the pit.'

The Report, dramatically illustrated by specially-drawn pictures, aroused the public conscience and prompted Parliament to intervene. The Mines Act of 1842 was the first of a number of Acts which sought to improve conditions in the mines:

1842 Act: Women, girls and boys under the age of ten prohibited from working underground. Mines inspectors appointed but not allowed underground.

1850 Act: Mines inspectors allowed underground. Colliery owners to be fined if they obstructed the inspectors. Fatal accidents to be reported to the Home Office.

1855 Act: Seven safety rules drawn up applying to all mines. The first said, 'An adequate amount of ventilation shall be constantly produced in the colliery, to dilute and render harmless noxious gases. . . .'

1860 Act: Boys not allowed underground until they were twelve unless they could produce a certificate for reading and writing. Miners to appoint their own checkweighman to inspect the full corves of coal and keep an account of how much work the men had done.

1862 Act: Single shaft mines not to be worked.

1872 Act: The number of safety rules increased to thirty. Workmen allowed to inspect the mines. Colliery managers to have a certificate of competency.

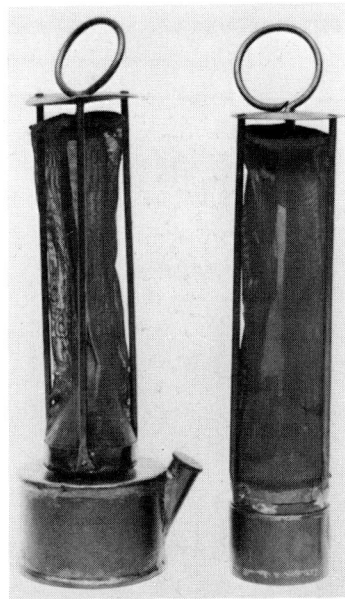

An early Davy lamp

One particularly significant development was the appointment of mines inspectors. By 1875 twenty-six such inspectors were employed to report on conditions in the mines, to enforce the mining regulations laid down by Parliament and to give advice as to how accidents might be prevented. Their work helped to reduce the accident rate. Mining, however, remained a dangerous occupation.

Using the evidence: death in the mines

Some idea of the frequency of mining accidents can be gained from the following extract from a newspaper article headed 'Colliery Disasters in the North'. This article, which was probably published in the late nineteenth century, seeks to provide a complete list of colliery explosions in Northumberland and Durham.

(1) On August 11 1756, about two o'clock in the morning, a dreadful accident happened at Chatshaugh Colliery, on the Wear. The foul air in one of the pits ignited, by which four men were instantly killed and torn to pieces. The explosion was so violent that a corf full of coals was blown up the shaft from a depth of 80 fathoms [180 metres] into the open air....

On June 5 1757, fifteen men and a boy were suffocated in a coal mine near Ravensworth by a gust of foul air, which took fire, and burnt up to the pit's mouth.

On June 15 1760, an explosion at Long Benton resulted in one death, besides several injuries more or less serious.

On December 1 1761, an explosion occurred at Hartley, by which the viewer Mr Curry, and four others perished.

On the first of April 1765, a terrible explosion took place at Walker Colliery, near Newcastle. The workings of this mine were about 100 fathoms [180 metres] below the surface of the earth. The foul air fired in an instant and the explosion which immediately followed made a report as loud as thunder. There were no lives lost, but the workmen were in most miserable condition, being fearfully scorched and burnt. As soon as it could be done, all possible assistance was given to the sufferers, who, on being drawn up, were sent to the infirmary. On the day following, several over-men and others descended to examine the state of the mine, when it fired a second time, and killed eight persons and seventeen horses, who were all burnt in a shocking manner.

On March 18 1766, an explosion took place in Walker Colliery, by which ten lives were lost.

On April 16 1766, an explosion took place in South Biddick Colliery by which 23 lives were lost.

The same article explains why this record of accidents is likely to be incomplete:

(2) Until comparatively recent days great pressure was put upon newspapers to prevent the publication of details, and, except when the tragedy was independently notorious, the very fact of an accident. A careful search through our own files suffices to render it probable that small mischances involving only two or three lives were ignored, and, speaking generally, that coal owners, being naturally anxious to conceal their own negligence, exerted all the influence they could command to stifle both inquiry and publicity. More generally, however, their motive in seeking to soften or veil the horrors of a calamity from the public eye was the fear of so alarming industrious men that a sufficient number of miners would not be procurable.... Their disinclination for inquiry was evidently, to some extent, shared in by the authorities, and perhaps also – though that is scarcely credible – by newspaper editors, so that when the coroner was compelled to go into the matter (and the intervention of the coroner in such cases is itself a modern innovation) care was taken that the published report of the proceedings should be confined to the two or three sample cases on which the inquiry was conducted. In this way, it frequently occurs that an explosion which really caused the death of scores, besides the

A pit cage in which late nineteenth-century miners travelled down the mine shaft everyday to the workings

Miners relaxing about 1900

crippling of scores more, finds record in our old columns as if it had proved fatal to only one or two, while not a word appears as to the blinded and maimed.

A strong tradition developed in the mining villages and many of the songs sung by the miners were about the tragic accidents which occurred so regularly. The following song was written in 1882 a few days after the explosion which killed seventy-four miners at the Trimdon Grange Colliery in Durham:

A miner and his family about 1900

(3) Oh, let's not think of tomorrow lest we disappointed be,
  Our joys may turn to sorrows as we all may daily see.
  Today we may be strong and healthy, but soon there comes a change
  As we may see from th' explosion that has been at Trimdon Grange.

  Men and boys left home that morning for to earn their daily bread,
  Nor thought before the evening they'd be numbered with the dead.
  Let's think of Mrs Burnett, once had sons but now has none –
  By the Trimdon Grange explosion, Joseph, George and James are gone.

  February has left behind it what will never be forgot;
  Weeping widows, helpless children may be found in many a cot.
  They ask if father's left them, and the mother hangs her head,
  With a weeping widow's feelings tells the child its father's dead.

  God protect the lonely widow and raise each drooping head;
  Be a father to the orphans, never let them cry for bread.
  Death will pay us all a visit, they have only gone before,
  We'll meet the Trimdon victims where explosions are no more.

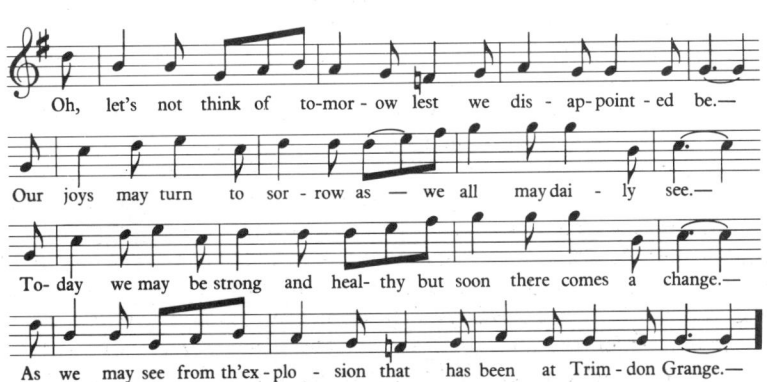

Oh, let's not think of to-mor-row lest we dis-ap-point-ed be.—
Our joys may turn to sor-row as — we all may dai-ly see.—
To-day we may be strong and heal-thy but soon there comes a change.—
As we may see from th'ex-plo-sion that has been at Trim-don Grange.—

A miner washing after work about 1900

The dangers faced by the miners made them very superstitious. Here is an extract from an article published in 1883 which describes a number of mining superstitions:

(4) Among the numerous superstitions which enter into the miner's daily life may be noticed his dislike to hearing whistling underground, a rule which, we are informed, is rarely infringed by even the youngest boy. Great faith is attached by the miner to the horseshoe, which he not only regards as a preservative against witchcraft, but as a safeguard against evil influences. It is considered, too, the height of ill luck for a miner to meet a woman either on his way to work in the morning or on leaving the pit mouth; and should he on his return home at night meet a stranger, and receive no answer from him in return to his customary greeting 'Good night!' it is considered an omen of misfortune. Indeed, like sailors, miners firmly believe in warnings, and assert that colliery explosions are generally preceded by a foreboding of some kind.

T. Dyer, 'Miners – Their Customs and Superstitions'

Questions and further work

1 How did the following contribute to the development of the iron and steel industries: (a) Darby's process (b) the steam engine as developed by Boulton and Watt (c) the puddling and rolling process (d) the Bessemer converter?

2 Document 1 deals with fire-damp explosions. What else made coal mining an extremely dangerous job?
Give two reasons why the number of mine workers killed increased during the nineteenth century.

3 Using Document 1 make a summary chart of colliery explosions which took place in Northumberland and Durham between 11 August 1756 and 16 April 1766.
You could set it out like this:

Place	Date	Number killed	Extra detail

4 Read Document 2. What reasons are given to explain why the list of colliery explosions in Document 1 is likely to be incomplete?

5 What does the first verse of the song about the Trimdon Grange explosion (Document 3) tell us about the miner's attitude to life? This song does not provide a detailed description of the Trimdon Grange disaster. What, however, do the second and third verses tell us about the accident?

6 Try to discover some more mining songs. What kind of information do they give about life in the mines? (A very useful book is *Folk Song in England* by A. L. Lloyd. A number of records are available which include *The Big Heaver*, a radio ballad by Ewan MacColl and Peggy Seeger (Argo Record Company), and *The Collier's Rant* by Louis Killen and Johnny Randle (Topic Records Ltd).)

7 Here are three statements about coal miners:
(a) Miners and their families often lived in small isolated villages.
(b) Mining was extremely dangerous work. Tragic accidents occurred frequently.
(c) There was often a very strong sense of community in mining villages.
Suggest reasons why (a) and (b) might help to explain (c).

8 Can you think of explanations for any of the superstitions listed in Document 4? How many superstitions can you think of? Why are people superstitious? Why might miners in particular be worried about superstitions?

13 Britain and the world

On the first of May 1851 the Great Exhibition opened in London. This was a display of goods of every possible kind from all over the world. It was housed in the Crystal Palace, a massive structure of iron and glass designed for the occasion by Joseph Paxton and built in Hyde Park in a mere seventeen weeks. The Exhibition was a spectacular success. Over six million people visited it during the six months it remained open. Queen Victoria, whose husband, Prince Albert, had worked unceasingly on the project during the months of preparation, wrote: 'I never remember anything before that everyone was so pleased with, as is the case with the Exhibition.'

The exhibits provided a dazzling display of human skill and ingenuity. They also highlighted Britain's position as the world's leading industrial nation. No other country could match the range of goods and machines displayed by British exhibitors. Together with exhibitors from Britain's colonies, they occupied half of the total Exhibition area. For home visitors this was all very reassuring and if the American display did not fill the space allotted to it they could afford to smile:

By packing up the American articles a little closer, by displaying Colt's revolvers over the soap and piling up the Cincinnati pickles on the top of the Virginian honey, we shall concentrate all the treasures of American art and manufacture into a very few square feet, and beds may be made up to accommodate several hundreds in the space claimed for, but not one quarter filled by, the products of United States industry.

The opening of the Great Exhibition

Part of the machinery display at the Great Exhibition

This jibe appeared in *Punch*. The mood of 1851 was one of optimism. Britain's future seemed bright. As the *Illustrated London News* put it in the issue which reported the opening of the Great Exhibition: '... we may reasonably anticipate, if no war arise in our time to destroy the auspicious work that has been begun, that the next twenty years will afford us triumphs still more substantial and more brilliant than those we already enjoy.'

Trading rivals

Developments in foreign trade during the next twenty years certainly justified these hopes. During this period Britain exported cotton and woollen goods, iron and steel, machinery, hardware and coal at a greater rate than ever before. The world demand for these goods was increasing and Britain, because of the Industrial Revolution, could supply them.

Ever since the end of the eighteenth century Britain had sold abroad the products of her rapidly expanding industries. She had taken advantage of her contacts with a large number of foreign markets and as a result her share of world trade was far greater than that of any other country. So long as Britain was the only industrial nation of any importance her goods inevitably sold well since no other country could supply them as cheaply or in such large quantities.

This situation, however, could not last for ever. Already a number of other countries were industrialising. By exporting goods such as iron and steel, machinery, rails, locomotives and coal as well as the skills of those British manufacturers, craftsmen and navvies who worked abroad, Britain assisted this development. As the United States of America, Germany, France, Belgium and other countries developed their own industries they inevitably had less need of British goods. They even tried to keep them out by charging duties on imported goods. In addition they began to compete with Britain in other markets. After about 1870 this foreign competition had a noticeable effect upon Britain's trading position. The export boom ended and British manufacturers found themselves having to look for new overseas markets. They found them in the less-developed parts of the world such as Africa, Asia and Australasia.

Nor was foreign competition confined to overseas markets. Manufactured goods from abroad, and in particular from Germany and the USA, began to appear at home. This caused some alarm as the following extract from a pamphlet published in 1896 shows:

Roam the house over, and the fateful mark will greet you at every turn, from the piano in your drawing room to the mug on your kitchen dresser, blazoned though it be with the legend, A Present from Margate. Descend to your domestic depths, and you shall find your very drainpipes German-made. You pick out of the grate the paper wrappings from a book consignment, and they also are 'Made in Germany'. You stuff them into the fire and reflect that the poker in your hand was forged in Germany. As you rise from the hearthrug you knock over an ornament on your mantelpiece; picking up the pieces you read, on the bit that formed the base, 'Manufactured in Germany'. And you jot your dismal reflections down with a pencil that was made in Germany. . . .

The mood of this pamphlet is very different from the confident predictions of 1851. The fact was that Britain was now one of a group of industrial countries. Indeed, she was no longer the leading member of the group. The American display at the Great Exhibition may have led to amused comment but by the 1880s the USA was manufacturing more goods than Britain. Soon after 1900 the same was true of Germany.

Changing trade patterns, as reflected in British exports to different parts of the world

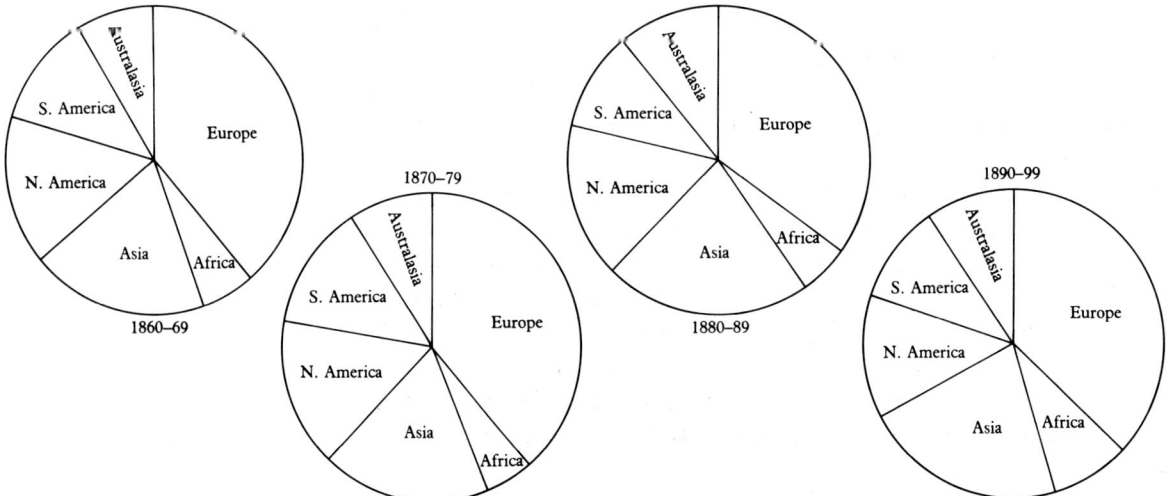

The British in India

India: ruler and ruled

India was undoubtedly Britain's most prized possession. In 1833 the historian Macaulay, who later worked in India, spoke in the House of Commons of the wonder he felt that Britain should rule India: '... that we should govern a territory ten thousand miles from us – a territory larger than France, Spain, Italy and Germany put together ... a territory inhabited by men differing from us in race, colour, language, morals, religion – these are prodigies.... Reason is confounded.' Moreover, India was economically the most important part of the Empire. It became in the nineteenth century the chief overseas market for Lancashire cottons, its own village-based cotton industry suffering in the process. At the same time it supplied goods such as raw cotton and tea.

British rule in India was established by the East India Company (a trading company which until 1813 had a monopoly of all trade in the East Indies) in the hundred years following the defeat of the French in India. India during this period was weak and divided. By the middle of the nineteenth century the British controlled the whole of India, directly in the case of the territories taken over by the Company, indirectly in the case of the 562 Princely States, where the Indian rulers continued to govern subject to British advice and control of foreign policy.

As their influence grew, the British administrators tried to alter the

Indian way of life. Slavery was abolished as were *suttee*, the Hindu custom of burning widows on the funeral pyres of their husbands, and *thuggee*, ritual murder carried out in the name of the goddess Kali. The law was reformed and English-speaking high schools and colleges were set up to develop: 'a class of persons, Indian in blood and colour, but English in taste, opinion, morals and intellect'. Such changes were not always welcomed by the Indians. British rule had brought benefits, notably the preservation of law and order, but now the British seemed to be imposing too many of their own ideas upon people they obviously considered inferior. It was, therefore, against a background of mounting unease that, in 1857, the Indian Mutiny broke out.

This was a revolt by the Indian troops serving in the Company's Bengal Army. It was sparked off by the issue of new rifles, the cartridges for which had to be bitten before being inserted. The cartridges were rumoured to be greased with either cow fat, which offended the Hindu troops to whom the cow was sacred, or with pig fat, which offended the Muslim troops to whom the pig was unclean. This came at a time when feelings were already running high among the Hindus in the army because they were now required to serve overseas. Fighting started in May 1857 and lasted for the rest of the year.

The Mutiny was marked by atrocities on both sides. At Cawnpore 200 British women and children were massacred by Indian troops. For their part the British fought grimly and dealt harshly with any captured mutineers. One officer wrote home: 'We have come along this far, doing

The British Residency at Lucknow after the Mutiny

The first steam locomotive to reach Indore, central India

a little business on the road such as disarming regiments and executing mutineers. The death that seems to have most effect is being blown from a gun . . .'. By the beginning of 1858 the rebellion was over.

After the Mutiny the Company was abolished and the British Government assumed direct control over Indian affairs. From now on it interfered little with the customs and religious beliefs of the Indian people. (They had little respect for them, however. The days when it was not unusual for British officials to dress in Indian clothes or to study Indian literature and art had long since gone.)

At the time of the Mutiny there were about 300 kilometres of railway in India. By 1900 there were about 40 000 kilometres. The railways stimulated the development of the coal and steel industries. They also opened up the interior of the country and made it easier for the government of India to tackle the problem of starvation in times of famine. In its efforts to fight famine the government also embarked on a number of irrigation projects designed to bring water to districts which had been dry. In this way the amount of land under cultivation was increased.

These were important advances. At the same time, however, the British, who felt betrayed by the Mutiny, grew increasingly apart from the Indians. More than ever they felt superior to the natives and convinced that they themselves were born to rule. They were reluctant to share responsibility with the increasing numbers of Indians trained in the schools and colleges they had set up and, as a result, opposition to the British began to develop among educated Indians.

Officers of the First Punjab Cavalry, 1879

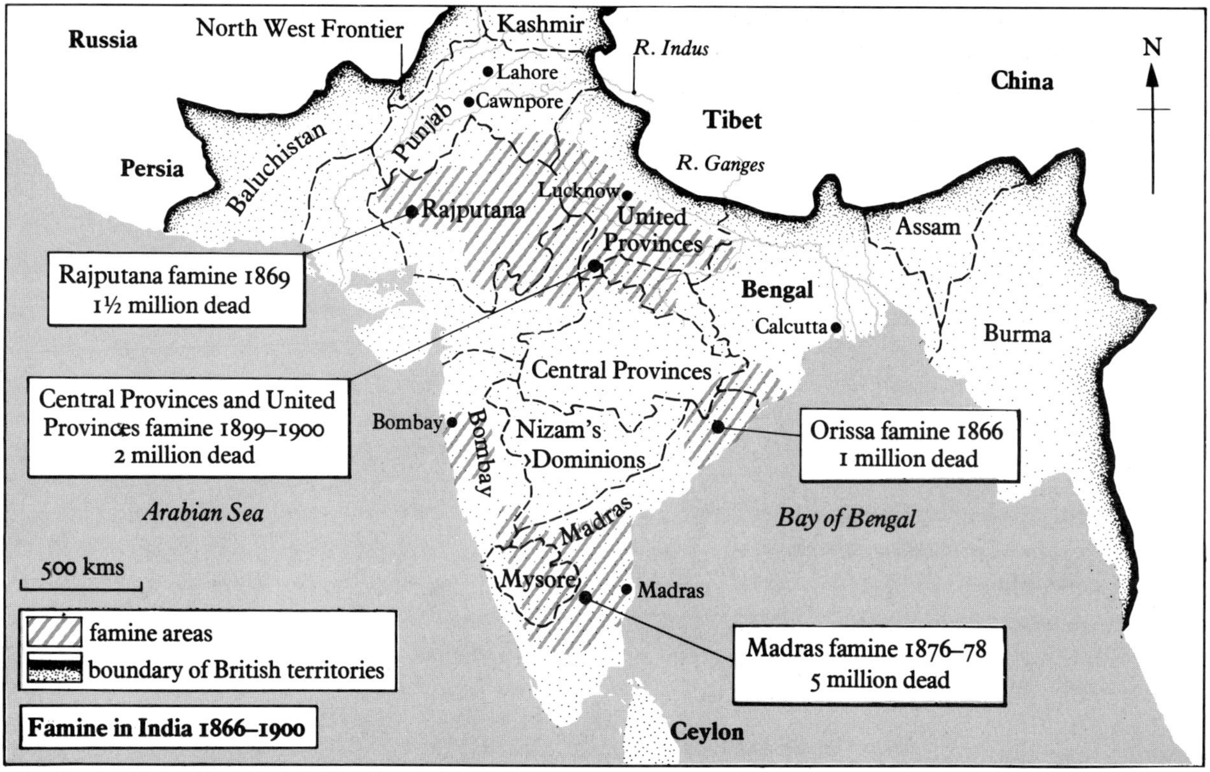

Famine in India 1866–1900

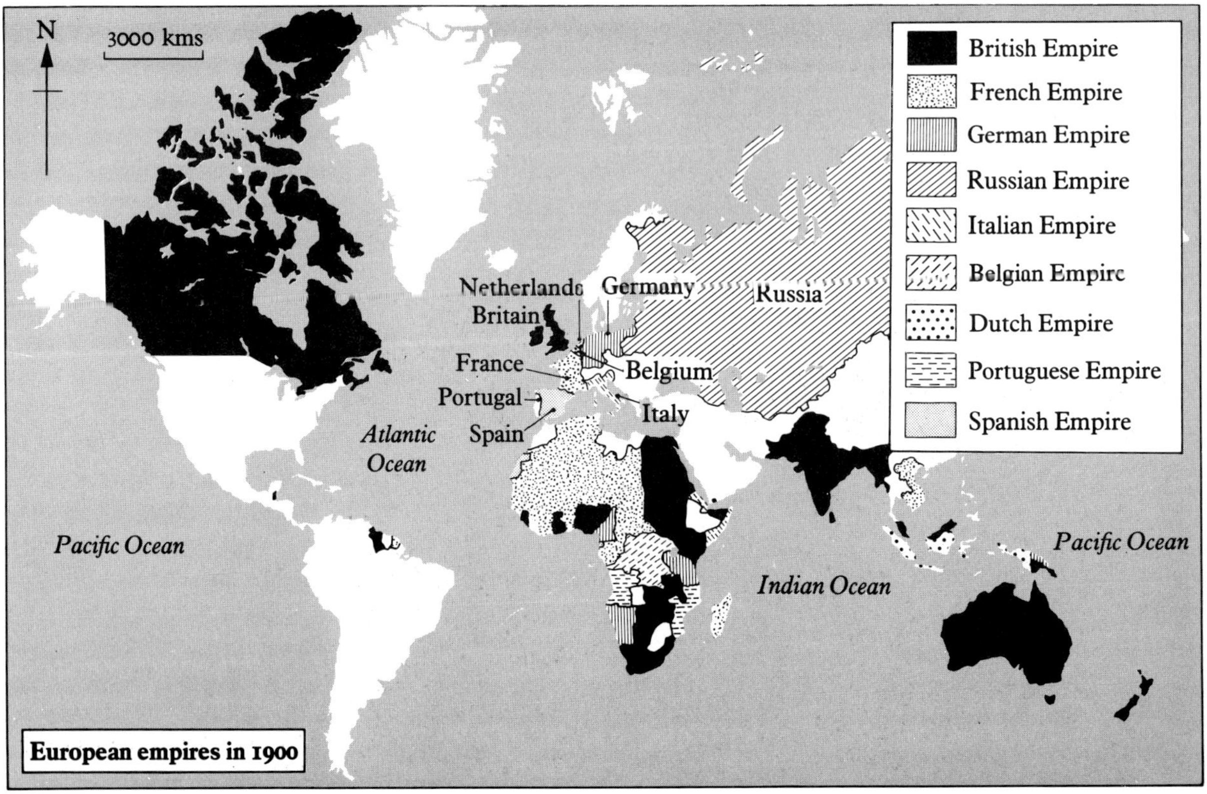

Russia

North West Frontier

Kashmir

R. Indus

China

Lahore

Cawnpore

Punjab

Baluchistan

Tibet

Persia

R. Ganges

Rajputana

Lucknow

United Provinces

Assam

Rajputana famine 1869
1½ million dead

Bengal

Calcutta

Burma

Central Provinces

Central Provinces and United
Provinces famine 1899–1900
2 million dead

Bombay

Nizam's
Dominions

Orissa famine 1866
1 million dead

Arabian Sea

Madras

Bay of Bengal

500 kms

Mysore

Madras

famine areas
boundary of British territories

Madras famine 1876–78
5 million dead

Ceylon

European empires in 1900

N

3000 kms

British Empire
French Empire
German Empire
Russian Empire
Italian Empire
Belgian Empire
Dutch Empire
Portuguese Empire
Spanish Empire

Netherlands

Germany

Britain

Russia

France

Belgium

Portugal

Spain

Italy

*Atlantic
Ocean*

Pacific Ocean

Indian Ocean

Pacific Ocean

Few in Britain at the end of the nineteenth century could foresee the end of British rule in India. Some were more perceptive. In 1911 one former high-ranking official suggested: 'It is not impossible that the twentieth century may see the complete withdrawal of Europe from Asia.'

The British Empire in 1900

The map shows the extent of the European empires at the end of the nineteenth century. Compare it with the map on page 35. European influence had extended considerably during this period. This had largely come about between 1870 and 1900 when a scramble for overseas possessions in Africa, Asia and elsewhere took place.

The largest of the European empires in 1900 was the British Empire. This occupied about one quarter of the world's land surface and included between one quarter and one-fifth of the world's population.

It included two types of colony. Canada, Australia and New Zealand, together with the South African states of Cape Colony and Natal, were self-governing colonies which meant that they controlled their own internal affairs. They were also colonies of settlement, for throughout the nineteenth century European settlers, most of them British, were attracted to these sparsely populated lands. In Canada, Australia and New Zealand white settlers made up the bulk of the population, far outnumbering the Indians, Aborigines and Maoris who were the original inhabitants of these lands.

Britain's remaining possessions were Crown Colonies. Some were administered by the British government, some by their own rulers under British protection. By and large these parts of the Empire, such as the West Indies and India, already had substantial populations and so were not as attractive to would-be emigrants. In these areas Britain came to feel that it was her duty to lead the native peoples along the path

Sheep-shearing in Australia in the 1890s

of progress. As Joseph Chamberlain, who was Colonial Secretary between 1895 and 1903, put it: 'We feel now that our rule over these territories can only be justified if we can show that it adds to the happiness and prosperity of the people . . .'. Rudyard Kipling stressed the same idea, that possessing an empire involved obligations to the peoples ruled:

> Take up the White Man's burden –
> Send forth the best ye breed –
> Go, bind your sons to exile
> To serve your captives' need. . . .

In the first place, however, the Empire existed for the benefit of trade, as it had in the eighteenth century. Trade with the colonies was no longer closely regulated but the colonies still supplied Britain with foodstuffs and raw materials while she in turn supplied them with manufactured goods. After 1870, when it became more difficult to sell British goods abroad, Britain came to rely more on her colonial markets. In 1885 Britain's exports to the Empire were valued at £26¼ million; in 1905 this figure was £113½ million. Referring to Britain's new African territories, Lord Salisbury, who was Prime Minister for the greater part of the period 1885–1902, said: 'It is our business in all these new countries to make smooth the paths for British commerce, British enterprise, the application of British capital, at a time when . . . other outlets for the commercial energies of our race are being gradually closed. . .'.

The acquisition of vast new territories after 1870 (over eleven million square kilometres and sixty-six million people were added to the Empire between 1871 and 1900) was accompanied at home by mounting public interest in and enthusiasm for the Empire. These feelings reached their climax in 1897 during the celebrations held to mark Queen Victoria's Diamond Jubilee.

The Cutty Sark

From sail to steam

In the nineteenth century it was the British who were 'the Carryers of the World' and the carrying trade was one area where Britain remained supreme after 1870. In 1890 there was more shipping registered in Britain than in the rest of the world put together.

The bulk of these ships were steam-driven but the switch from sailing ships to steamships had been a gradual process. One reason for this was that sailing ships became much faster with the development of the clipper ships. These were first built in the 1840s by the Americans who for a short while, until the outbreak of the American Civil War in 1861, succeeded in taking over from the British the bulk of the Anglo-American carrying trade. The most famous clipper of all was the *Cutty Sark*, built to bring tea from China. She was launched in 1869 and can be seen today in dry dock at Greenwich. The progress of the steamship was also delayed by the fact that, until the development of more economical engines from the 1860s onwards, the ships used vast amounts of coal. Once this problem was solved then the days of the sailing ship were numbered.

Using the evidence: crossing the Atlantic

The middle years of the nineteenth century saw a big increase in the number of people leaving Britain to seek their fortune in Canada, Australia, New Zealand and the United States of America. Britain may have been more prosperous than ever before but not all parts of the country shared in this prosperity. Ireland, always poverty-stricken, was in 1845 and 1846 devastated by the ravages of the potato blight. This

Emigrants embarking at Liverpool

disease, which crossed from the USA in 1845, reduced the staple food of the Irish to a black, rotting mush. The famine which resulted is thought to have claimed about one million Irish lives and following this disaster many of those who survived were prompted to leave their country for good. About two million people left Ireland between 1845 and 1855. They made up the bulk of the people leaving Britain during these years and the greater part of them decided to settle in the USA. This was no easy undertaking. The journey across the Atlantic was dangerous, extremely uncomfortable and very long.

Some of the dangers still exist. When he took part in the Single-

'The Last of England'. A painting of emigrants by Ford Madox Brown.

Handed Transatlantic Race of 1960 Francis Chichester encountered 160 kilometre per hour winds. He told of other hazards:

(1) By this time I was over the Grand Banks, and in fog nearly always, thin fog, thick fog or dense fog, always some kind of fog . . . I had expected 300 miles [480 kilometres] of fog, but actually I sailed through no less than 1430 miles [2400 kilometres]. . . .

Then there was ice. I dreaded icebergs, . . . I could not get any ice information with my radio, and could only guess at the ice area from the information got together before the race. Once a cold clammy air entered the cabin, and I thought there must be a big berg near. I climbed into the cockpit to keep watch, but found dense fog on a pitch black night. I could not see twenty-five yards ahead with a light.

The Lonely Sea and the Sky

Fifty-nine emigrant ships bound for the USA were lost between 1847 and 1853. One of them, the *Ocean Monarch*, caught fire and sank only a few hours after leaving Liverpool, with a loss of 176 lives. An eyewitness described the terrifying scene:

(2) The flames were bursting with immense fury from the stern and centre of the vessel. So great was the heat in these parts that the passengers, men, women and children, crowded to the fore part of the vessel. In their maddened despair women jumped overboard; a few minutes more and the mainmast shared the same fate. There yet remained the foremast. As the fire was making its way to the fore part of the vessel, the passengers and crew, of course, crowded still further forward. To the jib-boom they clung in clusters as thick as they could pack – even one lying over another. At length the foremast went overboard, snapping the fastenings of the jib-boom, which, with its load of human beings, dropped into the water amidst the most heartrending screams both of those on board and those who were falling into the water.

Compared with modern ocean-going ships, the wooden sailing ships, in which most emigrants still travelled, were light and small. The majority of passengers travelled in the space between decks known as the steerage. In 1852 a Passenger Act ordered that all single men were to be berthed in a separate part of the steerage. Until then men, women and children were herded indiscriminately together in very cramped conditions:

(3) The steerage

Most berths were less than two metres square and were intended for four people. Lieutenant Hodder, an emigration officer, explained the sleeping arrangements to a House of Commons Select Committee:

(4) **Questioner.** The single men and women all sleep alongside of one another...?
Hodder. Yes, there is no privacy whatever.
Quest. But supposing an emigrant comes and finds that there is no room on board the vessel, except in a berth holding four, one half of which is already occupied?
Hodder. He would have to go into that; his contract is, that he shall have eighteen inches [45 centimetres] space.
Quest. And if that is occupied by a married couple, the emigrant, whether a single man or a single woman, would be put into that berth alongside the married couple?
Hodder. I do not see anything to prevent it.

Bad weather made conditions in the steerage far worse. In 1849 an ex-sailor called Herman Melville wrote a novel in which an emigrant ship met stormy conditions in the Irish Sea:

(5) That irresistible wrestler, seasickness, had overthrown the stoutest of their number, and the women and children were embracing and sobbing in all the agonies of the poor emigrant's first storm at sea. [It was bad enough for the cabin passengers.] How then, with the friendless emigrants, stowed away like bales of cotton, and packed like slaves in a slave ship; confined in a place that, during storm time, must be closed against both light and air; who can do no cooking, nor warm as much as a cup of water; for the drenching seas would instantly flood their fire in their exposed galley on deck? We had not been at sea one week, when to hold your head down the fore hatchway was like holding it down a suddenly-opened cesspool.

Redburn: His First Voyage

Contagious diseases spread like wildfire among the steerage passengers. The most common was ship fever, or typhus, a disease transmitted by lice. In 1847, when more emigrants died at sea than in any other year during the nineteenth century, 7000 passengers died of the fever before reaching America and many more died soon after disembarking. Here is a description of the disease:

(6) Typhus is a disease of the blood vessels, the brain, and the skin. The onset is sudden. The symptoms are shivering, headache, congested face, bloodshot eyes, muscular twitchings, and a stupid stare, as if the sufferer were drunk. The disease takes its name from the Greek *tuphos* (mist) which describes the vague mental state of the patient. The pulse goes as high as 130 and as low as thirty-five. The skin becomes dark, and sometimes the illness was called *fiabhras dubh*, or black fever. About the fifth day a rash comes out, and the delirium becomes a stupor. It is a disease greatly encouraged by starvation, dirt, and overcrowding.

Terry Coleman, *Passage to America*

The emigrant's boat ticket entitled him to more than his passage across the Atlantic:

(7) In addition to any Provisions which the Passengers may themselves bring, the following quantities, at least, of Water and Provisions will be supplied to each Passenger by the Master of the Ship, as required by Law, and also Fires and suitable places for cooking:– 3 Quarts [3·4 litres] of Water daily, 2½ lb [1·1 kilograms] of Bread or Biscuit, not inferior to quality of Navy Biscuit; 1 lb [0·5 kilograms] of Wheaten Flour, 5 lb [2·3 kilograms] of Oatmeal; 2 lb [0·9 kilograms] of Rice; ½ lb [0·2 kilograms] Sugar, ½ lb [0·2 kilograms] of Molasses; 2 oz [0·1 kilograms] of Tea – per week.

Extract from a ticket issued in 1851

In practice, however, many captains did not fulfil their obligations and many emigrants complained about the quantity and the quality of the food they received. In 1850 William Mure, the British consul at New Orleans, reported that passengers from Liverpool were being issued with condemned bread. Three years later an article in *The New York Times* told of steerage passengers being given coffee made with water from the Atlantic. Nor was this all:

(8) [The captain of the *Bache McEver*] conducted himself harshly and in a most improper manner to some of the female passengers ... having held out the inducement of better rations to two who were almost starving in the hope that they accede to his infamous designs.

Letter from William Mure (1850)

On top of everything else the Atlantic crossing was long. From Liverpool to New York is 5025 kilometres and by sail this took six weeks. Imagine the emigrants' feelings of relief when their boat finally docked in New York harbour:

(9) *The* Kossuth *arrives at New York in 1851 with 592 emigrants aboard*

Questions and further work

1 Why did Britain's trade with her empire increase towards the end of the nineteenth century?

2 What did Kipling mean by the phrase 'White Man's burden'? (See page 160.)

3 Read Documents 1 and 2. List the problems the Atlantic still poses for sailors. Why are modern ships better-equipped to deal with these problems than nineteenth-century ones? What extra risk was more common for those who sailed in the times when Document 2 was written?

4 What information in Document 4 shows that it was written before 1851? Why do you think that most emigrants travelled in the cramped conditions of the steerage?

5 Read Document 5. Why would the steerage be 'closed against light and air' during a storm? Why could it be likened to a cesspool at that time? What could happen as a result of living in such conditions (see Document 6)?

6 Give one reason for and one against relying on Melville's book (Document 5) being used as a source of evidence about life aboard the emigrant ships.

7 Look carefully at Illustration 9. Suggest possible answers to the following questions.
(a) What is the woman to the left of the picture being told?
(b) What is the relationship between the man and the woman to her right?
(c) What is the relationship between the two men in the foreground of the picture?
Judging by this picture what kind of criminal did the new arrivals have to be on their guard against?

8 Using the evidence in the documents and illustrations, what advice might an emigrant give to someone back in Britain who was about to set out on the voyage to New York?

Europe
and
beyond

14 The French Revolution

1789

The revolt of the middle classes

Louis XVI summoned the States General in the desperate hope that it might find a way of solving the country's financial problems (see chapter 5). The elected representatives who assembled at Versailles for the official opening on 5 May 1789 were divided into three groups. Three hundred of the representatives were members of the clergy or First Estate, while 291 belonged to the nobility or Second Estate. The remaining 610 came from the Third Estate which was the class to which everyone in France who was not a clergyman or a nobleman belonged.

By tradition these three groups met in separate chambers. Proposals were passed if two of the chambers voted in favour. In practice this had meant that the two most privileged groups, the clergy and the nobility, had always been able to outvote the Third Estate.

Most of the Third Estate representatives in 1789 were members of the French middle classes. Many were lawyers or minor officials in local government who saw the meeting of the States General as an opportunity to make France a fairer and more democratic country. If the traditional method of voting continued, the clergy and nobility would be able to block any reforms proposed by the Third Estate. For this

The opening session of the States General, 5 May 1789

reason the Third Estate argued that all the representatives should meet in one hall. Decisions could then be reached by a straightforward count of hands.

The Tennis Court Oath as painted by David

The Third Estate delegates asked the clergy and nobility to join them and, when they refused, decided to take the law into their own hands and proceed with their reforms. They had the right to do this, they argued, since they represented the whole nation except for the clergy and nobility. To emphasise this they decided, on 17 June, to call themselves the National Assembly. Three days later, in the famous Tennis Court Oath, they expressed their determination not to disperse until they had brought about changes in the way France was governed.

The King was bewildered by this show of defiance. Reluctantly, he gave way and on 27 June agreed that all three estates should meet as one body. The Third Estate had won a great victory and the National Assembly, which after 9 July was known as the Constituent Assembly, was ready to begin the job of reform.

The storming of the Bastille

At this stage violence erupted in Paris. By the middle of 1789 many people in France were desperately hungry. The harvest of 1788 had been destroyed by hail (there were reports of hailstones 'sixteen inches [forty centimetres] in circumference') and now bread was scarce and expensive. Disorder followed. One newspaper wrote:

Each baker's shop was surrounded by a crowd that received a very mean ration and the next day's supply was never sure. The complaints of those who had queued all day without getting anything increased the alarm of the rest. There were frequent fights for bread.

The people of Paris were soon more than hungry. News of troops being assembled near the city led to rumours that the King intended to dismiss the Constituent Assembly and was prepared to use force if necessary. Fear and anger swept through the capital. Street orators urged people to arm themselves and to be prepared to fight for reform and soon crowds were surging everywhere seeking arms.

On 14 July a crowd surrounded the Bastille. This was a prison but it was also a royal fortress which contained arms. The mob soon penetrated to the inner court and when a detachment of mutinous troops arrived and trained five cannon on the main gate of the fortress itself Governor de Launay decided to surrender. Before long his head was being paraded round Paris on a pike. Several other defenders were killed and the rest were hustled off to prison. One survivor wrote:

The streets through which we passed and the houses flanking them (even the roof-tops) were filled with masses of people insulting and cursing me. Swords, bayonets and pistols were being continually pressed against me. I did not know how I should die but felt that my last moment had come. Those who had no arms threw stones at me and the women gnashed their teeth at me and threatened me with their fists.

Following the fall of the Bastille the offending troops were moved from around Paris. Once again Louis had been forced to give way.

Now, moreover, it was clear for all to see that the king of France was no longer an all-powerful monarch and that momentous changes were in the air. For years the word 'Bastille' had struck terror into people's hearts and yet now the people had actually overwhelmed this hated prison. If this could happen then all things were possible.

The revolt of the peasants

Dramatic though the events of 14 July were they formed only part of a wave of violence which swept the country during the summer months of 1789.

Many peasant landowners had hoped that the States General would abolish feudal dues. So far they had waited in vain and now, spurred on by hunger, they decided to take action themselves. *Seigneurs'* homes throughout much of France were attacked and the official documents concerning the dues they were entitled to collect were destroyed. Much property was burned down and although there was little if any personal injury, rumours about supposed acts of savagery soon began to spread. Arthur Young (see page 58) wrote of 'the *seigneurs* hunted down like wild beasts, their wives and daughters ravished'.

During late July the violence grew as rumours spread among the peasants that noblemen were employing bands of brigands to restore order. Drastic action was needed and between 4 and 11 August the

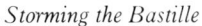
Storming the Bastille

A contemporary cartoon showing (on the left) a wealthy clergyman of the old regime and (on the right) his changed status after the events of 1789

Constituent Assembly responded by abolishing feudal dues.

Having got what they wanted the peasants now returned to their work. For them the Revolution was over.

1789–91

The Constituent Assembly

The Constituent Assembly now started on its programme of reform.

Numerous changes were made. With the publication in August 1789 of the Declaration of Rights, all Frenchmen, no matter how poor, were guaranteed certain basic rights. From now on nobody was to be imprisoned without trial. The days of the *lettres de cachet* were over. Shortly

L'arrestation du Roi a eu lieu à Varennes, à cinq lieues de France, vers une heure après minuit, au moment où l'on venait d'en être prévenu par M. Drouet, maître de poste de Sainte-Menehould, qui a rendu un service essentiel à la France, qu'elle surprise pour les fugitifs de se voir arrêtés au milieu de la nuit, par deux braves gardes nationaux

LA RÉCOMPENSE ACORDÉE A Mʳ
DROUET EST DE 50 MILLE LIVRE
ET A Mʳˢ SAUCE 20 MILLE LIVRE

qui ont bravé les menaces d'un détachement de hussards, qui avoit été commandé par le traître Bouillé! M. Sauce, Procureur de la Commune, a invité le Roi d'entrer chez lui et de s'y reposer lui et sa famille Le généreux citoyen de Varennes n'a point accepté les offres du Roi, disant qu'il devoit tout à sa patrie.

The flight to Varennes. On 21 June 1791 Louis and Marie Antoinette tried to escape from France. They went by heavy coach and made only slow progress. At Varennes they were recognised and forced to turn back.

The Constitution of 1791 as illustrated on a playing card

afterwards torture was abolished and the following year trial by jury was introduced. A temporary solution to the country's financial problems was found by confiscating and selling all the Church's lands and by issuing a new paper currency known as the *assignats*. Another change concerned local government which was reorganised and made more democratic. Previously it had been dominated by the thirty-three *intendants* appointed by the king. In future officials would be voted into office.

The right to vote in local government elections was restricted to four and a half million 'active' citizens. These were men who paid direct taxes equivalent to a labourer's wages for three days. These same 'active' citizens were later given the right to elect magistrates and judges and even priests and bishops.

In some ways the middle-class delegates who made up the Third Estate wanted to make France a fairer and better country for everybody. They also thought that it should be governed more democratically – not, however, too democratically. They wanted power to pass to the middle classes, not to the peasants or the town workers.

This was reflected in the Constitution which it was the Assembly's main job to produce (this was why it was called the Constituent Assembly). This was completed in 1791. It stated that the king's powers were to be reduced considerably by the permanent presence of an elected Legislative Assembly. Only 'active' citizens, however, would have the right to vote in the elections for this Assembly.

Would this Constitution mark the end of the French Revolution? This was the question in people's minds as the Constituent Assembly, its work now finished, dispersed to make way for the new Assembly.

1791–3

The end of King Louis

They soon knew the answer because the Legislative Assembly lasted less than a year. Too many people disliked the new Constitution. The King

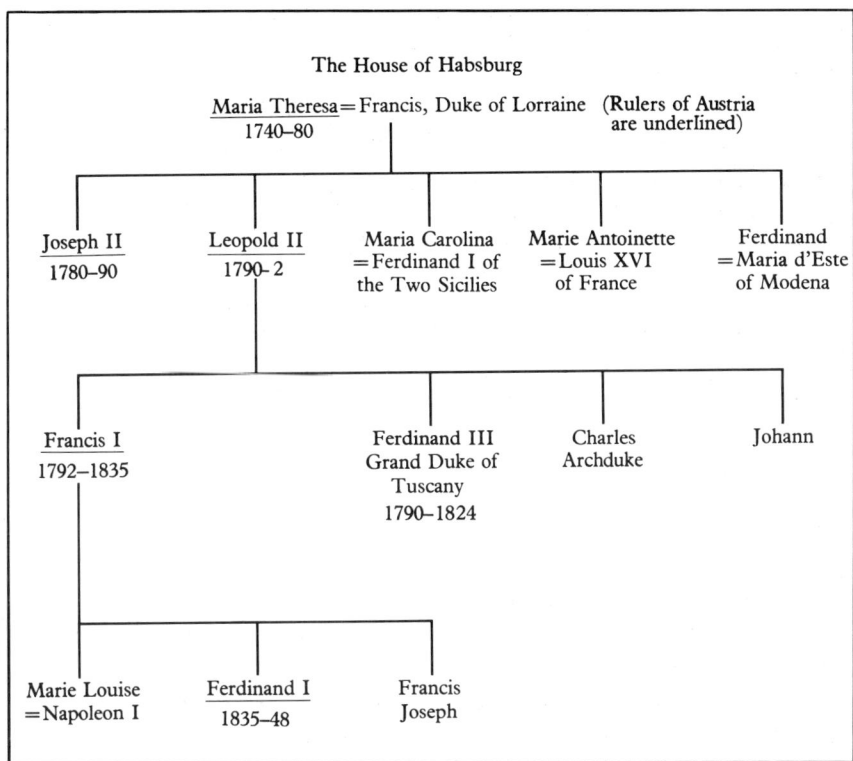

The House of Habsburg

Maria Theresa = Francis, Duke of Lorraine (Rulers of Austria
1740–80   are underlined)

- Joseph II 1780–90
- Leopold II 1790–2
- Maria Carolina = Ferdinand I of the Two Sicilies
- Marie Antoinette = Louis XVI of France
- Ferdinand = Maria d'Este of Modena

Children of Leopold II:
- Francis I 1792–1835
- Ferdinand III Grand Duke of Tuscany 1790–1824
- Charles Archduke
- Johann

Children of Francis I:
- Marie Louise = Napoleon I
- Ferdinand I 1835–48
- Francis Joseph

and his supporters thought it too democratic. For the working men of Paris and extremist political groups such as the Jacobins it was not democratic enough.

Then, in April 1792, war broke out between France and Austria. The war went badly for France. In May Austria was joined by Prussia and before long Austrian and Prussian troops were advancing steadily towards Paris. News of this caused panic in the French capital and led to rumours that the King was in league with the enemy. These rumours were not without foundation because Louis and his wife, Marie-Antoinette, had, since the early days of the Revolution, been secretly trying to persuade the Austrian emperor to invade France in order to restore Louis to his former powers. Tension mounted during the summer until on 10 August an angry crowd marched on the royal palace of the Tuileries. Fighting broke out in which nearly 1200 lives were lost. After such a terrifying outburst of violence the Legislative Assembly was in no mood to refuse the demand of the Paris workers that yet another Assembly, elected by all Frenchmen and to be known as the National Convention, should decide whether or not the King was to continue in office.

In this way the Legislative Assembly was replaced by the National Convention. This promptly dethroned Louis and declared France a Republic. To emphasise the break with the past it also decreed that the year should be changed and that 22 September 1792 was to mark the beginning of Year One of the Republic.

Marie Antoinette, who was sent to the guillotine in October 1793

Above: the execution of Louis XVI

Below: a sans culotte

Then in November an iron chest was discovered at the Tuileries which contained details of the royal correspondence with the Austrians. This sealed the King's fate. He was tried for treason by the Convention, found guilty and, on the morning of 21 January 1793, executed in Paris in front of a vast crowd.

1793–4

The Reign of Terror

Towards the end of 1792 the military situation began to improve for France. In a fit of enthusiasm the Convention extended the war so that by March 1793 France was at war with most of Europe including Britain. Success turned to failure and soon France was again on the verge of complete defeat.

Matters were made worse by events at home. Food shortages and soaring inflation (caused by the over-issue of *assignats*) were creating unrest and in March a serious revolt broke out in the department of La Vendée following the Convention's attempt to enforce conscription.

To cope with an increasingly desperate situation a special committee,

One of the many mock trials held during the September Massacres, 1792. The war against Austria and Prussia was not going well, and there was a rumour that royalists imprisoned in Paris intended to break out of prison and join forces with the invaders. Paris workers savagely attacked the prisons: between 1100 and 1400 prisoners were murdered.

the Committee of Public Safety, was set up. Control of this Committee, and with it France, soon passed to the Jacobins, the party with most popular support in Paris. They ruled for one year, a period known as the Reign of Terror.

The Committee of Public Safety consisted of gifted but ruthless men. The most important among them was Maximilien de Robespierre. A passionate believer in what the French Revolution had achieved he saw the Terror as the only way of saving France. If the foreign enemies were to be defeated then order had to be restored at home, whatever the cost in human lives.

The revolt in La Vendée and the revolts which during the summer broke out in other parts of the country were, therefore, ruthlessly suppressed. All known opponents of the Revolution were rooted out and guillotined and any who dared to question the Committee's policies were dealt with in the same way. In Paris alone over 2000 people were guillotined during the Terror.

Maximilien de Robespierre, 1758–94

To deal with the foreign threat the Committee organised a massive war effort. All bachelors and childless widowers between the ages of eighteen and twenty-five were enlisted for military service, thus creating a fighting force of over 850 000 men. Church bells were confiscated to provide metal for cannon and new arms factories were established.

These measures worked. Towards the end of 1793 France's young generals, freshly promoted from the ranks and spurred on by the example of unsuccessful colleagues who had been guillotined, led the French armies to a series of dramatic victories.

In doing this they paved the way for the end of the Terror. As defeat turned to victory there no longer seemed any need for the violent methods of Robespierre and eventually, on 26 July, the moderate politicians in the Convention found the courage to denounce him and vote his arrest. His former supporters, the Paris workers, still plagued by food shortages and rising prices, failed to help him and on 27 July he was guillotined along with twenty-one close supporters.

The Reign of Terror was over and so was the French Revolution.

Napoleon Bonaparte

Born in Corsica in 1769, Napoleon Bonaparte emerged during the 1790s as France's most gifted general. He seized power in 1799, and five years later crowned himself Emperor. His main concern was the war against Britain, Austria, Prussia and Russia. During his early years in power, however, he introduced a number of important reforms in France. The most significant was a revised system of laws, known as the Civil Code. Among other things this guaranteed religious toleration and the equality of all Frenchmen before the law.

Top Napoleon at the battle of Friedland, 1807, at which the Russian forces were defeated. The years 1805–7 saw some of Napoleon's greatest victories. In addition to Russia, Austria and Prussia were also defeated and a large part of the continent of Europe came under his control. In 1805, however, his navy had been defeated at Trafalgar by the British under Nelson. Britain remained his main opponent for the rest of the war.

Middle 'The Third of May' by Goya. This painting shows French troops executing Spanish rebels in 1808. After Trafalgar Napoleon decided to try to cripple Britain economically by ordering those countries under his influence to stop trading with Britain. One country not under Napoleon's control which had important trading links with Britain was Portugal. In 1807, therefore, Napoleon decided to invade Portugal and on the way he seized control of Spain. This provoked a revolt of the Spanish people which Napoleon found himself unable to crush. Britain sent troops under Sir Arthur Wellesley (later the Duke of Wellington) to help the Spanish guerrillas and by 1813 the French had been driven out of Spain.

Bottom Napoleon watching Moscow burn in 1812. For three years after her defeat at Friedland Russia obeyed Napoleon's instruction about not trading with Britain. However, Russia's own economy suffered and in 1810 Tsar Alexander I opened the country's ports to British ships. Napoleon therefore decided to invade Russia and in 1812 advanced east with a huge army of over 600 000 men. The Russians retreated, destroying their crops and villages as they went. Moscow itself was set on fire as soon as the French entered it. Napoleon had still not destroyed the Russian army and his troops were short of supplies. After a

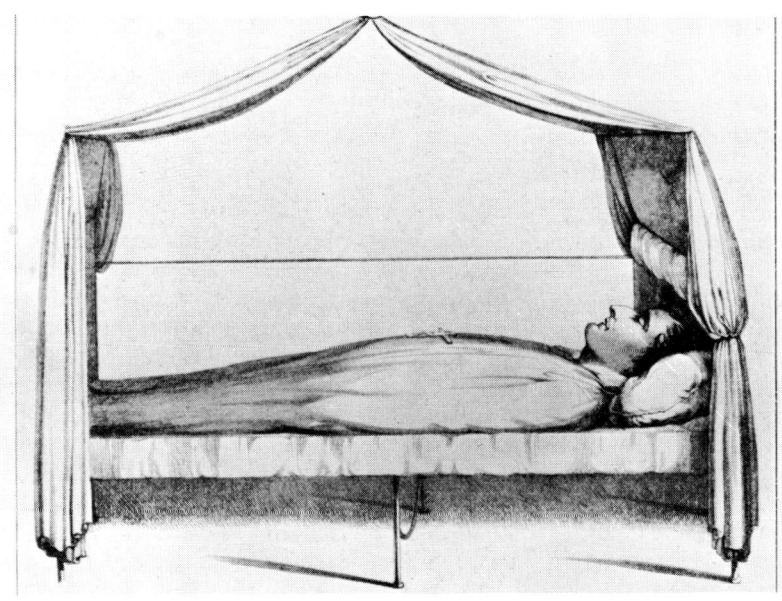

month in Moscow Napoleon was forced
to order the retreat. Soon, however, the
winter set in and thousands of his troops
died of exposure. Thousands more were
killed by Russian peasants and the
Cossacks. In the end, a mere 30 000
survived.

Napoleon after his death in 1821. After
the setbacks in Spain and Russia,
Napoleon's position was weaker. In
1813 Britain, Austria, Prussia, Russia
and Sweden allied themselves against
France and in October of that year
Napoleon was defeated at Leipzig (the
'Battle of the Nations'). Shortly
afterwards, in 1814, Napoleon was
forced to abdicate and was sent to live on
the island of Elba. He escaped in 1815
but was finally defeated at the battle of
Waterloo. He ended his days in exile on
the Atlantic island of St Helena.

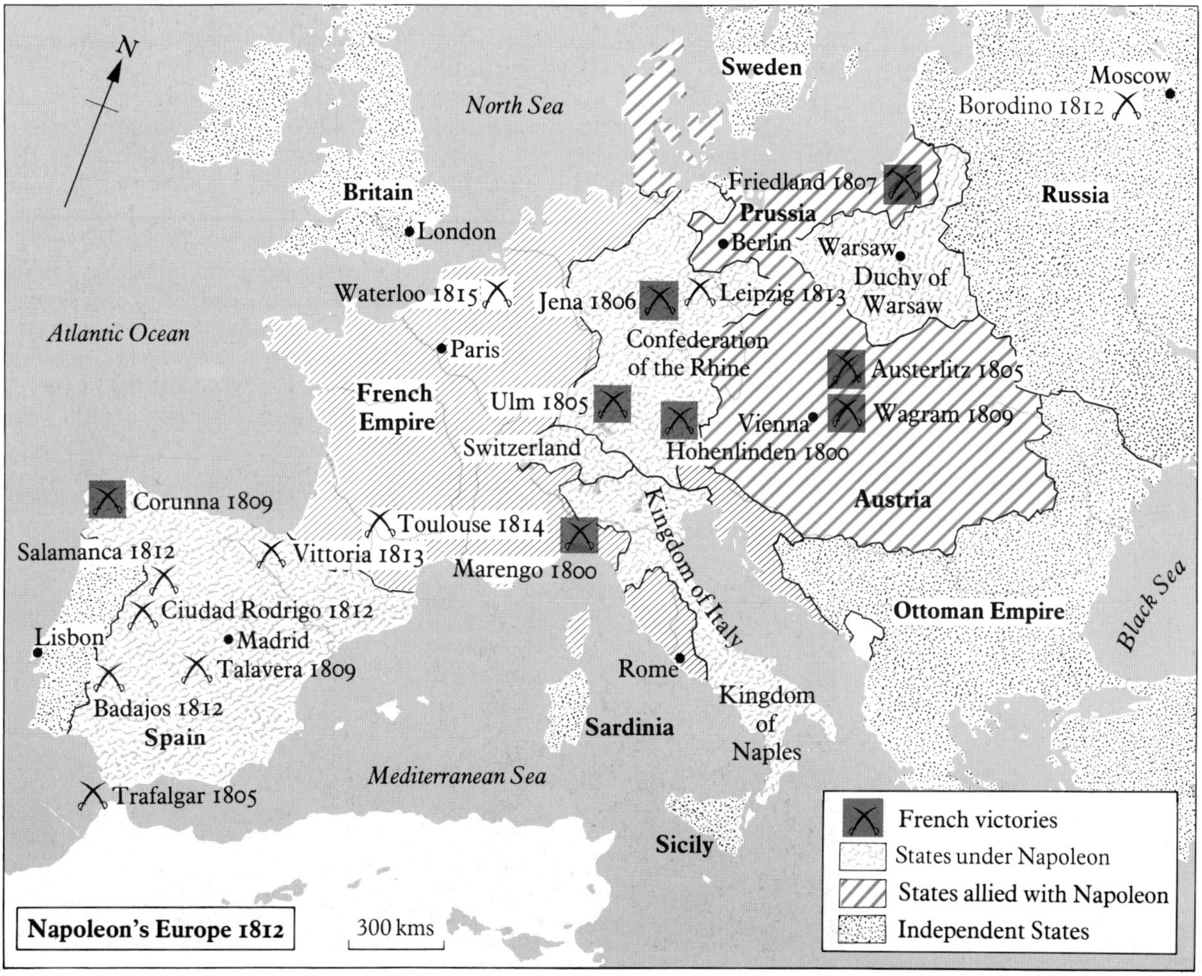

Napoleon's Europe 1812

Sweden

North Sea

Moscow

Borodino 1812 ✗

Britain

Friedland 1807 ✗

Prussia

Russia

London

Berlin

Warsaw

Waterloo 1815 ✗

Jena 1806 ✗ ✗ Leipzig 1813

Duchy of
Warsaw

Atlantic Ocean

Confederation
of the Rhine

Paris

Austerlitz 1805 ✗

French
Empire

Ulm 1805 ✗

Wagram 1809 ✗

Switzerland

Vienna

Hohenlinden 1800

Corunna 1809 ✗

Austria

Toulouse 1814 ✗

Kingdom of Italy

Salamanca 1812 ✗

✗ Vittoria 1813

Marengo 1800 ✗

Ottoman Empire

Black Sea

Ciudad Rodrigo 1812 ✗

Lisbon

Madrid

Rome

Talavera 1809 ✗

Kingdom
of
Naples

Badajos 1812 ✗

Sardinia

Spain

Mediterranean Sea

Trafalgar 1805 ✗

Sicily

300 kms

✗	French victories
	States under Napoleon
⧄	States allied with Napoleon
⠿	Independent States

Using the evidence: the coronation of Napoleon

Napoleon crowned himself Emperor in Notre-Dame Cathedral on 2 December 1804. Here is an account of the event provided by an eyewitness, Madame Junot:

(1) On his arrival at Notre-Dame, Napoleon ascended the throne, which was erected in front of the grand altar. Josephine took her place beside him, surrounded by the assembled sovereigns of Europe. Napoleon appeared singularly calm. I watched him narrowly, with the view of discovering whether his heart beat more highly beneath the imperial trappings, than under the uniform of the guards; but I could observe no difference, and yet I was at the distance of only ten paces from him. The length of the ceremony, however, seemed to weary him; and I saw him several times check a yawn.... When the Pope anointed him ... on his head and both hands, I fancied, from the direction of his eyes, that he was thinking of wiping off the oil rather than of anything else.... During the ceremony of anointing, the Holy Father delivered that impressive prayer which concluded with these words: 'Bless, O Lord ... Napoleon ... whom ... *we this day anoint Emperor, in your name*.' Napoleon listened to this prayer with an air of pious devotion; but just as the Pope was about to take the crown, called the *Crown of Charlemagne*, from the altar, Napoleon seized it, and placed it on his own head.... He had removed the wreath of laurel which he wore on entering the church.... The crown was, perhaps, in itself, less becoming to him; but the expression excited by the act of putting it on, rendered him perfectly handsome.

When the moment arrived for Josephine to take an active part in the grand drama, she descended from the throne and advanced towards the altar, where the Emperor awaited her.... He looked with an air of complacency at the Empress as she advanced towards him; and when she knelt down – when the tears, which she could not repress, fell upon her clasped hands, as they were raised to Heaven, or rather to Napoleon – both then appeared to enjoy one of those fleeting moments of pure felicity, which are unique in a lifetime.... The Emperor performed, with peculiar grace, every action required of him during the ceremony; but his manner of crowning Josephine was most remarkable; ... his manner was almost playful. He took great pains to arrange this little crown, which was placed over Josephine's tiara of diamonds; he put it on, then took it off, and finally put it on again, as if to promise her she should wear it gracefully and lightly.

The French painter David was a great admirer of Napoleon and painted numerous portraits of him. Here is his version of the coronation:

(2)

In contrast to the French, the British found the coronation of Napoleon something to make fun of in various ways:

(3) Napoleon's coronation procession as drawn by Gillray

(4) Soon made they every preparation
For a most brilliant coronation: ...
Brave Bonaparte and Josephine,
Preceded by the Pope, walked in;
His Holiness the crown anointed,
And Boney Emperor appointed.
Then Corsica's impatient son,
Snatch'd up the Crown, and put it on.
The Crown was decked with French frippery,
And with the oil, was rendered slippery;
Nap kept it on, tho', without dread,
To let them know *he had a head*,
And as to dally he was loth,
He rapidly pronounc'd the oath –
As soon as he the oath had swallow'd,
Another Coronation follow'd –
Fair Josephine advanced, and lo!
Nap put on her a crown also.
'Ah me!' thought she, 'there's something wrong,
I fear it will drop off 'ere long.'
Of holy oil, it seems, the fair
Had got too plentiful a share.
This pantomimic business o'er,
Now marched they grandly as before....

Questions and further work

1 What does Madame Junot tell us in Document 1 that might lead us to expect an accurate description of the coronation? If she had only wished to flatter Napoleon, which details of the coronation might she have missed out?

2 Look closely at Illustration 2. Give one reason for supposing Napoleon is about to crown himself. What evidence from Document 1 might imply he is about to crown Josephine?

3 What details in the picture make it clear David wanted people to admire Napoleon? Why do you think Napoleon's mother (shown seated in the background) was included in the picture even though she did not attend the coronation?

4 Later this picture was altered to make the Pope (seated on the right) look as though he was giving his blessing. Why do you think this was done? In what ways can paintings be an unreliable source of evidence?

5 How do Illustration 3 and Document 4 try to make fun of Napoleon and Josephine?

6 Why do you think that Napoleon crowned himself?

15 Railways, revolutions and wars

'The Charge of the Light Brigade'

Half a league, half a league,
Half a league onward.
All in the valley of Death
Rode the six hundred.
'Forward the Light Brigade!
Charge for the guns!' he said:
Into the valley of Death
Rode the six hundred.

'Forward the Light Brigade!'
Was there a man dismay'd?
Not tho' the soldier knew
Someone had blunder'd:
Theirs not to make reply,
Theirs not to reason why,
Theirs but to do and die:
Into the valley of Death
Rode the six hundred.

Cannon to right of them,
Cannon to left of them,
Cannon in front of them
Volley'd and thunder'd;
Storm'd at with shot and shell,
Boldly they rode and well,
Into the jaws of Death,
Into the mouth of Hell
Rode the six hundred.

Flash'd all their sabres bare,
Flash'd as they turn'd in air

Sabring the gunners there,
Charging an army, while
All the world wonder'd:
Plunged in the battery-smoke
Right thro' the line they broke,
Cossack and Russian
Reel'd from the sabre-stroke
Shatter'd and sunder'd.
Then they rode back, but not
Not the six hundred.

Cannon to right of them
Cannon to left of them,
Cannon behind them
Volley'd and thunder'd;
Storm'd at with shot and shell,
While horse and hero fell,
They that had fought so well
Came thro' the jaws of Death,
Back from the mouth of Hell,
All that was left of them,
Left of six hundred.

When can their glory fade?
O the wild charge they made!
All the world wonder'd.
Honour the charge they made!
Honour the Light Brigade,
Noble six hundred!

The Charge of the Light Brigade

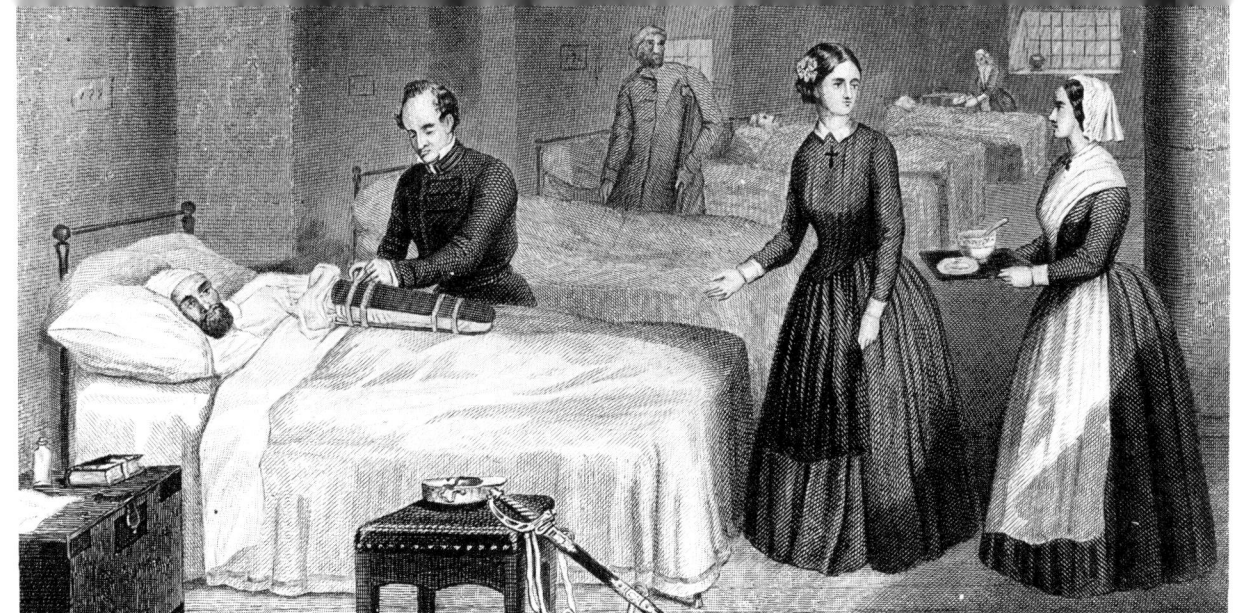

Florence Nightingale at work in the military hospital at Scutari

The heroic but disastrous charge of the Light Brigade so vividly described by Lord Tennyson was the result of a misunderstood order.

It occurred during the Crimean War (1854–6) which broke out when Britain and France decided to defend Turkey against a Russian attack. The Russian forces soon withdrew from those parts of the Turkish Empire they had occupied but Britain and France decided to continue the war by attacking the Russian naval base of Sebastopol in the Crimea. Hopes of a quick victory soon faded and Sebastopol was not taken until September 1855.

The charge took place on 25 October 1854. It formed part of the action known as the Battle of Balaclava.

In September the allies had defeated the Russians at the Battle of the River Alma but, instead of then pressing on to Sebastopol, they had moved south in order to establish a base at the small port of Balaclava. (This failure to attack Sebastopol immediately enabled the Russians to strengthen the city's weak defences and so make the task of the allies considerably more difficult.) On 25 October the Russians began to advance on Balaclava but were halted by the Heavy Brigade of the British cavalry which with under 600 men charged and put to rout a Russian cavalry force of nearly 3000 men. The Russians retreated over the Causeway Heights and reformed in the North Valley in a position which was defended by artillery on three sides.

Suddenly from his position high above the battle the British commander, Lord Raglan, saw that the Russians were preparing to take away the British guns which they had captured on the Causeway Heights. Captured guns were traditionally proof of victory and so Raglan sent a message to Lord Lucan, the cavalry commander, ordering him to, 'advance rapidly to the front – follow the enemy and try to prevent the enemy carrying away the guns'. Lucan was mystified by the order. From where he was he could see neither enemy nor guns. He asked Captain Nolan, who had brought the message from Raglan, to

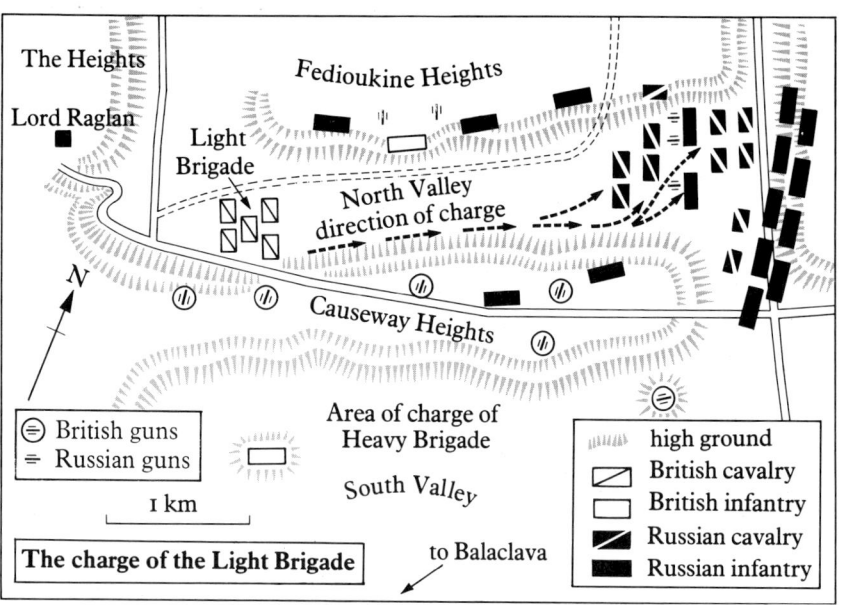

The charge of the Light Brigade

The Earl of Cardigan
1797–1868

clarify the order. This was the crucial moment. Pointing not to the Causeway Heights but to the guns at the far end of the North Valley Nolan replied: 'There, my lord, is your enemy, there are your guns.'

That the cavalry should be ordered to attack such a position seemed incredible. Nevertheless an order was an order and Lucan felt he had no option but to obey. He therefore ordered his brother-in-law, Lord Cardigan, who commanded the Light Brigade, to advance down the valley while he himself would follow in support with the Heavy Brigade.

The valley was about two kilometres long. As the Light Brigade advanced into it at a steady trot a hush descended upon the battlefield so that the jingle of the horses' bits could be clearly heard. Raglan and those with him could scarcely believe their eyes. They could see all too clearly the deadly trap into which the Light Brigade was riding.

The Russian guns quickly opened fire and were soon relentlessly punching holes in the Brigade's ranks. (Nolan was an early casualty.) To begin with the orderly advance was maintained but as the Russian fire grew fiercer Cardigan found it impossible to restrain his men and the pace quickened into a headlong gallop.

Horrified by the scene of destruction ahead of him, Lucan decided to halt the advance of the Heavy Brigade. He remarked: 'They have sacrificed the Light Brigade: they shall not the Heavy, if I can help it.'

Cardigan and what was left of the Light Brigade reached the guns only to find themselves confronted by the Russian cavalry. They had no alternative but to fight their way out and retreat 'as fast as our poor tired horses could carry us'. From start to finish the charge had lasted only twenty minutes.

A roll-call was taken. Of the 673 men who had set out behind Lord Cardigan 195 had returned.

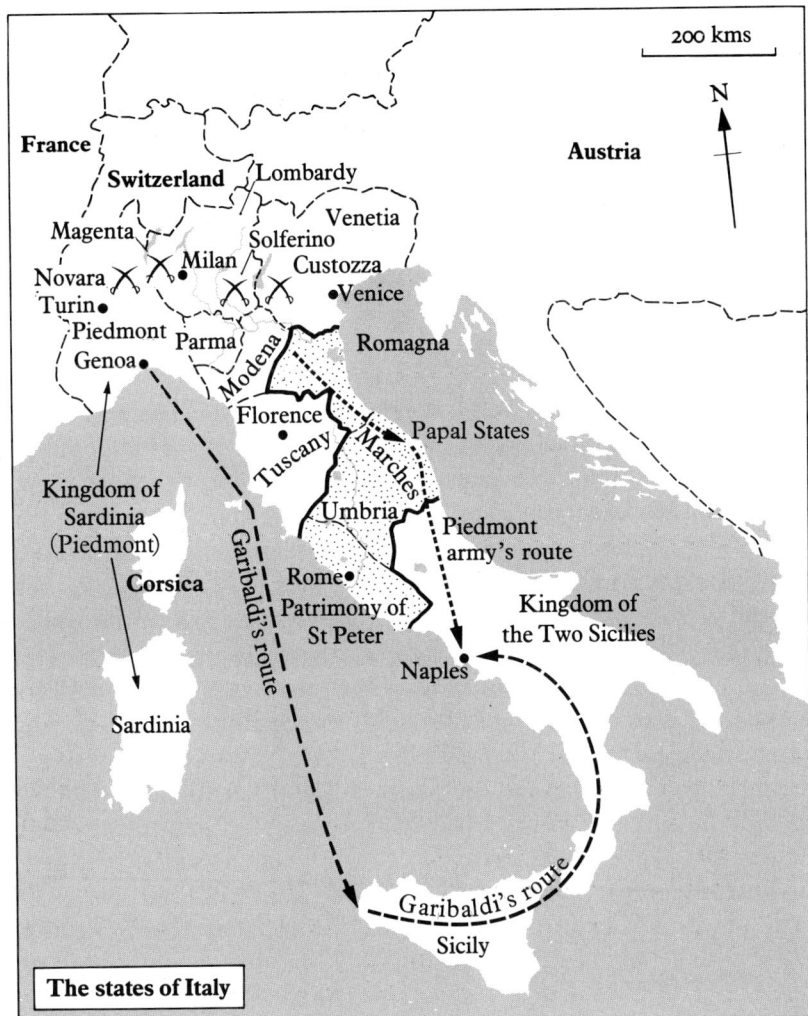

The states of Italy

Europe at War 1854–71

1854–6 **Crimean War**
 Russia v. Britain
    France
    Piedmont
    Turkey

1859 **Italian War**
 Austria v. France
     Piedmont

1864 **Danish War**
 Denmark v. Prussia
      Austria

1866 **Austro-Prussian War**
 Austria v. Prussia
     Italy

1870–1 **Franco-Prussian War**
 France v. Prussia

The Crimean War was Europe's first war for nearly forty years. After 1871 a major conflict was avoided until the outbreak of the First World War in 1914. The wars listed above brought about important changes in central Europe where in 1859 both Italy and Germany still consisted of numerous separate provinces. France's victory in that year over Austria made possible the unification of Italy, while the three wars fought by Prussia resulted in the proclamation of the German Empire in 1871.

Italy 1815–70: an example of change

Throughout the eighteenth century Italy was divided, despotically governed and influenced by foreign rulers. There seemed to be little prospect of change until Napoleon swept the Austrians out of the peninsula and proceeded to place the whole of Italy under his control. He abolished all the boundaries between the former Italian states and instead divided the peninsula into three main parts. He ruled more efficiently and more fairly than the governments he replaced. French rule was short-lived and in the end, because of heavy taxes and the conscription laws, it became highly unpopular but it showed the Italian people that change was possible.

Napoleon's defeat in 1815, was followed in Italy by the return of the old boundaries, the old ways of government, and an Austrian presence which was stronger than ever. Appearances were, however, deceptive. Many people in Italy were anxious for change. Merchants and manufacturers wanted Italy's eight states to unite economically. They argued

Giuseppe Mazzini, 1805–72

Count Camillo de Cavour, prime minister of Piedmont 1852–9 and 1860–1

that internal customs barriers should go and that all Italians should use the same currency. Together with lawyers and other middle-class people they also wanted more say in the government of their own particular state. They were annoyed by the inefficiencies of the peninsula's various governments. The desire for good government was not confined to the middle classes. Most Italians were peasants and they were desperately anxious for some improvement in the way they lived. Increasingly, after 1815, they were prepared to resort to violence to achieve this.

Giuseppe Mazzini

Mazzini was a revolutionary who believed that one day Italians would cast out their rulers and join to form a democratically governed republic of Italy. To bring about this *risorgimento* or reawakening of his country he formed in 1831 a society called Young Italy. Of this society he wrote: 'Young Italy is a brotherhood of Italians who believe in a law of progress and duty, and are convinced that Italy is destined to become one nation, convinced also that she possesses sufficient strength within herself to become one . . .'.

In the poverty-stricken conditions of the time it was easy enough for Mazzini and his small band of followers to persuade Italians to take up arms against their rulers. Virtually every year revolts broke out somewhere in Italy. They all failed. In 1848 revolutions erupted throughout the peninsula and for a time, with Austria paralysed by revolutions in other parts of her empire, enjoyed considerable success. Ruler after ruler, including the Pope, fled for safety. They soon returned. By August 1849 the Austrian hold upon Italy was firmly re-established.

Garibaldi and Cavour

The events of 1848–9 showed clearly that Mazzini was wrong in thinking that Italy could unite herself. One patriot who had been in the thick of the fighting was Giuseppe Garibaldi. He now wrote: 'We have been dishonoured and the name of Italian will be a laughing-stock for foreigners in every country. I am disgusted to belong to a nation of so many cowards.' Outside help was needed if the Austrians were to be shifted. Ten years later this help came, from France. Napoleon III did not, however, send his troops into northern Italy at the request of Mazzini and his fellow revolutionaries. French intervention against Austria was the result of an agreement reached with the Prime Minister of Piedmont, Count Camillo de Cavour, a man who was not remotely interested in the idea of Italian unity.

When in 1852 Cavour became Prime Minister of the only Italian state to be governed at all democratically, his main aim was to make Piedmont the dominant power in northern Italy. Like Mazzini but for a very different reason he wanted to be rid of the Austrians. Piedmont, however, had already tried once to expel the Austrians and had failed miserably. Amid the turmoil of 1848 Piedmont had declared war on

The Austrian-held town of Magenta, captured by the French in 1859

Austria. Her troops had been humiliated first at Custozza in 1848 and then at Novara in 1849. Cavour knew well that foreign help was needed. He was fortunate that Napoleon III, who was keen to reduce Austrian power, was willing, in return for Nice and Savoy, to provide it.

War broke out in 1859. The French defeated the Austrians first at Magenta and then at Solferino. Austria had lost Lombardy but was still in possession of Venetia when Napoleon, worried by signs that Prussia was preparing to intervene on Austria's side, decided to back out of the war. Cavour was bitterly disappointed but the failure to secure Venetia was soon compensated by successes elsewhere. Revolution was now sweeping through central Italy as Austria's misfortunes encouraged the inhabitants to try once again to rid themselves of their rulers. The dukes of Parma, Modena and Tuscany were all quickly deposed and the Pope was forced to abandon the Romagna.

Napoleon III, the nephew of Napoleon Bonaparte, Emperor of the French 1852–70

As the old rulers moved out so Piedmont moved in. Together with Lombardy, these areas were incorporated into Piedmont which by March 1860 included nearly half the population of Italy. In one year Piedmont had more than doubled its size. Cavour still wanted Venetia but he had no immediate plans for further expansion. He was certainly not considering the annexation of Naples and Sicily which together made up the Kingdom of the Two Sicilies. At this point, however, events passed out of his control.

A peasant revolt broke out in Sicily. The islanders wanted freedom from Naples but one man who shared Mazzini's vision of a united Italy saw in this uprising a chance to extend further the process of unification. Garibaldi set sail from Genoa with his thousand red-shirted followers in May 1860. Once landed in Sicily he was swiftly and dramatically successful. By July the royal forces were broken and Garibaldi was master of the island.

The people adored Garibaldi. The following extracts from a diary kept by one of Garibaldi's followers give some idea of the feelings he aroused:

Giuseppe Garibaldi, 1807–82

13 May, Salemi, from a convent balcony, facing the glory of the sun
When the General arrived, there was an outbreak of delirious enthusiasm. A band played madly. All that could be seen were raised arms and brandished rifles. . . .

Salemi, 14 May
The General has ridden through the city on horseback. When the populace see him they take fire. There is a magic in his look and in his name. It is only Garibaldi they want. . . .

In August Garibaldi crossed to the mainland. Once again he had massive popular support and within a month the capital city of Naples had fallen to him.

This was disturbing news for Cavour. If Garibaldi continued to advance northwards and marched on Rome he would clash with the French troops who had been stationed there since 1849, when they had helped the Pope to recover his lands. The last thing Cavour wanted was a breach with France and so Piedmontese troops were dispatched to intercept Garibaldi. They did this, seizing Umbria and the Marches from the Pope on their way. On 26 October their king, Victor Emmanuel, met Garibaldi who greeted him with the words: 'Hail, to the King of Italy.' This indeed he soon became, for Garibaldi surrendered his conquests, and a kingdom of Italy was proclaimed which included the whole peninsula except for Rome and the area around it and Venetia.

Neither of these areas remained apart for long. Italy was given Venetia as her reward for joining Prussia when she fought and defeated Austria in 1866. Four years later the outbreak of the Franco-Prussian War was accompanied by the removal of the French troops garrisoned in Rome. Italian troops promptly marched in and Rome replaced Florence as the capital of Italy.

Italy was united although this had not come about in the way that Mazzini had foretold. In reality Piedmont had absorbed the whole of the peninsula.

Europe in an age of change

The French Revolution released ideas which threatened to topple other monarchs as they had toppled King Louis XVI of France. The rulers of Russia, Prussia and Austria were well aware of this. They hoped that in defeating France in 1815 they had defeated these ideas and that it would be possible to return to the world as it had been before 1789.

These were, however, unsettled times. The ambitions of middle-class people who wanted some share in government; the growth of national feeling in Italy, Germany and various parts of eastern Europe, and the poverty to be found in town and country alike, all help to explain this. The example of the French Revolution encouraged violence. It led people to think that revolutions might succeed in other countries. The unrest reached its climax in the revolutions of 1848, which involved most of Europe except for Britain and Russia. For a few months the old order seemed to have collapsed.

However, the revolutions of 1848 ended in failure, and the monarchies of Prussia, Austria and Russia survived until the First World War. There were changes. Germany, like Italy, was united so that in 1871 the King of Prussia became Emperor of Germany. In 1867 Hungary was given self-government within the framework of what became known as the Austro-Hungarian Empire. In Germany, and later in Austria (although not in Hungary), all men were allowed to vote in parliamentary elections. (How much power the elected parliaments had was, however, another matter.) Serfdom, which had disappeared in Prussia in 1807, was abolished in the Austrian Empire in 1848 and in Russia in 1861.

These changes partly explain why there were so few political revolutions between 1848 and 1914. A different kind of revolution did, however, take place – an industrial revolution. Parts of Europe were now transformed, as Britain had been earlier, by the large-scale development of industry, the growth of towns and the building of the railways. As in Britain these changes brought serious problems. They also brought increased wealth and power. In the late nineteenth century Europe's influence in the world at large seemed greater than ever. This supremacy did not last for much longer. By 1914 the USA was producing more iron and steel than the whole of Europe put together.

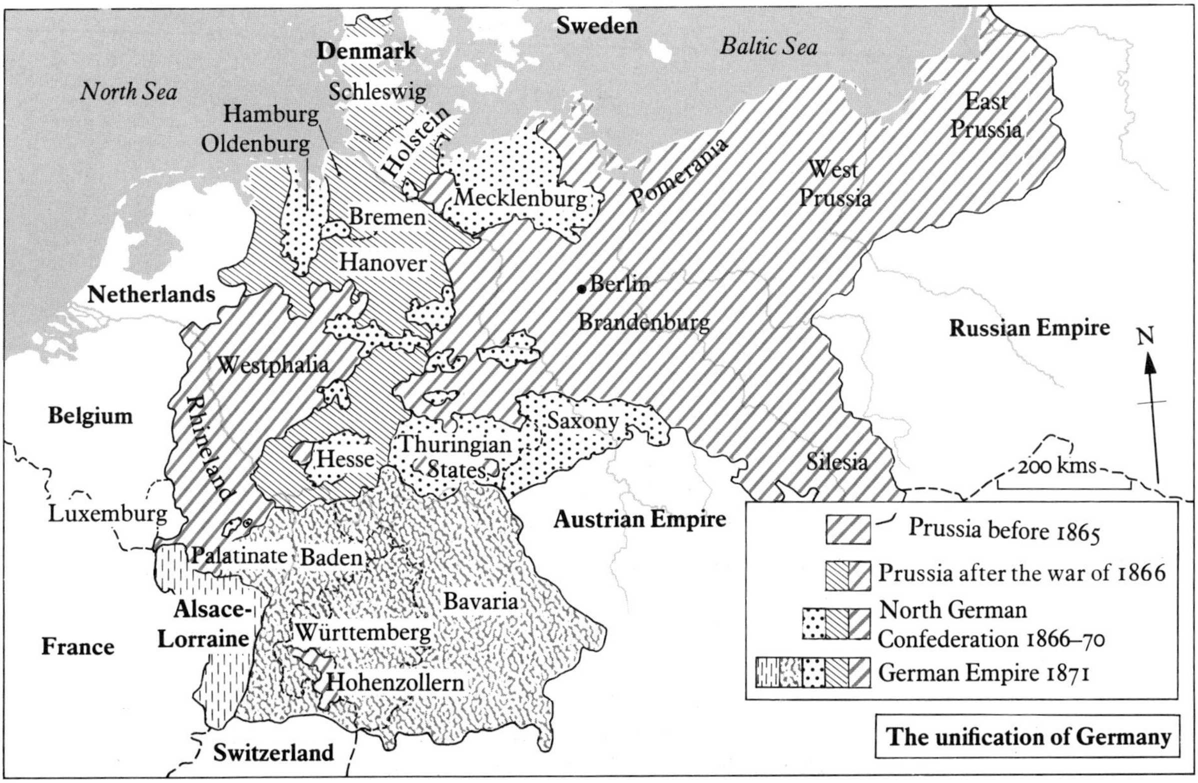

Otto von Bismark, prime minister of Prussia 1862–71 and chancellor of Germany 1871–90. It was Bismark who ensured that the unification of Germany was achieved under Prussian leadership.

Sweden

Denmark

Baltic Sea

North Sea

Schleswig

Hamburg
Oldenburg

Holstein

East
Prussia

Mecklenburg

Pomerania

West
Prussia

Bremen

Hanover

Berlin

Brandenburg

Netherlands

Russian Empire

N

Westphalia

Belgium

Rhineland

Saxony

Hesse

Thuringian
States

Silesia

200 kms

Luxemburg

Austrian Empire

Palatinate Baden

Alsace-
Lorraine

Bavaria

France

Württemberg

Hohenzollern

Switzerland

Prussia before 1865

Prussia after the war of 1866

North German
Confederation 1866–70

German Empire 1871

The unification of Germany

Using the evidence: the industrialisation of Europe, 1850–1900

The following figures highlight some aspects of the economic growth of six European countries during the period 1850–1900.

(1) Populations (in millions)

	1850	1860	1870	1880	1890	1900
Germany	35·9	38	41	45	49	56
Austria-Hungary	30·7	31·7	35·8	38	41	45
France	35·8	37·4	36	37	38	39
Great Britain	27·6	29	31	35	38	41
Italy	24·3	25	26	28	30	32
Russia	57	63	77	89	95	103

(2) Pig-Iron Production (in million tonnes)

	1850	1860	1870	1880	1890	1900
Germany			1·3	2·5	4·1	7·5
Austria-Hungary			0·4	0·5	0·7	1·5
France	0·4	0·9	1·2	1·7	2	2·7
Great Britain	2·2	3·9	6	7·8	8	9
Russia			0·4	0·4	0·9	2·9

(3) Steel Production (in million tonnes)

	1850	1860	1870	1880	1890	1900
Germany			0·3	0·7	2·3	6·7
Austria-Hungary					0·5	1·2
France			0·3	0·4	0·7	1·6
Great Britain			0·7	1·3	3·6	4·9
Russia					0·4	1·5

(4) Railways (kilometres of track open)

	1850	1860	1870	1880	1890	1900
Germany	5856	11 089	18 876	33 838	42 869	51 678
Austria-Hungary	1579	4543	9589	18 507	26 519	36 330
France	2915	9167	15 544	23 089	33 280	38 109
Great Britain	10 662	16 798	24 759	28 876	32 223	35 204
Italy	620	2404	6429	9290	13 629	16 429
Russia	501	1626	10 731	22 865	30 596	53 234

(5) Coal Production (million tonnes)

	1850	1860	1870	1880	1890	1900
Germany	6	12	34	59	89	149
Austria-Hungary	1·2	2·3	8·6	15	26	39
France	4·5	8·3	13·3	19·4	26·1	33·4
Great Britain	57	80	110·4	147	181·6	225·2
Italy						0·5
Russia		0·15	0·75	3·2	6	16·2

(6) Coal Production (as percentage increases)

	1850–60	1860–70	1870–80	1880–90	1890–1900
Germany	100	183·3	73·5	50·8	67·4
Austria-Hungary	91·7	273·9	74·4	73·3	50
France	84·4	60·2	45·9	34·5	28
Great Britain	40·4	38	33·2	23·5	24
Russia		400	326·7	87·5	170

'Fritz', a huge steam hammer installed by Alfred Krupp at his Essen ironworks in 1861

Questions and further work

1 Using the map on page 183 to help you, draw a map of Italy as it was in 1815. Label the different states clearly. Then use different colours to show:
  (a) which parts were united by March 1860
  (b) which parts were added between March and October 1860
  (c) which part was added in 1866
  (d) which part was added in 1870.
2 Mazzini, Cavour, Napoleon III and Garibaldi each played an important part in the unification of Italy. Which of them:
  (a) made sure that Italy included Naples and Sicily
  (b) first tried to inspire the Italians with the idea of a united country
  (c) united half of Italy under Piedmont by March 1860
  (d) was responsible for driving the Austrians out of Lombardy?
3 Study Tables 1 to 6. Reproduce the information in each table as a line graph, using a different colour for each country (one graph for each table).
4 Compare the economic development of the countries listed. Which country had become a clear rival to Britain by 1900?
5 Here are two statements based on Table 5.
  (a) In 1850 Germany produced six million tonnes of coal while Britain produced fifty-seven million tonnes.
  (b) In 1850 Germany was second only to Britain in terms of coal production.
  Both these statements are correct but why does the second statement give a somewhat misleading view of Germany's coal production in 1850?
6 These tables are based on ten-yearly figures. Why could it be misleading not to know what happened between the dates given?
7 Compare Tables 5 and 6, looking closely at the figures for Britain and Russia. Why is it important to check actual increases in production as well as looking at percentage-increase figures?
8 Why are tables a useful source of information? What must the historian consider when using tables as evidence? (Look at your answers to questions 5 and 6.)

16 A documentary history of the American West

Just as people from Europe uprooted themselves and sailed across the Atlantic in order to start life afresh in the USA, so, throughout the nineteenth century, Americans moved west. Primarily they went in search of land. The existence of vast lands to the west gave people hope of a prosperous future. They were drawn there as if by a magnet and it mattered little that the Indians had to be driven out to make way for them.

Early days

The attraction of the West was nothing new. One reason the Thirteen Colonies rebelled against Britain was that the colonists resented the British Government's attempt to stop them moving beyond the Appalachians in search of more fertile soils.

The peace settlement of 1783 gave the USA control over the lands up to the Mississippi. It was not long before many families were making their way along one of the roughly-made roads which crossed the Appalachians, prior to sailing down the Ohio which would take them to the heart of the newly-gained territory.

To ease this migration the government built a new road across the mountains. This was the National Road, the first stage of which, from Cumberland on the Potomac to Wheeling on the Ohio, was opened in 1818. It was wide, cambered and had a good surface. Not surprisingly it attracted many travellers:

(1) As for the emigrants, it would astonish you to witness how they get along. A covered one-horse wagon generally contains the whole wordly

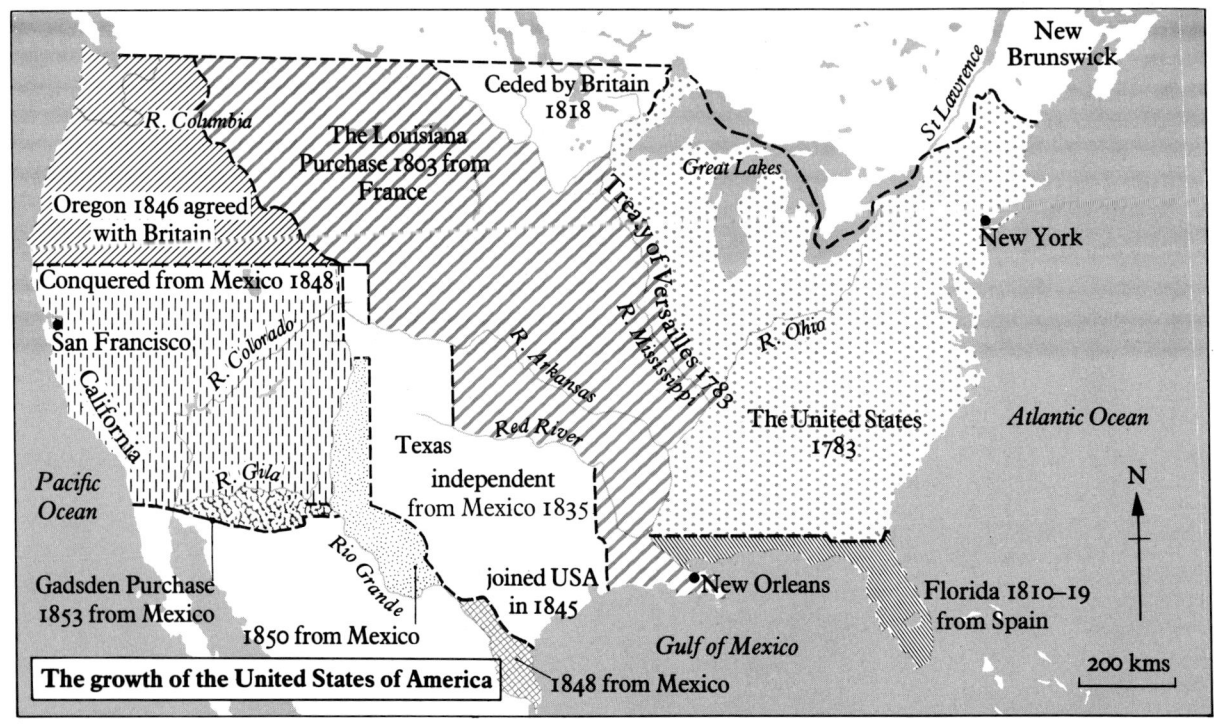

The growth of the United States of America

Ploughing in the 1880s

substance of a family consisting not unfrequently of a dozen members.... The strength of the poor animal is, of course, half the time unequal to the demand upon it, and you will, therefore, unless it be raining very hard, rarely see any one in the wagon, except perhaps some child overtaken by sickness, or a mother nursing an infant. The head of the family walks by the horse, cheering and encouraging him on his way. The good woman, when not engaged as hinted above, either trudges along with her husband, or, leading some weary little traveller by the hand behind, endeavours to keep the rest of her charge from loitering by the wayside. The old house-dog – if not chained beneath the wagon to prevent the half-starved brute from foraging too freely in a friendly country – brings up the rear.

The attractions of the lands beyond the Appalachians were described by Morris Birkbeck, a wealthy farmer from Britain who settled in Illinois:

(2) Our soil appears to be rich, a fine black mould, inclining to sand, from one to three or four feet [one metre] deep, lying on sandstone or clayey loam; so easy of tillage as to reduce the expense of cultivation below that of the land I have been accustomed to in England, notwithstanding the high rates of human labour. The wear of plough-irons is so trifling, that it is a thing of course to sharpen them in the spring once for the whole year. Our main object will be livestock, cattle, and hogs, for which there is a sure market at a good profit. Twopence a pound [1p for half a kilo] you will think too low a price to include a profit, but remember, we are not called upon, after receiving our money for produce, to refund a portion of it for rent, another portion for tithe, a third for poor's rates, and a fourth for taxes; which latter are here so light as scarcely to be brought into the nicest calculation. You will consider also, that money goes a great deal farther here, so that a less profit would suffice....

The idea of exhausting the soil by cropping, so as to render manure necessary, has not yet entered into the estimates of the western cultivator. Manure has been often known to accumulate until the farmers have removed their yards and buildings out of the way of the nuisance. They have no notion of making a return to the land, and as yet there seems no bound to its fertility.

For about half the capital that is required for the mere cultivation of our worn-out soils in England, a man may establish himself as a proprietor here, with every comfort belonging to a plain and reasonable mode of living....

Shooting grizzly bears. A drawing by one of the members of Lewis and Clark's expedition.

Lewis and Clark holding a meeting with Indians

New territories

The western frontier of the USA was by now far beyond the Mississippi. In 1803 she had bought Louisiana from France for fifteen million dollars. (France had obtained the area from Spain in 1800.) This action doubled the size of the USA and it was small wonder that the country's president, Thomas Jefferson, boasted that he had bought enough land to last Americans for a thousand years. The following year, at his request, Meriwether Lewis and William Clark set out with a party of about thirty people to explore the new lands and in particular to see what lay between the headwaters of the Missouri and Columbia rivers. Jefferson knew that the Rocky Mountains were there but he did not know how big they were. If they did not prove too much of an obstacle then an easy trade route might be established through to the Pacific. Lewis and Clark's findings shattered these hopes.

In his diary Lewis recorded his mixed feelings on seeing the Rockies for the first time:

(3) While I viewed these mountains I felt a secret pleasure in finding myself so near the head of the heretofore conceived boundless Missouri; but when I reflected on the difficulties which this snowy barrier would most probably throw in my way to the Pacific, and the sufferings and hardships of myself and party in them, it in some measure counterbalanced the joy I had felt in the first moments in which I gazed on them. . . .

A mountainman with his Indian squaw. The mountainmen lived in the Rockies trapping beaver and selling the skins.

Lewis's misgivings were justified but, in spite of many difficulties, the explorers crossed the Rockies and reached the Pacific.

The expedition strengthened the USA's claim to Oregon which lay between Louisiana and the Pacific, a claim which was disputed by Britain. In 1846 an agreement was reached which resulted in the northern half of Oregon being added to Canada while the southern half became part of the USA. Two other substantial pieces of territory were added to the USA in the 1840s so that by 1848 the country had very largely assumed the shape that we know today.

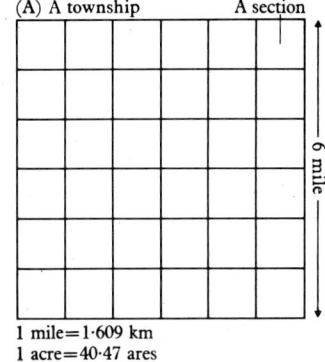

(A) A township   A section

1 mile = 1·609 km
1 acre = 40·47 ares

Organising the settlement of the land

The government tried, often unsuccessfully, to prevent settlers from moving into new territory until it had negotiated the removal of all Indians. When it had done this, its surveyors divided the land into townships ten kilometres square. As soon as the sections were worked out the land could be sold off. In this way the government hoped to impose some sort of order on the move west.

To begin with, a section of 267 hectares was the smallest unit of land a settler could buy from the government. Later legislation helped the poorer settlers by allowing them to purchase smaller portions of land. The Homestead Act of 1862 allowed settlers to claim free of charge, apart from the legal fees, a quarter-section if they worked this land for a minimum of five years.

Thomas Jefferson would have approved of the Homestead Act. He dreamt of a land of small, independent farmers. Even with favourable legislation, however, the small man did not always find it easy to secure the land he needed. Land speculators bought up much of the land in order to sell it at a higher price later on.

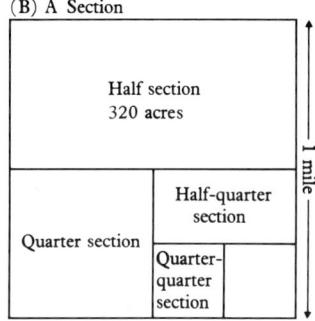

(B) A Section

Half section
320 acres

Quarter section

Half-quarter section

Quarter-quarter section

Wagons West

By the 1840s the fertile lands of the Ohio and the Mississippi were getting crowded. Settlers were forced to look elsewhere. The Great Plains did not attract them. There was so little rain over most of this region that it was known as the Great American Desert. On the other hand fur traders were bringing news of the good soils and the favourable climate to be found beyond the Rockies. Encouraged by such talk people began to move to Oregon and California.

Until the coming of the railways the most popular way of reaching the far West was by covered wagon. The Indian threat encouraged families to join together to form wagon trains. The most important assembling point was Independence, Missouri. From there to the far West was about 3300 kilometres and the journey usually lasted five or six months.

The pattern was set by the Great Emigration of 1843 when some two hundred families left Independence bound for Oregon. Many settlers had brought cattle and eventually the party split in two when those without cattle decided to go on ahead. Jesse Applegate

Settlers on the Oregon trail in the 1840s

led the cow column which followed behind. Here he describes the preparations for a day's travelling:

(4) It is four o'clock a.m.; the sentinels on duty have discharged their rifles – the signal that the hours of sleep are over; and every wagon and tent is pouring forth its night tenants, and slow-kindling smokes begin largely to rise and float away on the morning air. Sixty men start from the corral, spreading as they make through the vast herd of cattle and horses that form a semi-circle around the encampment, the most distant perhaps two miles [three kilometres] away.

The herders pass to the extreme verge and carefully examine for trails beyond, to see that none of the animals have strayed or been stolen during the night. This morning no trails lead beyond the outside animals in sight, and by five o'clock the herders begin to contract the great moving circle, and the well-trained animals move slowly towards camp.... In about an hour, five thousand animals are close up to the encampment, and the teamsters are busy selecting their teams and driving them inside the corral to be yoked. The corral is a circle one hundred yards deep, formed with wagons connected strongly with each other....

From six to seven o'clock is a busy time; breakfast is to be eaten, the tents struck, the wagons loaded, and the teams yoked and brought up in readiness to be attached to their respective wagons. All know when at seven o'clock the signal to march sounds, that those not ready to take their proper places in the line of march must fall into the dusty rear for the day....

It is within ten minutes of seven; the corral but now a strong barricade is everywhere broken, the teams being attached to the wagons. The women and children have taken their places in them. The pilot (a borderer who has passed his life on the verge of civilization, and has been chosen to the post of leader from his knowledge of the savage and his experience in travel through roadless wastes) stands ready in the midst of his pioneers.... Ten or fifteen young men, not today on duty, form another cluster. They are ready to start on a buffalo hunt.... The cow-drivers are hastening, as they get ready, to the rear of their charge, to collect and prepare them for the day's march.

It is on the stroke of seven, the rushing to and fro, the cracking of whips, the loud command to oxen, and what seemed to be the inextricable confusion of the last ten minutes has ceased. Fortunately every one had been found and every teamster is at his post. The clear notes of a trumpet sound in the front, the pilot and his guards mount their horses; the leading division of wagons move out of the encampment, and take up the line of march; the rest fall into their places with the precision of clockwork. . . .

Gold fever

Until 1848 the numbers settling in Oregon and California were still relatively small. In that year, however, gold was discovered in California and a rush to the far West developed in which Americans were joined by, among others, Mexicans, Australians, and Chinese. Some Americans went by boat, either round Cape Horn or via the Isthmus of Panama. Most used the overland route and, as the following newspaper report shows, many of them were ill-prepared for the long and difficult journey ahead of them.

A miner panning for gold

(5) Fort Kearney, 26 May, 1849
Since my last, the army of gold diggers has received mighty and powerful reinforcements. It now numbers over 10 000 men, and has a baggage train of 2527 wagons. The prairie is dotted with them as far as the eye can reach; not an instant for the last two weeks has there been, that emigrants and emigrant wagons have not been in sight from this post. For two or three days past, the weather has been most disagreeable, and the effect has been somewhat to *dampen* the ardor of the emigrants, particularly so as the rain has been falling in torrents most of the time. I have heard hundreds wish themselves home, and several have actually turned back at this point. The great majority now crossing the plains were profoundly ignorant of what was before them when starting – had no idea of what an outfit consisted of, and, in short, looked upon crossing the prairies as nothing but a pleasure trip where killing buffalo, wolf hunting, etc., formed the prominent features. The result of such want of experience was, that almost every wagon that left the frontiers was overloaded, not with articles absolutely necessary, but with such things as each might fancy he might need while on the prairies, or after he reached the end of his journey. Sawmills, pick axes, shovels, anvils, blacksmith's tools, feather beds, rocking chairs, and a thousand other useless articles for such a trip, filled the wagons as they left the Missouri River. Soon it was found that the loading was too great for the teams, and now overboard goes everything. The road is lined with various articles – even *gold vases* and *gold washers* are abandoned by the roadside. Quantities of provisions share the same fate, which it is to be feared will be sadly wanted by those who threw them away, before they reach the Pacific.

Several serious accidents have occurred on the road from the careless use of firearms. Three men have been shot dead, and yesterday a young man was brought to the hospital dangerously shot through the shoulder.

'Pawnee', *Missouri Republican*, 16 June 1849

When they arrived some of the migrants struck lucky and made quick fortunes. Most of them, however, were doomed to disappointment. It was the same story in each of the various 'rushes' which occurred in different parts of the West over the next thirty years.

The coming of the railways

The railways transformed the journey west. What had been a matter of months now became a matter of days.

Until the 1860s the railways stopped at the Mississippi and the Missouri. Then in 1862 the government ordered the building of a line between Omaha and San Francisco. The Union Pacific Railway Company was to start building in the east while the Central Pacific Railway Company was to start building in the west. Seven years later the two lines were joined at Promontory Point in Utah and the first transcontinental railway was complete.

A photograph was taken of the workers and officials of the two companies as they celebrated their historic meeting.

(6)

An advertisement for the Union Pacific Railway Smoky Hill Route

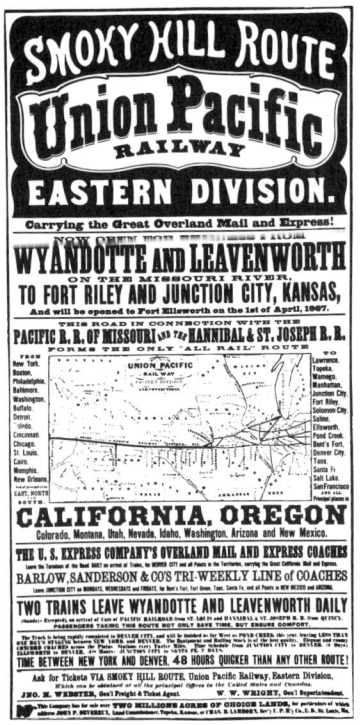

Thanks to the electric telegraph (invented by Samuel Morse in 1837) the event could be celebrated simultaneously throughout the country.

(7) The event was celebrated in all the large cities, and everywhere hailed with demonstrations of delight. In New York, Trinity Church was thrown open at mid-day, an address was delivered by Rev. Dr Vinton, and a large crowd united 'to tender thanks to God for the completion of the greatest work ever undertaken by man'. In Philadelphia, bells were rung and cannon were fired. At Chicago a great impromptu demonstration took place, in which all citizens joined; at Buffalo a large crowd gathered to hear the telegraph signals, sang the 'Star-Spangled Banner', and listened to speeches from distinguished citizens; and at every important point the announcement of the completion of the work was received with unbounded joy.

Other transcontinental lines soon followed, as well as a multitude of local lines.

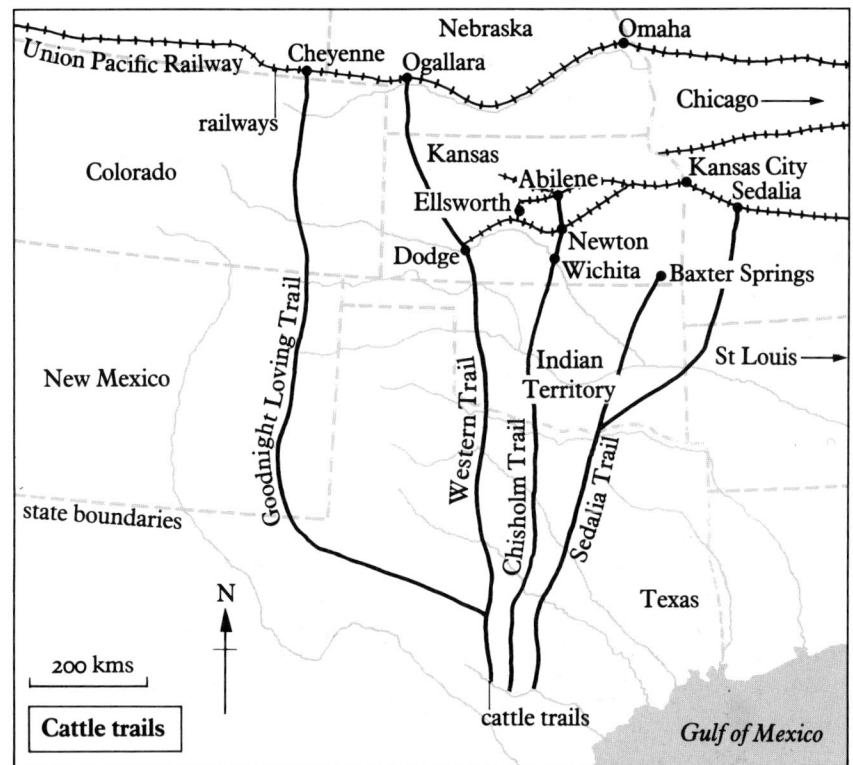

The cowboys

Among those who benefited from the railways were the Texas cowboys. For some time Texas had been a cattle kingdom (it is estimated that there were 3 535 000 longhorns in Texas in 1860). The cowboys earned their living by driving herds of cattle to areas like the Mississippi and the Missouri lands, which were well-settled. The new railways opened up the prospect of cattle worth only two to three dollars a head in Texas being sold for twenty times as much in the cities of the East. All the cowboys had to do was to round up the cattle and drive them 1000 kilometres to the railheads in the north.

Between 1867 and 1887 the cowboys drove fifty-five million head of cattle to towns like Abilene, Ellsworth and Dodge City. Their work was hard and dangerous as the following account shows.

(8) When skies were clear and the air bracing, the task of cattle-driving was a pleasant and healthful one. But there came rainy days, when the cattle were restless, and when it was anything but enjoyable riding through the steady downpour. Then especially were the nights wearisome, and the cattle were ready at any time to stampede.

No one could tell what caused a stampede.... A flash of lightning, a crackling stick, a wolf's howl, little things in themselves, but in a moment every horned head was lifted, and the mass of hair and horns, with fierce, frightened eyes gleaming like thousands of emeralds, was off. Recklessly, blindly, in whatever direction fancy led them, they went, over a bluff

A cattle drive

[steep slope] or into a morass [marsh] it mattered not, and fleet were the horses that could keep abreast of the leaders. But some could do it, and lashing their ponies to their best gait the cowboys followed at breakneck speed. Getting on one side of the leaders the effort was to turn them, a little at first, then more and more, until the circumference of a great circle was being described. The cattle behind blindly followed, and soon the front and rear joined and 'milling' commenced. Like a mighty mill-stone, round and round the bewildered creatures raced until they were wearied out or recovered from their fright. . . .

A stampede always meant a loss, and rendered the herd more likely to be again panic-stricken. Hysterical leaders were often shot because of their influence on the remainder of the column. Another danger was that of the mingling of two herds; while in the earlier days the presence of buffalo was a decided peril. A herd of buffalo roaring and tearing its way across the plain was almost certain to cause a panic, if within hearing, and out-riders were necessary to watch for these enemies and turn their course from the trail. Besides, marauding Indians were always to be feared, and many a skirmish was had between the cowboys and redskins. An understanding with the chiefs was, however, usually sufficient to ensure safety. Thus accompanied by incidents that brought into play all the strength and strategy of their guards, the horned host moved on. Rivers were crossed by swimming in the same order that had been followed on land.

Cowboys preparing for the night. While some slept, others would remain on guard. In the background is the chuck wagon which carried all the food, tools and other supplies needed by the cowboys.

The cowboy's life was not all excitement. Plenty of days in the saddle were only hot, dusty and long. The dangers of the trail, however, caught the popular imagination. So, too, did the wild goings-on at the end of the trail when the cowboys spent money like water in the saloon bars and dance halls of the cow towns. The cowboy became a hero and has remained one ever since.

With all attention focused on his skill as a rider, his six-shooters, his hard drinking and his reckless gambling the cowboy has been over-glamorised. We can see the process beginning in this drawing by Frederick Remington:

(9)

The cowboy era lasted little more than twenty years. As cattle ranchers fenced in more and more of the open range and as the railways brought an increasing number of settlers to the area the cowboy's job became increasingly difficult. He depended on being able to drive his cattle through open country. The last of the big drives was in 1886 and it was not very long before cattle trailing had dwindled away completely.

The settlement of the Great Plains

Until the 1870s the Great Plains were still largely unsettled. As the far West filled up, however, settlers were driven to consider cultivating the open grasslands of the Great American Desert. Daunting though the prospect was, the railways made it possible to think of moving into this region. The journey there presented no problems and any special equipment and timber which might be needed to establish a farm in this dry, treeless area could now be brought in as required.

It was in the interests of the railway companies to encourage settlers to fill up the West's empty spaces. Some companies, as a result of generous government grants, owned a great deal of un-occupied land which they now wished to sell. Every company wanted as much traffic as possible running along its lines. Railway companies began, therefore, to mount intensive advertising campaigns in which the West was painted in very rosy colours. Here is a sample. It is part of a circular put out by the Burlington and Missouri River Railroad:

Above: the town of Helena in the State of Montana, 1870

(10) Ho for the West! Nebraska ahead! The truth will out! The best farming and stock-raising country in the world! The great central region, not too hot or too cold.

The facts about Western Iowa and Southern Nebraska are being slowly but surely discovered by all intelligent men. The large population now pouring into this region, consists of shrewd and well-informed farmers, who know what is good, and are taking advantage of the opportunities offered.

The crops of Southern Nebraska are as fine as can be; a large wheat and barley crop has been harvested; corn is in splendid condition and all other crops are equally fine. The opportunities now offered to buy B. & M. R. R. lands on long credit, low interest, twenty-per-cent rebate for improvements, low freights, and fares, free passes to those who buy, etc., etc., can never again be found.

Chief Joseph

Before the end of the century, the Great Plains were settled. This marked the end of an era for Americans. For the first time in their history there were no large tracts of land for them to move into. The West was won.

The fate of the Indians

It was won at the expense of the Indians, who were forced to exchange their lands for the inadequate reservations allowed by the

US government. Some went peacefully. Others resisted and had to be forcibly removed.

The Plains Indians were the last to lose their lands. For them the building of the railways across the Great Plains marked the beginning of the end. The railways brought settlers. They also brought the men who virtually exterminated the animal around which the lives of the Plains Indians revolved. In 1840 perhaps forty million buffalo roamed the Great Plains. By 1890 about a thousand remained.

Many were killed by the men employed by the railway companies to supply their construction crews with meat. William Cody earned his nickname 'Buffalo Bill' by killing 4280 buffalo in the space of eighteen months on behalf of the Kansas Pacific Railway Company. Many more were killed for sport and by professional hunters who sold the hides to tanneries in the East for $1 to $3 apiece.

For almost thirty years the Plains Indians resisted the white man. Tribe by tribe, however, they were defeated and confined to reservations. Chief Joseph of the Nez Perce tribe surrendered in 1877.

(11) I am tired of fighting. Our chiefs are killed. Looking Glass is dead. The old men are all killed. It is the young men who say yes or no. He who led the young men is dead. It is cold and we have no blankets. The little children are freezing to death. My people, some of them, have run away to the hills, and have no blankets, no food; no one knows where they

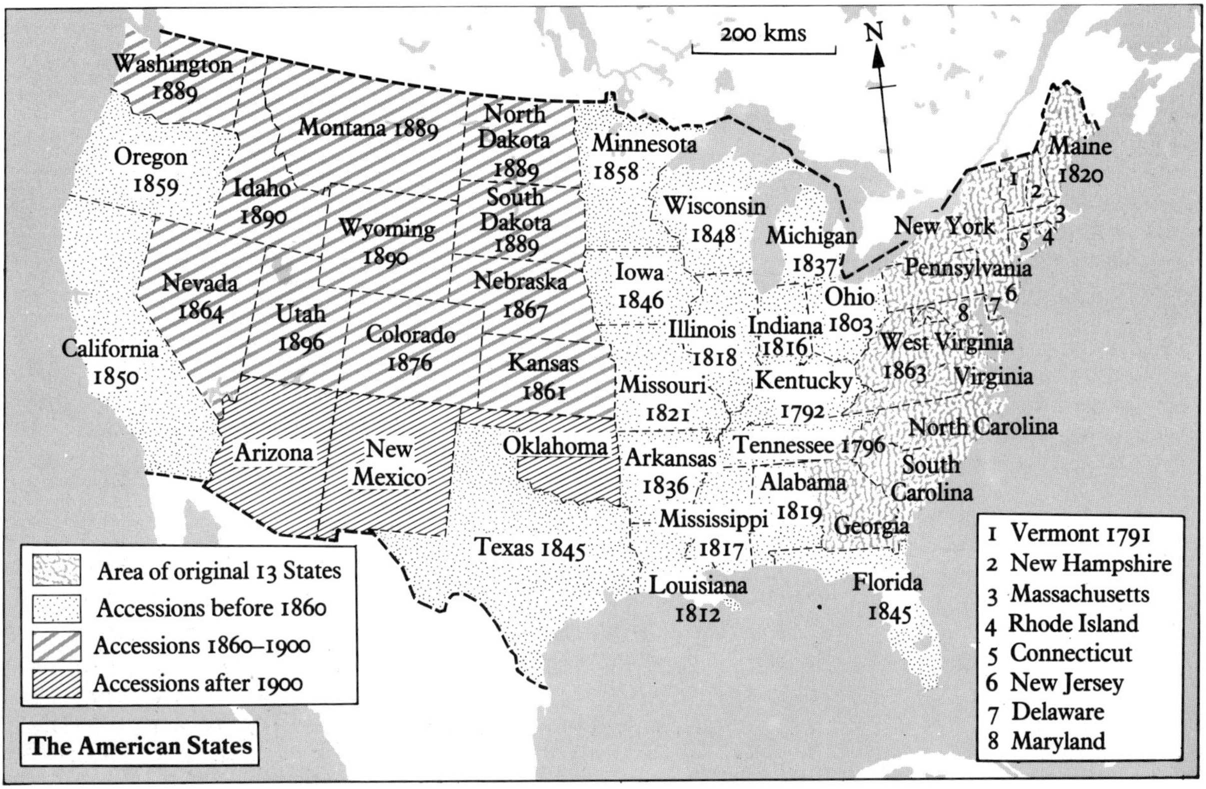

200 kms N

Washington 1889
Oregon 1859
Idaho 1890
Montana 1889
North Dakota 1889
South Dakota 1889
Minnesota 1858
Wisconsin 1848
Michigan 1837
Maine 1820
New York
Pennsylvania
Nevada 1864
Utah 1896
Wyoming 1890
Nebraska 1867
Iowa 1846
Ohio
Indiana 1803
Illinois 1818
West Virginia 1863
Virginia
California 1850
Colorado 1876
Kansas 1861
Missouri 1821
Kentucky 1792
North Carolina
Arizona
New Mexico
Oklahoma
Arkansas 1836
Tennessee 1796
Alabama
Mississippi 1817
South Carolina
Georgia
Texas 1845
Louisiana 1812
Florida 1845

Area of original 13 States
Accessions before 1860
Accessions 1860–1900
Accessions after 1900

The American States

1 Vermont 1791
2 New Hampshire
3 Massachusetts
4 Rhode Island
5 Connecticut
6 New Jersey
7 Delaware
8 Maryland

The Indian Territory, 16 September 1893. This was the biggest of the 'rushes' for land.

are, perhaps freezing to death. I want time to look for my children and see how many of them I can find. Maybe I shall find them among the dead. Hear me, my chiefs, I am tired; my heart is sick and sad. From where the sun now stands I will fight no more forever.

The last battle of the Indian wars was fought in 1890. Fearing another uprising the US Army attacked the Sioux on their reservation. The Indians fled and were massacred in what is known as the Battle of Wounded Knee.

The end of the Indian Territory

The Indian Territory to the west of the Mississippi was the largest piece of land left to the Indians. Numerous tribes were settled here by the US government. As land grew scarce, white settlers looked greedily at this region and in 1889 the government declared the unoccupied central part of the Territory open to settlement. On 22 April thousands of settlers lined up along the edge of this region. They had come on horseback, in wagons, on bicycles and even with wheelbarrows. When the bugles sounded at noon they raced in to stake their claim. Within twenty-four hours the whole area had been staked out.

Other 'rushes' followed and in 1907 the Territory became Oklahoma.

Postscript: industrial America

The USA did not remain, as Jefferson hoped it would, a nation of farmers. It was a country fabulously rich in natural resources such as coal, iron ore and oil. Already by the end of the nineteenth century vast industries were developing in cities like Pittsburgh, Philadelphia and Chicago. Rather than go west increasing numbers of Americans chose to work in these and other industrial centres. In 1860 only sixteen cities had populations of over 50000. By 1890 this number had reached fifty-eight. The days were gone when the West was the only place to go for those hoping to improve their lives.

Questions and further work

1 Trace the map on page 201. Using six different colours shade in (a) the Thirteen Colonies (b) those states admitted to the Union by 1800, 1825, 1850, 1875 and 1900. Which states had still to be admitted to the Union to make up the USA as it is today?

2 What advantages, according to Birkbeck in Document 2, did the farmers of Illinois have over the farmers in Britain?

3 Using the information in Document 4, draw up a list of instructions about early morning procedure which the leader of a wagon train might give to the people in his charge.

4 Write a short newspaper report about the celebrations which took place at Promontory Point when the Union Pacific and the Central Pacific railways met (Illustration 6). Why did the event arouse such interest and enthusiasm throughout the country?

5 What part did the railways play in the development of the West?

6 How did cowboys earn their living? What were the four dangers mentioned in Document 8 that a cowboy might encounter on a cattle drive?

7 Look carefully at Illustration 9. Describe the image of the cowboy it presents.
   Try to find some more pictures by Remington and some by Charles Russell to compare with this one.

8 What Westerns have you seen on television and at the cinema? Which ones do you think present (a) a glamorised picture (b) a realistic view of the West?

9 Which statements in Document 10 show that it is an example of propaganda? Why do you think this kind of persuasion was used to get settlers into the area? Can you think of any present-day examples?

10 The advance of the white man forced the Indians out of the territories they had lived and hunted in for generations; drastically reduced their main food supply of buffalo, and finally made them live in reservations in the poorest parts of the country. Imagine you are now a reservation Indian. Describe what happened to you as the white man advanced.

17 The Rising Sun

The end of Japanese isolation

On 8 July 1853 the inhabitants of the Japanese fishing village of Uraga suddenly caught sight of something strange and terrifying on the horizon. Sailing towards them were four great ships, two of which were pouring out clouds of menacing black smoke in a manner the villagers had never seen before. The sight caused the utmost consternation. Fishermen out in their junks rowed crazily for the shore while in the village temple bells rang and people raced to take cover. The 'black ships' did not, however, bring destruction. They dropped anchor about one and half kilometres offshore and waited.

They were American warships. Their commander was Commodore Matthew Perry who had been sent by President Fillmore to communicate to the Japanese the American government's wish to establish trading relations with them. Like everybody else except the Dutch, who had been allowed to occupy the tiny island of Decima in Nagasaki Bay, the Americans knew very little about the Japanese. For over two hundred years Japan had pursued a policy of deliberately keeping foreigners out, and she seemed a likely market for American goods.

On 9 July local officials from Uraga were rowed out to the warships. Through Dutch intermediaries they asked the Americans to leave. The request was turned down and Perry, who had not left his cabin (his aloofness impressed the Japanese who referred to him as the High and Mighty Mysteriousness), let the officials know that he personally would speak to no one other than the Governor of Uraga.

Accordingly, the Governor went out to the Commodore's flagship. The meeting went well and it was agreed that Perry should come ashore in order to deliver the letter he had brought from President Fillmore. The landing took place on 14 July. Both sides were out to impress. Rows of Japanese soldiers in full armour lined the beach as the Americans, splendidly uniformed, marched, complete with band, from the shore to the specially constructed Audience Hall. Here Perry met

Commodore Matthew Perry
1794 1958

Perry's landing 1853

representatives of the *Shogun* who was Japan's chief official. The President's letter, together with various other documents including a letter from Perry himself, was handed over and the Commodore explained that he would return the following spring for the Japanese reply. It was clear that he expected the reply to be favourable. The meeting only lasted twenty minutes. When it was over the Americans returned to their ships and three days later they sailed away.

For some years the Japanese had debated whether or not they should continue to exclude foreigners. Now a decision was needed and opinion was very much divided. In reality, though, the Japanese had no choice. They were a weak nation. When Perry returned he brought a squadron of nine ships which between them carried about 250 mounted guns. How could the *Shogun* turn him away?

Accordingly, therefore, on 31 March 1854 a Treaty of Friendship between Japan and the USA was signed. A new era in Japanese history had begun.

A village chief

Traditional Japan

In 1854 Japan was an agricultural country heavily dependent upon the cultivation of rice. Its thirty million or so people were still rigidly divided into four classes. First in importance were the *samurai* or warriors, next came the peasants or farmers (by far the biggest group), then the craftsmen and finally the least respected group of all, the merchants. The most important *samurai* were those who held land. To these feudal lords the peasants had to pay a proportion of their rice crop. The majority of peasants were extremely poor and violent protests about the amount of rice being demanded were not uncommon. Very often such action brought concessions from the lord but those known to have stirred up the violence could expect little mercy.

The lord was not a person to offend. The following episode recounted in the diary of a *samurai* illustrates this very clearly:

Japanese samurai

The lord of Iyo [in Shikoku] lost a favourite hawk, and sought for it throughout his domain. One day a certain farmer went out to tend his fields, while his wife stayed at home with her weaving. A hawk flew in and perched on her loom. The wife took her shuttle and struck the bird, which straight away died. The farmer returned home and was told by his wife how a beautifully marked bird had settled on her loom, how she had struck at it without intending to kill it, but how the bird had unfortunately died. Her husband looked at it and saw it was a hawk. He was greatly alarmed, for he knew that the lord was searching for such a bird. With much fear he told the village headman about what had happened, and the occurrence was reported to the bailiff. The latter, in great anger, had the husband and wife bound, and taken before his lord for trial. The lord, too, was enraged, and had the wife crucified, but pardoned the husband because he was not at home at the time in question.

The ruling Tokugawa family apart, the most powerful feudal lords were the *daimyo*. These families held large estates and over the years their influence grew while that of the Tokugawa declined. Ever since 1603 this family had, in addition to controlling more land than any other family, monopolised the position of *Shogun* or supreme general. Residing in their castle in Edo (renamed Tokyo in 1868) the Tokugawa ruled as emperors in all but name. There continued to be an emperor but he had no real power. By the time Commodore Perry arrived, however, the authority of the *Shogun* was on the wane and it was not long before a group of *daimyo* conspired to put an end to Tokugawa rule.

The overthrow of the Shogun

Criticism of the *Shogun* mounted as a result of his concessions to the USA and other foreign powers. The Treaty of Friendship negotiated by Perry provided for the opening of two Japanese ports to American traders and for the appointment of an American consul to look after his country's interests in Japan. In 1858, however, the US government insisted on the drawing up of a further treaty which opened up more ports (including Edo) and gave to the American consul the right to deal with any American citizen who committed crimes on Japanese soil. Britain, Holland, Russia and France all demanded similar treaties and the *Shogun* had no option but to comply. The result in Japan was a wave of anti-foreign feeling. The demand that consuls in Japan should have judicial powers, which implied that Japanese law was not good enough for foreigners, was particularly resented. An 'expel the foreigner' movement developed and its supporters were prepared to resort to violence. Sir Rutherford Alcock, the first British consul in Japan, wrote at this time:

... no officer of the Missions of either Great Britain or America can walk out of their official residence without risk of rudeness. ... Stones are thrown, blows are struck, swords are drawn on gentlemen passing along the thoroughfare inoffensively and peaceably. ...

In one particularly serious incident the American consul's secretary was attacked and murdered by a group of fanatical anti-foreigners.

All this weakened the position of the *Shogun* because he had let the foreigners in. Opposition to his rule did not come only from those who wanted rid of the foreigners. It also came from certain *daimyo* families, notably the Satsuma and the Choshu, who appreciated Japan's need to learn from the West if she was ever to deal with them on equal terms but who also felt that the country now needed a much stronger government than that provided by the *Shogun*. These families decided to take action and it was they who, in 1868, overthrew the *Shogun* and entrusted the government of the country to the young Emperor Meiji.

The age of change

On the face of things the Emperor was restored to his former powers in 1868. In practice the business of government was carried out by a gifted group of ministers chosen from, in particular, the Satsuma and Choshu families. These men were the new rulers of Japan and they now embarked on a remarkable programme of modernisation.

Their over-riding aim was to ensure that Japan did not share the fate of India and China, of being completely dominated by the western powers. They were determined to do all they could to ensure that Japan survived as an independent country.

An early step was the abolition of the powers and privileges of the feudal lords, a move which greatly strengthened the position of the central government and put it in a much better position to bring about radical change. This was in 1871. The same year a group of ministers set off on a mission to acquire 'knowledge from all over the world'. They visited the USA and numerous countries in Europe, including Britain. One of the party wrote of Britain:

In every city there are many factories. The shipyards in Liverpool, the spinning mills in Manchester and the cotton mills in Glasgow, in particular, are equipped with powerful machines which are in constant operation. Besides these, there

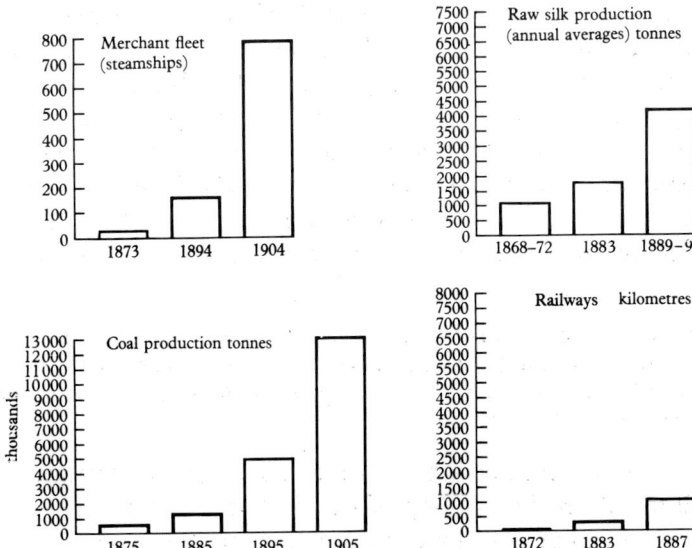

Japanese economic progress, 1870–1905

are countless large and small plants. When I saw them I realized how England had become such a powerful and wealthy nation. In remote places there are roads and bridges. Railways are in use, not to mention horse-drawn carriages, for transportation. I was impressed by the convenience of it all.

There was no mistaking the lesson to be learned here. Japan had to industrialise.

Accordingly, the government now initiated Japan's Industrial Revolution. Iron foundries and textile factories were built and coal mines were opened. The shipyards were expanded, railways were constructed and by 1880 all the major cities were linked by telegraph. Much of this enterprise was financed to begin with by the government. Later, industrialists began to play their part as the government sold off all its industrial interests except those connected with defence. The government did not encourage foreign investment, because it wanted the country to retain control over its own industries. Likewise it had no intention of becoming dependent on the foreign advisers whose services it recruited. An American visitor wrote in 1911:

The Japanese are dismissing as rapidly as possible all foreigners whom they have employed to train them in western ways, from professors and school-teachers, to engineers, draughtsmen and foremen in mills and factories. This is done partly from motives of economy, and partly because here, and as I believe in almost all other departments of life, they feel themselves to be capable of going it alone.

The government did not confine its attention to the economy. Schooling was extended, the legal system was overhauled and a western-style constitution was introduced which allowed for the election of a House of

Japanese policemen, 1877. Notice the western-style uniforms. Can you find any other signs of western influence in the picture?

Representatives. (In spite of this constitution power remained firmly in the hands of the Emperor's closest advisers.)

In the midst of all this change the west was copied even in superficial matters. In the towns western foods such as meat and dairy produce became popular as did western clothes, and such developments received official encouragement. In 1872, for example, the Emperor ordered men to wear western dress for all formal occasions at Court and a few years later the Empress announced her approval of western women's fashions. Such moves were considered necessary if Japan was to win the respect of the western powers.

The beginnings of empire

Westernisation was a means to the end of making Japan a powerful nation. From the start the armed forces received careful attention. Conscription was introduced, munitions works were established and orders were placed with British shipyards for a series of warships. As a result Japan rapidly became the strongest country in Asia. By 1894 she could mobilise an army of 200 000 men and had a navy of twenty-eight newly-built vessels.

The government's main object in foreign policy was to secure the renegotiation of the hated treaties forced upon the *Shogun* by the western powers. Not surprisingly these countries were reluctant to

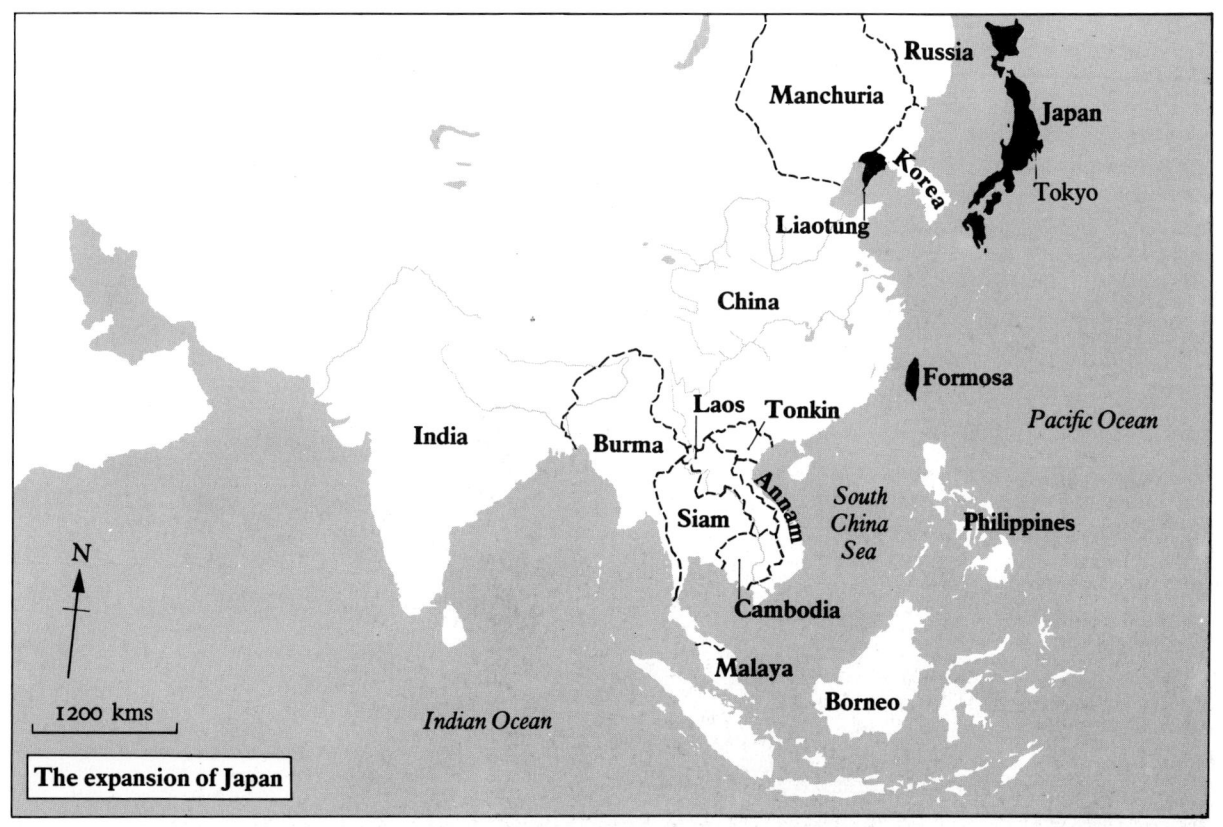

The expansion of Japan

abandon their privileges and it was not until the 1890s that the treaties were revised. By then Japan had started to build up her own overseas sphere of influence. In 1876 she had forced Korea to open certain ports to her traders and thereafter her interest in that country had steadily grown. Eventually this brought her into conflict with China which had long had close links with Korea. War broke out in 1894 and went extremely well for Japan. By the spring of 1895 Japanese forces were making for Peking, and China decided to surrender. Harsh terms were imposed on her. By the Treaty of Shimonoseki, China agreed to pay a large indemnity, to give up her claim to Korea (which was declared independent but came increasingly under Japan's control until formally annexed to her in 1910) and to surrender not only the island of Formosa but also part of the Liaotung peninsula on the Chinese mainland. In the event the terms were too harsh. Russia was very concerned about this sudden extension of Japanese influence and, backed by France and Germany, urged the Japanese government to abandon all thought of taking the Liaotung peninsula. Much though she resented this latest example of western interference, Japan was not yet strong enough to refuse such a request. Reluctantly she agreed and imposed an extra indemnity instead. (Determined not to be humiliated in this way again, the government immediately ordered further substantial increases in both military and naval strength.)

In spite of this setback, the foundations of the Japanese Empire had been laid. (In yet another way Japan was copying the west.) It was not long, moreover, before Japan gained the international recognition she craved. In 1902 she concluded an alliance with Britain and so gained entry to the diplomatic circle of the great powers. Two years later the Russo-Japanese War broke out and, to the astonishment of the world, Japan's forces were dramatically successful.

The Japanese fleet in action during the war with Russia, 1904–5

The full extent of the change that had come over Japan in the half-century since Commodore Perry's visit was now clear for all to see.

Drinking sake, *a traditional Japanese drink made from rice*

Using the evidence: Japan and the west

The great issue in Japan in the nineteenth century was whether or not the country should open its doors to foreigners. Writing in 1825 Aizawa Seishisai argued forcefully that Japan should keep foreigners out. Here are two extracts from his *New Proposals*:

(1) ... now we must cope with the foreigners of the west, where every country upholds the law of Jesus and attempts therewith to subdue other countries. Everywhere they go they set fire to shrines and temples, deceive and delude the people, and then invade and seize the country. Their purpose is not realized until the ruler of the land is made a subject and the people of the land subservient.

(2) The earth ... appears to be perfectly round, without edges or corners. However, everything exists in its natural bodily form, and our Divine Land is situated at the top of the earth. Thus, although it is not an extensive country ... it reigns over all quarters of the world. ... The various countries of the west correspond to the feet and legs of the body. That is why their ships come from afar to visit Japan. As for the land amidst the seas which the western barbarians call America, it occupies the hindmost region of the earth; thus, its people are stupid and simple, and are incapable of doing things.

Sakuma Shozan believed equally strongly that in order to survive, Japan had to learn from the west. He was particularly concerned about the inadequacies of Japan's defences. In 1854 he was imprisoned for encouraging a pupil to stow away on one of Commodore Perry's ships. After his release, one year later, he put forward his case in a book called *Reflections on My Errors*. The book made many criticisms of the existing regime and was not published until after the overthrow of the *Shogun* of 1868.

(3) Formerly, with one or two friends, I took a trip. ... In the course of this trip I stopped at about ten places where barricades had been set up in preparation against an invasion from the sea. However, the arrangement of them made no sense, and none of them could be depended on as a defence

The Emperor opening Japan's first railway in 1872

fortification. Upon discovering this, I unconsciously looked up to Heaven and sighed deeply; I struck my chest and wept for a long time. . . . If barbarian ships arrived in force, how could we either defend against them or defeat them? After my trip, I felt the urge to write a petition discussing the things that should and should not be done in maritime defence, with the hope that I might be of assistance in this time of emergency. I completed my manuscript and requested my former lord for permission to submit it. He refused and I gave up my plan. . . .

The main requirement for maritime defence are guns and warships, but the more important item is guns. . . .

What do the so-called scholars of today actually do? . . . Do they, after having learned the rites and music, punishment and administration, the classics and governmental system, go on to discuss and learn the elements of the art of war, of military discipline, of the principles of machinery? Do they make exhaustive studies of conditions in foreign countries? Of effective defence methods? Of strategy in setting up strongholds, defence barriers, and reinforcements? . . . if they do, I have not heard of it! . . .

. . . learning a barbarian language is not only a step toward knowing the barbarians, but also the groundwork for mastering them.

One of the Emperor Meiji's leading ministers was a man called Okuma Shigenobu. In 1908 he completed his book *Fifty Years of New Japan* in which he described and defended the policy of westernisation pursued since 1868:

(4) Her [i.e. Japan's] general progress, during the short space of half a century, has been so sudden and swift that it presents a spectacle rare in the history of the world. This leap forward is the result of the stimulus which the country received on coming into contact with the civilisation of Europe and America, and may well, in its broad sense, be regarded as a boon conferred by foreign intercourse. . . . We possess today a powerful army and navy, but it was after western models that we laid their foundations by establishing a system of conscription in pursuance of the principle 'all our sons are soldiers', by promoting military education, and by encouraging the manufacture of arms and the art of shipbuilding. We have reorganised the systems of central and local administration, and effected reforms in the educational systems of the empire. All this is nothing but the result of adopting the superior features of western institutions.

JAPAN. THE EMPEROR MUTSUHITO AND THE EMPRESS HARUKO

The Emperor Mutsuhito and the Empress Haruko

Questions and further work

1 Explain the following:
   (a) *samurai*
   (b) *diamyo*
   (c) *Shogun*
2 What does the story on page 206 tell you about traditional Japan?
3 Imagine that you were an inhabitant of Uraga when Commodore Perry's ships arrived. Describe your feelings when you first caught sight of the strange black monsters on the horizon. Explain what you saw and what you thought was arriving.
4 Read Document 1 carefully. What did Aizawa fear would happen if Japan allowed foreigners in? In Document 2 he likens the world to a human body. Draw the picture he describes. How does this help us to understand the Japanese attitude towards foreigners at this time?
5 Read Document 3. What does Sakuma Shōzan have to say about:
   (a) the state of Japan's defences and
   (b) what needed to be done to improve them?
   What aim did he share with Aizawa, the author of Documents 1 and 2?
6 What is Okuma Shigenobu's attitude towards the west (Document 4)? How does this compare with Aizawa's views in the first two documents?
7 List the changes which contact with the west brought to Japan. What disadvantages did this contact bring?
8 Japan has become a wealthy and important country in the twentieth century because of industrialisation. What evidence is there of Japan's influence on our way of life today?

18 The second wave of inventions

The introduction of electric lighting was one of many important scientific and technical developments in the years 1850–1900.

Brunel's Great Eastern *laying the Atlantic telegraph cable in 1866. (Samuel Morse invented the telegraph in 1837.)*

> SAVOY – Electric Light on the Stage
> SPECIAL MATINÉE THIS DAY, at 2

When this notice appeared in *The Times* on 28 December 1881 only a handful of buildings in Britain were lit by electricity. It was a brand new form of lighting. Electric incandescent lamps had, however, been used in the auditorium of the Savoy Theatre, London, since its opening just over two months earlier. Because of technical problems the management had been forced initially to use gas lamps on the stage. Now it was ready to use electric lamps throughout the theatre.

The very special matinée performance was fully reported in *The Times*:

An interesting experiment was made at a performance of *Patience* yesterday afternoon, when the stage was for the first time lit up by the electric light. . . . The success of the new mode of illumination was complete, and its importance for the development of scenic art can scarcely be overrated. The light was perfectly steady throughout the performance, and the effect was pictorially superior to gas, the colours of the dresses . . . appearing as true and distinct as by daylight. The Swan incandescent lamps were used, the aid of gaslight being entirely dispensed with. . . .

The comparative safety of the new system was pointed out to the audience by Mr D'Oyly Carte, the manager of the Savoy Theatre, who enveloped one of the lamps in a piece of highly inflammable muslin. On the glass being broken and the vacuum being destroyed, the flame was immediately extinguished without even singeing the muslin. The occasion of which we speak is, we believe, the first on which an entire theatre has been illuminated by electricity alone, and the marked success of the experiment augurs well for the future of the new light on the stage.

And, the reporter might have added, for the use of electric lighting generally.

Above left: Baron von Reuter, 1816-99, founder of Reuter's News Agency which he established in London in 1851.

Above right: Alexander Graham Bell making the first telephone call between New York and Chicago in 1892. Bell patented the telephone in 1876 and by 1900 1 350 000 Bell telephones were in use in the USA.

Right: Guglielmo Marconi with his wireless in 1901. In December of this year he sent wireless messages across the Atlantic.

By 1900 cycling was a very popular pastime. These bicycles were known as 'safety' bicycles in contrast to 'ordinary' bicycles which had the front wheel much larger than the back. Notice the chain-driven back wheels and the pneumatic tyres.

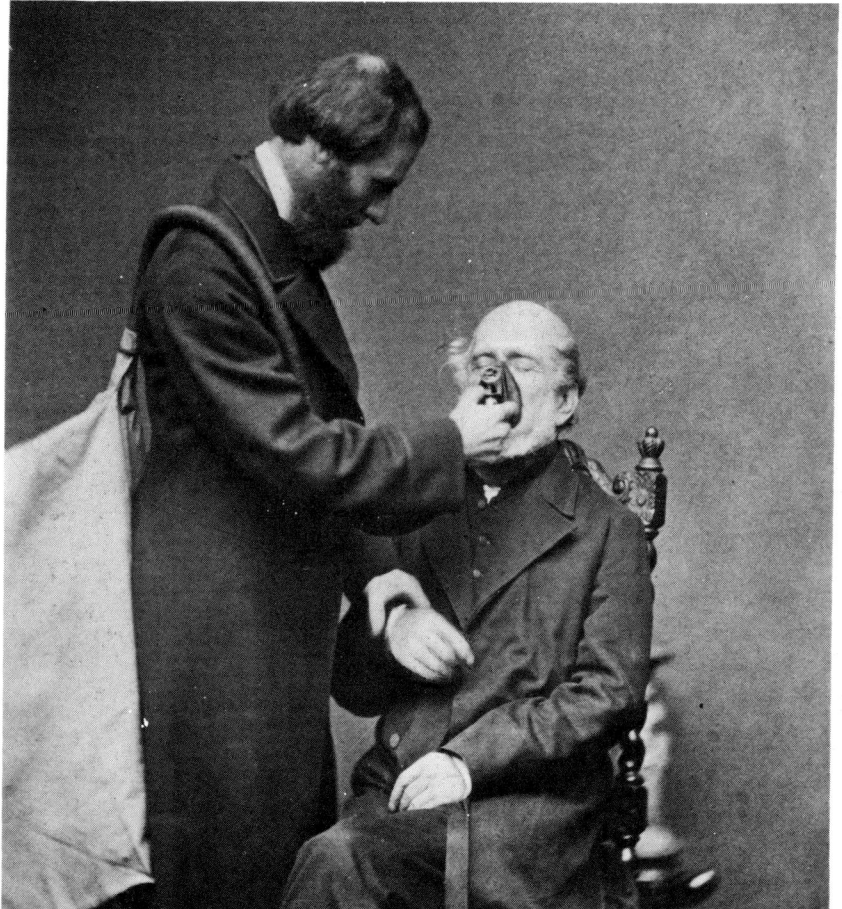

*Above: a Benz motor car, 1895.
Karl Benz from Mannheim in
Germany played a very important
part in the early development of the
motor car. He produced a three-
wheeled petrol-driven car in 1885
and his first four-wheeled version in
1893.*

*Left: a chloroform bag in use.
Anaesthetics were first used in
surgery in the 1840s.*

*Right: a dyehouse laboratory
attached to a Manchester factory.
Until the 1860s all dyes used in
textile manufacture were of natural
origin. By 1900 artificial dyes were
widely used.*

Marie and Pierre Curie at work in their Paris laboratory in 1903. They discovered the radioactive element of radium.

W. H. Fox Talbot, 1800–77, one of the pioneers of photography

Left: a patent envelope machine, as displayed at the Great Exhibition of 1851

Right: a clockwork toy of the 1880s

The first Singer sewing machine, 1851

THE ILLUSTRATED LONDON NEWS, FEB. 3, 1900.— 172

WHAT WILL YOU DO

IN THE

LONG, COLD, DARK, SHIVERY EVENINGS,

WHEN YOUR HEALTH AND CONVENIENCE COMPEL YOU TO STAY

INDOORS ?

WHY !!! HAVE A PHONOGRAPH, OF COURSE.

It is the FINEST ENTERTAINER in the WORLD.

There is nothing equal to it in the whole Realm
of Art.

It imitates any and every Musical Instrument,
any and every natural sound, faithfully:

the HUMAN VOICE, the NOISE OF THE
CATARACT, the BOOM OF THE GUN,
the VOICES OF BIRDS OR ANIMALS.

From

£2 2s.

THE GREATEST MIMIC.

A Valuable Teacher of Acoustics. Most Interesting to Old or Young   A Pleasure
and Charm to the Suffering, bringing to them the Brightness and Amusements of
the outside World by its faithful reproductions of Operas, New Songs, Speeches, &c.

EVERY HOME WILL sooner or later have its PHONOGRAPH as a NECESSITY.

HAVE YOURS NOW; you will enjoy it longer.

Brought within the reach of every family by Mr. Edison's last production at £2 2s.

Send for our Illustrated Catalogues to

EDISON - BELL CONSOLIDATED PHONOGRAPH CO., LD.,

Or to our Licensees—   39, Charing Cross Road, W.C

EDISONIA LD., 25 to 22, Banner Street, and City Show-Rooms, 21, Cheapside, E.C., LONDON.

Using the evidence: technology and progress

*The phonograph was an early kind
of gramophone which used cylinders*

Like many of his contemporaries the nineteenth-century historian T. B.
Macaulay had no doubts about the benefits brought by the advance of
technology:

(1) It has lengthened life; it has mitigated pain; it has extinguished diseases; it
has increased the fertility of the soil; it has given new securities to the mariner;
it has furnished new arms to the warrior; it has spanned great rivers and
estuaries with bridges of form unknown to our fathers; it has guided the
thunderbolt innocuously from heaven to earth, it has lighted up the night with
the splendour of the day; it has extended the range of the human vision; it has
multiplied the power of the human muscles; it has accelerated motion; it has
annihilated distance; it has facilitated intercourse, correspondence, all friendly
offices, all dispatch of business; it has enabled man to descend to the depths of
the sea, to soar into the air, to penetrate securely into the noxious recesses of the
earth, to traverse the land in cars which whirl along without horses, and the
ocean in ships which run ten knots an hour against the wind. These are but a
part of its fruits, and of its first fruits. For it is a philosophy which never rests,
which has never attained, which is never perfect. Its law is progress. A point
which yesterday was invisible is its goal today, and will be its starting-post
tomorrow.

Critical and Historical Essays (1837)

Twenty-nine years later the cartoonist Daumier took a more jaundiced view:

(2) 'The Dream of the Inventor of the Needle Gun'

Questions and further work

1 Read Document 1 carefully and try to think which developments Macaulay was thinking about when he wrote this passage.
2 What is Daumier trying to say in his cartoon?
3 Consider the technical advances made during the years 1700–1900. What benefits did they bring? What problems did they create?
4 On balance do you think that the benefits technology has brought outweigh the problems, or the other way round?

Index

Acknowledgements

The author and publisher wish to thank the following who have kindly given permission for the use of copyright material:

Associated Book Publishers Ltd for an extract from UK Exports table from *Economic History of England* by William Ashworth, published by Methuen & Company Ltd and an extract from *Narrow Boat* by L. T. C. Rolt, published by Eyre & Spottiswoode Ltd; B. T. Batsford Ltd for extracts from *The Agricultural Revolution* by J. D. Chambers and G. E. Mingay and *Everyday Life in Traditional Japan* by C. J. Dunn; The Bodley Head Ltd for an extract from *My Autobiography* by Charles Chaplin; Cambridge University Press for figures from *British Economic Growth 1688–1959* by P. Deane and W. A. Cole, Japanese Industry and Trade figures from *Meiji Japan* by H. Bolitho, and Overseas Trade figures from *Abstract of British Historical Statistics* by B. R. Mitchell and P. Deane; Columbia University Press for an extract from *Sources of the Japanese Tradition* by de Bary; David and Charles Ltd and Michael E. Rose for extracts from *The English Poor Law 1780–1830*; Gerald Duckworth & Company Ltd for an extract from *The West in the East* by Price Collier; Paul Elek Ltd for an extract from *Age of the Grand Tour* by Anthony Burgess and Francis Haskell; Evans Brothers Ltd for extracts from *Canals 1720–1920* by Rhoda Pearce and *The Coming of the Railways* by J. R. S. Whiting; Faber and Faber Ltd for an extract from *The Story of Japan* by Ian Nish; E. P. Greenleaf for extracts from *The Luddites of West Yorkshire* edited by E. P. Greenleaf and J. A. Hargreaves, Banney Royd Teachers Centre, Kirklees; D. C. Heath & Company for extracts from *The American Pageant*, 5th edition, by Thomas A. Bailey and *America: A Modern History of the United States* by F. Freidel and H. N. Drewry, © 1970; Heinemann Educational Books Ltd for an extract from *Equiano's Travels* edited by Paul Edwards; Hodder & Stoughton Ltd for an extract from *The Lonely Sea and the Sky* by Sir Francis Chichester; Hulton Educational Publications Ltd for an extract from *Britain's Heritage*, Book 3 by P. J. Larkin; Hutchinson Publishing Group Ltd for extracts from *The Railway Navvies* and

Passage to America by T. Coleman; Lawrence and Wishart Ltd for extracts from *Folksong in England* by A. L. Lloyd; Longman Group Ltd for extracts from *Problem of Poverty 1660–1834* by Geoffrey Taylor and *Empire and Slavery* by P. Richardson; Oxford University Press for extracts from *The Diary of One of Garibaldi's Thousand* by G. C. Abba, translated by E. R. Vincent (1962), *The Settlement of the American West* by Joan Chandler (1971), *Lark Rise to Candleford* by Flora Thompson (1954), tables from *The Struggle for Mastery in Europe 1848–1918* by A. J. P. Taylor (1954), and two graphs from *English Overseas Trade Statistics* by E. B. Schumpeter; Routledge & Kegan Paul Ltd for extracts from *Social History of the French Revolution* by Norman Hampson, *London Life in the Eighteenth Century* by Dorothy George and *English Travellers in France 1698–1815* by Maxwell; Times Newspapers Ltd for an extract from a report published in *The Times*, December 1881; The University of Newcastle upon Tyne School of Education for an extract from Archive Teaching Unit No. 1: *Coals from Newcastle*; Ward Lock Educational Ltd for an extract from *Inland Waterways* by L. T. C. Rolt; Wayland Publishers Ltd for an extract from *The American Revolution* by Roger Parkinson; Weidenfeld & Nicolson Ltd for an extract from *Destination America* by M. A. Jones.

The author and publishers wish to acknowledge the following photograph sources:

Reproduced by Gracious Permission of Her Majesty the Queen, pp. 23 bottom, 49.
American History Picture Library, pp. 39, 70, 72 top.
Archiv Gerstenberg, p. 46.
Archiv für Kunst und Geschichte, pp. 48, 55.
Harold Arnold, p. 99.
Australian Information Service, London, p. 159.
Beds. C.C., p. 80 bottom.
British Library, pp. 25 bottom (MS/PM/OBJ. No. 52–121), 90, 147 top.
By courtesy of the Trustees of the British Museum, p. 42.
British Waterways Board, p. 97.
Leslie Bryce, p. 98.
Bulloz, pp. 61, 169, 172 bottom, 173, 174 top, 175 bottom.
Mrs Betty Cadbury – Playthings Past Museum, p. 219 left.
Camera Press Ltd, p. 19 bottom.

Cliché des Musées Nationaux – Paris, pp. 62/63.
Communist Party of Great Britain, James Klugmann Collection, pp. 108 top, 119.
Cooper-Bridgeman Library, p. 31 top.
Corporation of Bristol, p. 32.
Denver Public Library, Western History Dept., p. 195.
Giraudon, pp. 59 bottom, 60 bottom.
Greater London Council, pp. 23 top, 142.
Guildhall Library, p. 115 bottom.
Heinz Moos Verlag, Munich, p. 220.
Michael Holford, p. 176 centre.
Humberside County Council, p. 27, 28.
ICI, p. 10.
Illustrated London News, pp. 103 top, 105 top left, 132 bottom, 162 top, 163, 208, 219 right.
Ironbridge Gorge Museum Trust, p. 140.
A. F. Kersting, p. 11.
Keystone Press Agency, pp. 204, 205 top, 211.
Krupp Essen, pp. 188/189.
Lancashire Record Office, p. 102.
Mansell Collection, title page top, middle right, bottom, pp. 9, 12 top, 13, 16, 17, 19 top, 21, 24/25 bottom, 31 bottom, 34 bottom, 37, 38, 44, 47, 57 right, 58, 62, 75 top, 77, 80 top, 88, 89, 94 bottom, 103 bottom, 104 top, 104/105, 109, 115 top right, 118 bottom, 121, 122, 129 top, 138, 139, 153, 155, 156, 157 top, 160, 167, 172 top, 177, 178, 179, 180, 181, 184 top, 186, 213, 214, 215 top left, 217 top left, 218 top.
City of Manchester Art Galleries, p. 105 top right.
Manchester Public Libraries, pp. 106, 112.
Mary Evans Picture Library, pp. 74, 107.
Hugh McKnight, pp. 100/101.
Museum of British Transport, p. 133.
Museum of London, pp. 22, 24/25 top.
Photographs by courtesy of National Coal Board, pp. 114, 146 top, 148, 149, 150.
National Galleries of Scotland, p. 60 top.
National Maritime Museum, p. 161.
National Portrait Gallery, p. 116 bottom.
Crown Copyright – National Railway Museum, pp. 125, 129 bottom.
National Trust, p. 36.
Timothy Newark Collection – Historical Picture Service, pp. 205 bottom, 212.
Courtesy of the Oklahoma Historical Society, p. 202.
Post Office, p. 91.

Public Records Office, p. 116 top.
Punch, p. 132 top.
Radio Times Hulton Picture Library, pp. 12 bottom, 25 top, 65, 75 bottom, 108 bottom, 113, 114/115 top left, 117, 118 top, 126 top, 136, 157 bottom, 176 top/bottom, 182, 184 bottom, 185, 187, 206, 210, 215 top right, 215 centre, 217 top right.
Royal Commonwealth Society, pp. 33, 40, 41, 43 top.
Crown Copyright – Science Museum, London, pp. 87, 94 top, 127 bottom, 131, 134 bottom, 147 bottom, 215 bottom.
Singer, p. 218 bottom.
Edwin Smith, p. 52.

Snark International, pp. 56, 57 left, 168, 171, 174 bottom, 175 top.
Sunday Times, p. 72 bottom.
Tate Gallery, p. 162 bottom.
Ullstein Bilderdienst, title page middle left, pp. 45, 50/51 top, 53, 54.
University Library, Cambridge, p. 127 top.
University of Reading, Museum of English Rural Life, p. 81, 82 top, 83.
Crown Copyright – Victoria and Albert Museum, p. 152.
W. D. and H. O. Wells, p. 34 top.
Trustees of the Wedgewood Museum, p. 43 bottom.
Western Americana Picture Library, pp. 66, 67, 68, 69, 71, 191, 192, 194, 196, 198, 199, 200, 201.
Yorkshire Post Newspapers Ltd, p. 145.
From *A Country Camera* by Gordon Winter, p. 85.
Taken from the publication – T. Coleman – *Passage to America*, p. 165.

The *cover* illustration is reproduced by kind permission of Robert Harding Associates (private collection)

The publishers have made every effort to trace the copyright holders, but if they have inadvertently overlooked any, they will be pleased to make the necessary arrangement at the first opportunity.

Luddite trial verdict: the three accused were all found guilty and were hanged at York on 8 January 1813.